TOURING THE
NATURAL
WONDERS
OF NEW ZEALAND

First published in 2009 by New Holland Publishers (NZ) Ltd
Auckland • Sydney • London • Cape Town

www.newhollandpublishers.co.nz

218 Lake Road, Northcote, Auckland 0627, New Zealand
Unit 1, 66 Gibbes Street, Chatswood, NSW 2067, Australia
86–88 Edgware Road, London W2 2EA, United Kingdom
80 McKenzie Street, Cape Town 8001, South Africa

Publishing manager: Matt Turner
Project manager: Carolyn Lagahetau
Editor: Mike Wagg
Design: Trevor Newman
Maps: Barry Bradley

National Library of New Zealand
Cataloguing-in-Publication Data

Janssen, Peter (Peter Leon)
Touring the natural wonders of New Zealand : over 45
spectacular routes / text by Peter Janssen ; photography by
Andrew Fear ; cartography by Barry Bradley.
ISBN 978-1-86966-234-9
1. Automobile travel—New Zealand—Guidebooks. 2. New
Zealand—Guidebooks. I. Fear, Andrew. II. Bradley, Barry.
III. Title.
919.3044—dc 22

10 9 8 7 6 5 4 3 2 1

Colour reproduction by SC (Sang Choy) International Pte Ltd,
Singapore

Printed in China by SNP Leefung on paper sourced from
sustainable forests.

TOURING THE NATURAL WONDERS

OF NEW ZEALAND

OVER 45 SPECTACULAR ROUTES

PETER JANSSEN   PHOTOGRAPHY BY ANDREW FEAR

NEW HOLLAND

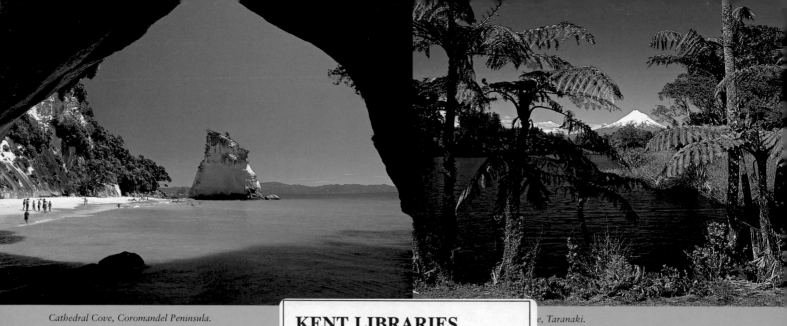

Cathedral Cove, Coromandel Peninsula.

e, Taranaki.

Contents

North Island

Pancake Rocks, West Coast.

Rakaia River and Mt Hutt Range, Canterbury.

South Island

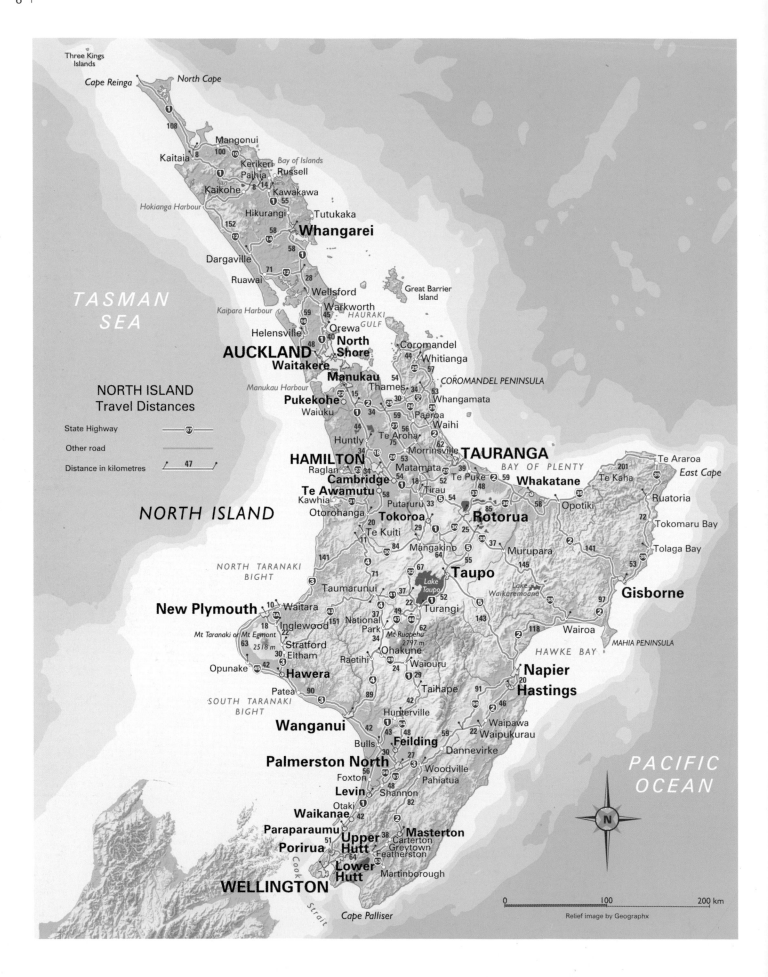

Three Kings
Islands

Cape Reinga   North Cape

① 108

Mangonui
100 ⑩
Kaitaia ⑧
Kerikeri   Bay of Islands
Paihia ① Russell
Kaikohe ⑧ 14
Kawakawa
① 55
Hikurangi   Tutukaka
152 58   **Whangarei**
⑫ ⑭
58 ①
Dargaville
71 ⑫
Ruawai   28
Wellsford
Kaipara Harbour   59 ⑯
Warkworth   HAURAKI
45   GULF
Orewa
Helensville ① 40   Great Barrier
Island
48 **North**
AUCKLAND   **Shore**   Coromandel
Waitakere   44   Whitianga
57
Manukau Harbour   **Manukau**   54   *COROMANDEL PENINSULA*
Pukekohe 22 15   Thames   53
Waiuku ① 34   30 34   Whangamata
59   Paeroa
44 56   Waihi
Huntly   Te Aroha   75
HAMILTON 34 ⑱   Morrinsville   **TAURANGA**   Te Araroa
Raglan 34   Matamata 39   *BAY OF PLENTY*   201   *East Cape*
Cambridge 54   52   Te Puke   Te Kaha   ㉟
Te Awamutu 18   Tirau ② 59   **Whakatane**   ㉟
Kawhia   58   33 54   48   Ruatoria
Otorohanga ㉛   Putaruru 33   85   58   Opotiki   72
20   **Tokoroa** ㉚   **Rotorua**   Tokomaru Bay
Te Kuiti 29   ① 25   37   Murupara   141   Tolaga Bay
11   84   Mangakino ⑤   145   ㉟ 53
141   64   Lake
NORTH TARANAKI   4   67 ㉜   Waikaremoana   ㊳   97
BIGHT   71   Lake   **Taupo**   143   Gisborne
Taumarunui   37   Taupo   52   ⑤
③   22   Turangi
New Plymouth 10 Waitara   4   49 46   62   118   Wairoa
⑱ 37   National 47   *HAWKE BAY*   *MAHIA PENINSULA*
18   Inglewood   Park   34   Mt Ruapehu
Mt Taranaki or Mt Egmont   22   2797 m
63   2518 m   Stratford   Ohakune
30   Eltham   Raetihi 49   Waiouru   **Napier**
Opunake ㊺ 42   24 ①   20   **Hastings**
Hawera   29 Taihape   91
Patea 90   89   50   46
③   42   Hunterville
SOUTH TARANAKI   43 48   22 Waipawa
BIGHT   59   Waipukurau
Wanganui 42   **Feilding** 27   Dannevirke
Bulls   ③
Palmerston North   Woodville
Foxton 56   66   Pahiatua
Levin 48   82
Otaki ① Shannon
Waikanae 42   ②
Paraparaumu 38   **Masterton**
51 **Upper**   Carterton
Porirua   **Hutt**   Greytown
64   Featherston
Lower
Hutt   Martinborough
WELLINGTON

TASMAN
SEA

NORTH ISLAND
Travel Distances

State Highway   ⑧⑦
Other road
Distance in kilometres   47

NORTH ISLAND

PACIFIC
OCEAN

N

Cook
Strait   Cape Palliser

0   100   200 km

Relief image by Geographx

KEY TO TOUR MAPS

Driving

Tour routes   **Other roads**

Motorway
State Highway ②
Other road, sealed
Minor road, unsealed
'Got Time?' (tour extension)

Walking

.... Country walks

By boat

Ferry or tour boat

Navigation

⇁   Route direction

15   Distance in kilometres

⑧ ✿   Place of interest

Other features

Urban area   Exotic plantation
○   Town   Wetlands
○   Locality   Snow & icefields
UREWERA   National Park   Forest Park *VICTORIA*

Land cover classes shown only when relevant to an individual tour

SOUTH ISLAND

TASMAN SEA

PACIFIC OCEAN

CANTERBURY BIGHT

KARAMEA BIGHT

Farewell Spit
Collingwood   Golden 27 Bay
Takaka
Tasman Bay
60   53
Motueka   **Nelson**
33
77   Havelock
14   Richmond   35   Picton
69   91   28
Blenheim
Westport   Murchison   35
47   41   12   Lake Rotoroa   25   Lake Rotoiti   Tapuae-o-Uenuku 2885 m   1
34   101   65   72   130
Reefton
7   79   44   83   Hanmer Springs 102   Kaikoura
Greymouth   18   9   76
Lake Brunner   7   24   79   75
Hokitika   22   7   56   Cheviot
6   186   43   1
73   Waipara
136   **Rangiora** 58
Pegasus Bay
Darfield   48   **CHRISTCHURCH**
25   Franz Josef Glacier
Fox Glacier   Aoraki/Mt Cook 55   Lake Ellesmere
121   3754 m   Methven   33   87   83
Haast   Aoraki/Mt Cook   1   Rakaia   76   Akaroa
Lake Pukaki   Lake Tekapo   51   **Ashburton**   BANKS PENINSULA
55   Tekapo   42   46   Geraldine
80   47   Fairlie   18   Temuka
Lake Ohau   11   Twizel   62   18   **Timaru**
Mt Aspiring   143   28   Omarama   37
Lake Hawea   Lake Benmore
Milford Sound   Milford Sound   Lake Wanaka   52   Kurow   63   68   Waimate
6   Wanaka   110   66   47
70   53   1
Doubtful Sound   **Queenstown**   95   87   **Oamaru**
94   57   Cromwell   Ranfurly   77   60
Lake Wakatipu   31   Alexandra
120   Lake Te Anau   107   72   135   Palmerston
Te Anau   21   Roxburgh   55
15   95   65   8
Lake Manapouri   Manapouri   Lumsden   **Mosgiel**
14   73   94   62   90   59
Ohai   49   64   Lawrence   1   **DUNEDIN**
50   62   6   25   Milton
Winton   48   13   **Gore**   71   Balclutha
Tuatapere   31   Mataura
99   83   1   53
30   **Invercargill**
FOVEAUX STRAIT
Bluff
Halfmoon Bay
Stewart Island/Rakiura

Cook Strait

SOUTH ISLAND
Travel Distances

State Highway ——㊲——
Other road ————
Distance in kilometres 47

N

0   100   200 km

Relief image by Geographx

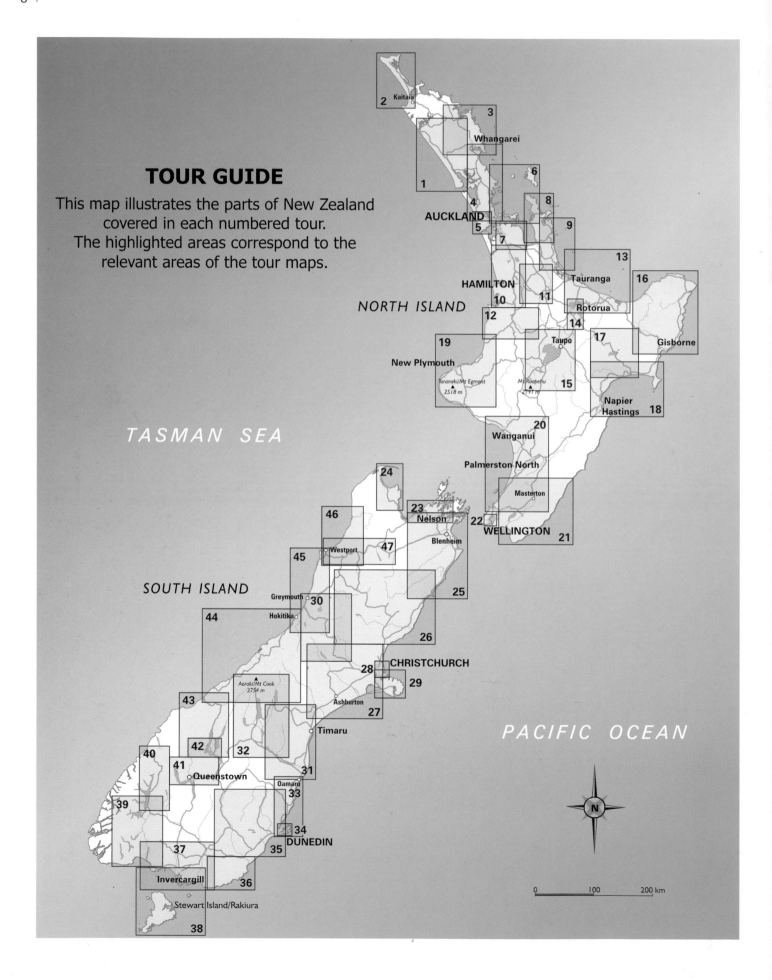

TOUR GUIDE

This map illustrates the parts of New Zealand covered in each numbered tour. The highlighted areas correspond to the relevant areas of the tour maps.

TASMAN SEA

PACIFIC OCEAN

NORTH ISLAND

SOUTH ISLAND

2 Kaitaia

3

Whangarei

1

6

4

8

AUCKLAND

5

9

7

13

HAMILTON

Tauranga

16

10

11

Rotorua

12

14

19

17

Gisborne

New Plymouth

Taupo

Taranaki/Mt Egmont
2518 m

Mt Ruapehu
2797 m

15

Napier
Hastings

18

20

Wanganui

Palmerston North

Masterton

24

23

Nelson

22

46

Blenheim

WELLINGTON

21

45

Westport

47

25

Greymouth

30

Hokitika

44

26

CHRISTCHURCH

28

29

Aoraki/Mt Cook
3754 m

Ashburton

43

27

Timaru

42

32

40

41

Queenstown

31

Oamaru

33

39

34

DUNEDIN

37

35

Invercargill

36

Stewart Island/Rakiura

38

N

0   100   200 km

Exploring natural New Zealand

This book offers almost 50 driving tours linking the country's most spectacular natural attractions. Route directions are given, as well as information on the flora, fauna and unique geology for which the country is rightly famous. To get the most out of your tour, it is worth familiarising yourself with the itineraries and with the travel tips and advice given below.

How to use this book

Below the title of each trip you will find key points of interest and a total distance. Note that it is not intended that these trips be covered in a single day, particularly if you choose to stop and spend time at each place, nor that the total distance be a limit to your adventuring. Depending on your own interests some trips can be covered in a shorter time, while others could be extended over several days. Often the trips only feature highlights, but offer plenty of opportunities for you to explore your surrounds independently. That said, these trips in my extensive travel experience are the key routes for anyone wanting to explore New Zealand's natural heritage.

The numbered destinations in each tour are marked on the maps, which highlight the main route in red. In many tours there is an extra side-trip or extension labelled 'Got Time?'. These are provided in the event you are eager to explore further and are prepared to venture onto some rougher, less travelled routes. The 'Got Time?' trips are marked on the maps in green; they are not included in the total distance.

A full map key can be found on page 7.

Highways and back roads

New Zealand has a good network of roads that are well maintained and signposted with excellent directional information. However, what might appear to be a main road on a map can turn out to be a very different story on the ground. With the greater part of the population clustered in cities and large towns, most of the 200 km of motorway exists within these centres, in particular Auckland. Outside of the tiny motorway system, the main roads are largely just two lanes, with passing lanes at varying intervals. And since so much of the country is hilly and rugged, on some main roads it's not

unusual to find winding sections with sharp corners, one-way bridges, and steep climbs. Gravel roads (that is, road surfaces that are not tarsealed) on minor routes are common even within a short distance of the largest cities, let alone in the less populated regions, and they are frequently narrow, twisting and rutted. In rural areas farmers often use the roads to move sheep and cattle, and while most farmers will endeavour to minimise any traffic hold-ups they might cause, you should slow down, be patient and not blow your horn, and let the animals pass quietly.

Whether on the main routes or back roads, the key to driving safely is to not drive too fast, drive to the conditions, and take care when passing.

Best time to travel

Summer is naturally the most popular time to tour the country's scenic attractions. New Zealand welcomes nearly two and a half million visitors a year, and while by international standards that is not a

high number, many places are, by local standards, becoming crowded. Mid-December to mid-March is going to be particularly busy, with most folks taking a break between Christmas and the end of January, a period that coincides with the annual school holidays. In addition, the town festivals and other major events that occur through January and February can often overwhelm the local accommodation and facilities.

The shoulder period, from March through to May, is a great time to tour the country. While the warmest weather might have passed, this period generally experiences settled conditions with pleasant days and cool nights. The peak of the summer holidays is past, the kids are back in school, accommodation is much easier to find and even the most popular tourist spots are not so crowded.

A word on the weather

New Zealand's temperate island climate lends itself to some extreme, unpredictable,

Mountain highway to Arthur's Pass and the West Coast, Canterbury.

and rapidly changing conditions. Whereas scorching-hot days with the temperature well over 30°C are common in summer, snow and driving cold winds off the Antarctic are equally frequent in winter. Although the north of the country often cops the tail end of tropical cyclones in the summer months, bringing rain, wind and flooding, fortunately this doesn't usually last long and it is warm not cold weather. In the east of the South Island summer fluctuates between searing heat and sudden cool wet changes springing from the south.

With clear skies and low latitudes, sunburn is a real problem. In the middle of the day, skin can burn in less than 15 minutes. Even if the sky is overcast you can still get burnt and a cool wind can also disguise the sun's true heat. So, before you venture out, make sure you put on good sunblock and take a hat.

Facilities

Not surprisingly for a country with a world-renowned reputation for hospitality, almost anywhere you go in New Zealand you can find good accommodation ranging from the most rudimentary camping ground through to backpackers, bed-and-breakfast establishments, motels, hotels and luxury lodges.

While most camping grounds have toilets, washing facilities and kitchens, some of the more remote grounds and those run by the Department of Conservation (DoC) are considerably more basic, so be prepared.

INFORMATION

Both local authorities and DoC run excellent, friendly and very knowledgeable visitor information centres. However, watch out for the 'information centre' lookalikes that primarily promote one or two operators, especially in the more popular tourist spots.

Out and about

Given the popularity of walking and tramping in New Zealand, the country has a vast number of tracks and walkways. However, they do vary considerably and range from beautiful paths where it would be impossible to get lost through to rough and muddy tracks that are poorly marked. The bush can be very dense and off the

track it is very easy to become disoriented and lost. A few tips to save a lot of problems follow.

- Preferably go with someone. If that's not possible or desirable then let somebody know where you are heading.
- If you're not sure of the local conditions, check out the tracks with the local information centre. The staff will have up-to-date and accurate information on track conditions and weather and can also advise on the options that will suit you best.
- Stay on the track. Some tracks can be confusing, so if you are uncertain retrace your steps until you know you are on the right track.
- Carry a small pack with more food and drink than you need in case your walk takes longer than anticipated.
- Wear good footwear. The bush is frequently wet and muddy, and while tramping boots are not always necessary, footwear with a good tread is essential.
- Invest in a waterproof jacket. It can rain heavily at any time and any place in New Zealand. Many jackets look good, but there are no prizes for being the best-looking corpse and a number are only wind- or shower-proof. Make no compromises here: opt for a totally waterproof jacket only.
- Protect yourself from the sun — slop on a high SPF sunblock and slap on a hat.
- In cold conditions make sure you keep your body warm and dry between the neck and waist.
- Mobile phones can be very useful if you are lost, but be aware that coverage is not always available in some of the more remote spots.
- On longer trips carry a first-aid kit and any personal medicine you may require.
- Drowning was once called the 'New Zealand death', so take care when crossing rivers and streams.

Security

An unfortunate fact of modern life is that car burglary is a common occurrence in isolated car parks. Some very popular attractions now even have security guards. Short of leaving someone with the vehicle at all times, there are a few things you can do to lessen the chances of a break-in. Lock

the doors, even when you are only doing a short walk. Double-check all windows are closed; it's easy to forget the back windows. Make sure all valuables are out of sight, and if possible carry your most valuable items with you (wallet, camera, phone, video equipment and so forth). A steering lock may not prevent your vehicle being broken into, but it will indicate to thieves that you are security conscious — and hopefully make them think twice about attempting to make off with it.

Sandflies

Small and nasty, sandflies may be tiny but they pack a mean bite. In certain parts of the country, such as Fiordland and the West Coast, these minuscule creatures are a real menace. You can't really enjoy the countryside without packing an insect repellent. These are readily available at any supermarket, chemist or general store.

Giardia

Giardia is a microscopic parasite accidentally introduced into New Zealand waterways. Symptoms of infection are loss of appetite, bloating and diarrhoea. Remember, while the water might look clean and pure even in alpine areas, it is best only to drink water that has been boiled, filtered or chemically treated.

Camper vans

Although camper vans provide a very popular and easy way to see the country, the sheer number of these vehicles is starting to cause some problems. Most regions of the country are relatively relaxed about 'freedom' camping and in general local authorities are reluctant to restrict camping and camper vans. However, many of the smaller sleeper vans are without toilet facilities and in some areas casual toilet arrangements are beginning to cause a predictable and unpleasant problem with regard to human waste. Some local authorities, such as the Queenstown Lakes District Council, have banned freedom camping altogether for those vans without sanitary facilities and this trend is likely to spread.

The solution is simple: either camp where there is a toilet or pack it up and take it with you until the waste can be disposed of properly.

North Island

1 The Kauri Coast • Kaipara Harbour to Hokianga Harbour

Kauri forests • Endless sandy coastline • Mangrove swamps • 205 km

It isn't hard to find solitude in the quiet harbours, vast forests and empty beaches of the west coast of Northland, despite its increasing popularity with independent travellers.

INFORMATION
Kauri Coast i-SITE,
67–69 Normanby St, Dargaville,
ph (09) 439 8360
Hokianga i-SITE, SH 12, Omapere,
ph (09) 405 8869
Waipoua Forest Information
Centre,
River Road, Waipoua Forest,
ph (09) 439 3011

Getting there
Travelling north on SH 1, the turnoff to the west on SH 12 is clearly marked just south of the bush-covered range known as the Brynderwyns. From the north the access is via Kaikohe or across the Hokianga Harbour by ferry at Rawene. The roads are good, with the key routes sealed, though the road through the Waipoua Forest is winding and narrow.

Best time to visit
Don't be fooled by the slogan 'The Winterless North'. While temperatures are definitely mild, frosts are not unusual inland during winter and it can rain heavily at any time of the year. The holiday period from mid-December to early February is pretty busy and popular spots like Kai Iwi Lakes Camping Ground and accommodation around the Hokianga are often booked out. March and April are usually very pleasant months weather-wise and there are fewer tourists.

Facilities
Dargaville is the main town and has a wide variety of shops, cafés, banks, motels, several historic hotels, camping grounds and a supermarket. While there is a good range of camping grounds in the area, outside of Dargaville other accommodation and facilities are rather light. The

Hokianga area in particular has limited accommodation, so if you are travelling in the peak summer period, plan ahead.

1 Tokatoka Peak and Maungaraho Rock
From the Brynderwyn turnoff on SH 1, follow SH 12 for 55 km to Tokatoka. Maungaraho Rock and Tokatoka Peak are the cores of old volcanoes that erupted millions of years ago. The rock and the peak are all that remain as the outer volcanic material has eroded away. Tokatoka Peak's distinctive shape is impossible to miss on the road from Ruawai to Dargaville, while Maungaraho Rock is a little further inland. There is a short track through regenerating bush to the top of Tokatoka Peak that takes around 20 minutes one way and the views are well worth it. Below, the sluggish, tidal Wairoa River threads through the flat and once swampy landscape, while far to the south is the wide expanse of the Kaipara Harbour. The track to Tokatoka Peak is 1.5 km up Tokatoka Road, and starts right next to the Tokatoka Tavern.

2 Kai Iwi Lakes
Situated 41 km north of Tokatoka Peak via Dargaville on SH 12 and then a further 12 km from SH 12 down Omamari Road.

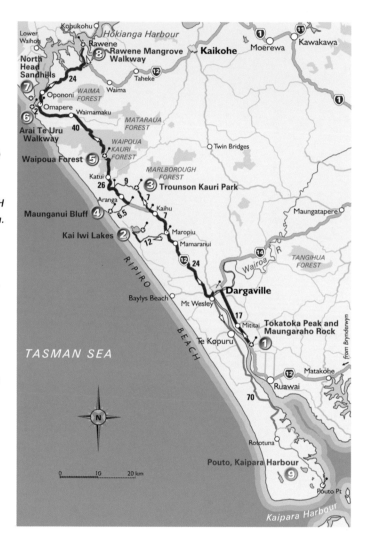

Formed during the Pleistocene period, these three small dune lakes have no inlets or outlets and rely entirely on rainwater to maintain their level. A hard ironstone pan prevents the lakes from draining and they are surprisingly deep. The largest, Lake Taharoa, reaches a depth of 37 metres and Lake Waikare descends 30 metres. The lakes are fringed by a shelf of pure white sand, with a dramatic change of water colour as the lake bed drops sharply into deeper water. Thermal stratification, where layers of water vary significantly

Kauri Trees

The New Zealand kauri, *Agathis australis*, is a conifer and is part of the ancient family *Araucariaceae*. Twenty species are spread through the tropics and three are found in the southern hemisphere, of which the New Zealand kauri is the most southerly. Even within this country the tree does not grow naturally further south than Kawhia on the west coast and Tauranga on the east coast. In Waipoua Forest, Tane Mahuta, the largest surviving kauri, towers over 51 metres high and has a girth of 13.8 metres, while nearby Te Matua Ngahere is estimated to be 2000 years old and has a girth of 16.5 metres although not the same impressive height. Other trees, long since disappeared, were much larger — the largest recorded specimen had a girth of 32 metres, double that of Te Matua. A visit to the Matakohe Kauri Museum will give the visitor a true appreciation of these giants of the forest. (Matakohe Kauri Museum, Church Road, Matakohe; situated on SH 12, 26 km from SH 1.)

The trunk of a mature kauri is very clean and straight, with a columnar appearance. Today timber is used from ancient forests in the form of trees felled tens of thousands of years ago by natural calamities and preserved by the boggy Northland soil. Items made from this timber are marketed under the name 'swamp kauri'. Kauri are not, however, New Zealand's tallest native trees. Both rimu and kahikatea grow much taller, with one kahikatea on the slopes of Mt Pirongia in the Waikato towering a massive 20 metres higher than Tane Mahuta.

the more secretive giant kauri snail. While Trounson doesn't have the big trees and attracts far fewer visitors than the Waipoua Forest further north, the dense stands of huge kauri give the forest a primordial appeal that is accentuated by a more peaceful atmosphere. The easy loop walk through the forest takes about 45 minutes and is ideal for all ages.

4 Maunganui Bluff

From the southern turnoff to Trounson Kauri Park on SH 12, continue north for 8 km then turn left and drive a further 6.5 km to the beach. The last section of road is gravel.
Maunganui Bluff acts as a giant 'full stop' for the marvellous sweep of Ripiro Beach that stretches for 100 km from the bluff right around to Pouto on the Kaipara Harbour. Rising to 460 metres, the bluff was formed by a lava flow from eruptions 11 to 15 million years ago, and today is cloaked by rare coastal forest. The views from the top are spectacular both north and south, and a trip to the summit will take less than three hours return. Apart from the tiny bach settlement at the foot of the bluff, the shore is virtually empty and open to the thundering swells off the Tasman Sea and a constant westerly wind. The beach is backed by high dunes and wading and seabirds are common.

in temperature, can be very noticeable in summer. The vegetation around the lakes is undergoing restoration. There is a large camping ground with basic facilities, but it is very popular in the December–January period, so booking ahead is essential (ph (09) 439 8360; info@kauricoast.co.nz).

3 Trounson Kauri Park

From the Kai Iwi Lakes turnoff, continue north along SH 12 for 7 km and then turn right (signposted) and continue a further 7 km to the park. The road forms a loop and rejoins SH 12.
Covering over 450 hectares, Trounson Kauri Park is a beautiful reserve of virgin kauri forest and was the first Department of Conservation (DoC) 'mainland island' project in Northland, with intense predator control seeing a resurgence of native fauna, including brown kiwi and

The kauri trees 'Darby' and 'Joan' flank SH 12, Waipoua Forest.

5 Waipoua Forest

From the turnoff to Maunganui Bluff, continue north on SH 12 for 26 km to Tane Mahuta in the heart of the Waipoua Forest.

Waipoua, along with adjoining forests, now covers over 13,000 hectares and is the most important and largest remaining kauri forest in New Zealand. It also contains the largest individual kauri trees and protects a diverse range of native flora and fauna. Saved from the axe in the early days of settlement by the inaccessible terrain, the forest was acquired by the government in 1876 and, despite public pressure to protect it, trees were regularly felled up to the end of the Second World War. Even the 1952 decision to set aside 9105 hectares as a protected reserve attracted considerable opposition from milling interests.

Among the forest's notable trees are the tallest surviving kauri, Tane Mahuta, standing at just over 51 metres high, and Te Matua Ngahere, the kauri with the largest girth at 16.5 metres — both estimated to be over 2000 years old. While the kauri are the main attraction, the reserve also protects magnificent rimu, towai, northern rata and taraire, and important fauna including the brown kiwi and the unique carnivorous kauri snail.

The walk to Tane Mahuta takes five minutes from SH 12, but just 1 km south of the big tree there are three other short walks to equally impressive kauri. While Tane Mahuta attracts all the coach tours, only a small proportion of visitors make it to the other parts of the forest. The visitor centre is a good starting point for those wanting to explore the surrounds further and for information on simple accommodation.

Waipoua River, Waipoua Forest Park.

6 Arai Te Uru Walkway, Hokianga Harbour

From Waipoua Forest, the south head of the Hokianga is 40 km north on SH 12. Access to the walkway is by Signal Hill Road, 4 km east of Omapere.

Rising sea levels since the last ice age slowly invaded this river valley and today the long finger of the Hokianga Harbour stretches over 30 km inland. The narrow channel at the ocean outlet creates a strong tidal flow and a rough and wild bar, while the upper reaches are characterised by numerous estuarine rivers such as the Mangamuka, Whirinaki, Waihou and Utakura, which drains Lake Omapere, Northland's largest lake.

At low tide, around half of the harbour's 115 sq km are exposed, creating a rich environment for aquatic and migratory birds. Along the south head the Arai Te Uru Walkway winds through stunted manuka, toetoe and flax and over wind-shaped sand to several lookout points with views inland along the harbour, over the entrance towards the north head, and out over the wild Tasman Sea.

7 North Head Sandhills, Hokianga Harbour

Depending on demand, Hokianga Express Charters runs a water taxi on the hour from Opononi Wharf to the sandhills.

In contrast to the south head, the northern side of the harbour is a vast expanse of rolling sandhills, golden coloured and rising to 300 metres in places. Over thousands of years the relentless wind off the Tasman Sea has sculpted the sand into deep gullies, wind-blasted cliffs and intriguing formations. Even the hardiest of plants have been unable to establish a toehold in this unforgiving landscape. It is a magnificent place to walk but these sandhills are much larger close up than they appear from a distance, and walking on the sand can be a strain, so don't be overambitious. They are also exposed to harsh winds, so make sure you take plenty of water in hot weather and thick clothing when it's cooler.

8 Rawene Mangrove Walkway, Hokianga Harbour

From the south head, travel east along SH 12, 26 km to Rawene.

New Zealand has just one single species of mangrove, *Avicennia marina* subspecies *australasica*, and like several other New Zealand plants it is the most southerly growing member of a usually tropical family. Frost-tender, mangroves grow as far south as Ohiwa Harbour on the east coast and Kawhia Harbour on the west, but the more southern plants are mere midgets compared with those in Northland, where they reach the size of small trees. Tangled trunks support tough leathery leaves designed to withstand salt water, while the trees' unique aerial roots spike sharply through the sludgy seabed, enabling them to breathe. Once considered to have very little value, mangrove swamps are now recognised as vital habitat for the young of many fish species that use the labyrinth of roots and trunks to evade larger predators.

The Te Ara Manawa Walkway at Rawene is a raised boardwalk that winds through a forest of mangroves. Located on Clendon Esplanade, the walkway is accessible at all tides, allowing the visitor to stroll through the otherwise impenetrable hidden world of the mangrove swamp. The walk takes about 20 minutes and there are information boards along the way with details of the fascinating life cycle of these unusual trees.

GOT TIME? (+70 KM)
9 Pouto, Kaipara Harbour

The Kaipara Harbour is huge, covering 520 sq km with 3200 km of coastline, making it the largest enclosed harbour in New Zealand with its catchment area covering around one third of Northland. But the Kaipara also has an unenviable reputation: muddy, tidal, inaccessible and just plain dull. However, while bush clearance and overfishing have undoubtedly taken a toll on this once pristine harbour, the Kaipara does have another face. The vast tidal area is an important habitat for migratory, wading, shore and seabirds. Over 30,000 birds, including 32 species from the Arctic, arrive here each summer to feed on the plentiful supply of shellfish, worms and crabs. Bird species include godwits, sandpipers, snipe and curlews. In addition, native shore birds also feed and breed in the area, including the endangered New Zealand dotterel and the banded dotterel.

At Pouto, on the north head, the Kaipara is quite different from the vast mud flats, shallow creeks and estuarine rivers that characterise it elsewhere. Here the water runs clear and fast, racing along deep channels and cutting into banks of white sand as vast volumes move through the relatively narrow entrance with each tide. Pouto settlement is sheltered from the worst of the westerly winds and is an excellent starting point for long walks on the sand around to the entrance. You can drive on the sand here, but you do have to know what you are doing and bear in mind that most rental cars are not covered by insurance when driven on a beach.

Pouto is 70 km south of Dargaville on the western bank of the Wairoa River, but the road is sealed for 50 km and is in good condition. While it's a long drive, Pouto is a quiet and magical place with long stretches of empty sandy shores, wild water and tranquil views over the vast harbour. Facilities are mainly limited to a camping ground and lodge, although there is a sheltered picnic area by the car park.

The entrance to the Hokianga Harbour, Northland.

2 The Far North • Kaitaia to Cape Reinga

Giant sand dunes • Dramatic seascapes • Untouched beaches • Unique flora • 185 km

The equable climate, empty beaches and clear blue waters at the northernmost extreme of mainland New Zealand — the Far North — make this a special place to visit.

> **INFORMATION**
> Kaitaia i-SITE, South Road, Kaitaia,
> ph (09) 408 0879

Getting there
SH 1 leads through the heart of the Aupouri Peninsula, directly north from Kaitaia. While the main highway is a good road, side roads are usually gravel and some are pretty rough.

Best time to visit
The summer months from November to April are the best time to enjoy the beaches and walks in this region. However, in summer the area is exposed to cyclonic weather from the tropics that can bring high winds and very heavy rain, although it won't be cold. A good time to visit is during March and April when the weather is still settled, the sea water is warm, and the summer crowds have thinned measurably. Kaitaia has never recorded a temperature below freezing.

Facilities
Most folk visit this area as a day trip from Kaitaia, and while Kaitaia itself is not a particularly attractive town, it has a wide range of accommodation, banks, cafés and shops. North of Kaitaia facilities are few and far between, with limited accommodation and just small shops selling the basics. Petrol is most likely to be considerably cheaper in Kaitaia than further north. Popular camping grounds such as Spirits Bay and Tapotupotu are often crowded in the height of summer.

Before you go — driving on the beach
Ninety Mile Beach is famous as an alternative to SH 1. While driving on the beach is a great experience, it does require some expertise and the following advice should be heeded:

- Only drive along the beach two hours either side of low tide. Stick to the hard sand close to the water.
- You can strike soft sand anywhere and will come to an immediate stop. If you are travelling too fast, then it is quite easy to roll the vehicle. Also, avoid gripping the steering wheel with your thumbs as the wheel can spin quite suddenly when you hit soft sand.
- Take care when crossing streams as this is the most likely spot to hit soft sand.
- If you hit soft sand, don't apply power as you are most likely to dig yourself into a hole. If you stop, try to reverse out on your fresh tracks.
- If you are stuck, clear the sand away from the tyres and use your car mats, old carpet or wood to get a grip.
- Salt water is very damaging to cars, so avoid driving in the sea water.
- Stay out of dune country and the sand above high tide. This is sensitive habitat and the nesting ground for shore birds.
- Drive with consideration for other beach users.
- Many insurance and rental car companies do not cover damage while driving on the beach so check your policy first.

1 Ninety Mile Beach
Ahipara is 14 km southwest of Kaitaia on the Kaitaia–Awaroa Road.

There are numerous other access points to the beach off SH 1 north of Kaitaia, including from Waipapakauri, Hukatere and the Te Paki Stream. Described by Dutch explorer Abel Tasman in 1640 as 'a desert coast', this beach has changed little in the intervening centuries. While only 55 miles in extent instead of 90 (the origins of the name are unclear), this beach is a magnificent sweep of sand backed by extensive dune country and is pounded by the relentless waves off the Tasman Sea. A number of small dune lakes can be found inland, the largest of which are Ngatu and Waiparera. As is to be expected, seabirds are common on this vast stretch of sand and include terns, black-backed gulls and

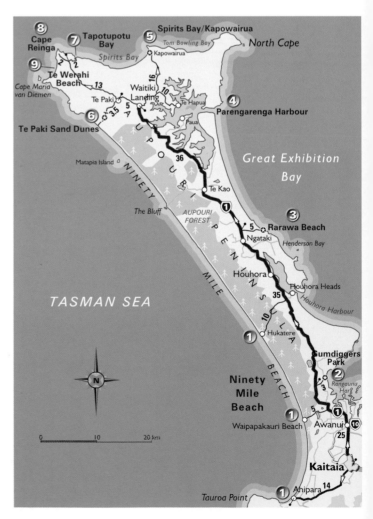

oystercatchers. Very little development has taken place along the shoreline — the only significant settlement is Ahipara at the very southern end, protected from the westerly winds by Tauroa/Reef Point. Vehicles frequently use the beach, though driving safely on sand does require experience.

2 Gumdiggers Park
Located 25 km north of Kaitaia at 171 Heath Road; signposted from SH 1.
While an old gum field may not appear to have immediate appeal for those seeking a natural environment, there is a fascinating story to be literally uncovered at Gumdiggers Park. Underlying the park are not one, but two ancient kauri forests. The deeper trees date back 150,000 years and belong to a forest that may have declined owing to climate change. The second forest, 45,000 years old, is much different. The felled trees lie in the same direction and appear to have fallen all at one time, leading to the theory that they were subjected to a more severe event such as a tsunami. The trees in this park are said to be the oldest preserved timber in the world. In addition to the old gum workings, Gumdiggers Park breeds the unique Northland green gecko (*Naultinus grayii*), which can be viewed in the Gecko House (ph (09) 406 7166, www.gumdiggerspark.co.nz; entry fee applies).

3 Rarawa Beach
Travel north for 35 km on SH 1, which will bring you 15 km north of Houhora. One km north of Ngataki turn into Rarawa Beach Road and follow the gravel road 5 km to the beach.
Empty, unspoilt and untouched, the sands of Rarawa Beach contain a high proportion of silica creating a bright sparkling expanse that will have you reaching for your sunglasses. Lapped by an azure sea and backed by dunes, the beach is protected by small rocky headlands to the north and south. Just to the south of Rarawa is Henderson Bay, another pristine beach, popular with surfers. However, instead of white sand, the sand here is golden despite the two beaches being only a few kilometres apart. Both beaches are popular with shell collectors, and while neither has any facilities there is a DoC camping ground at Rarawa.

4 Parengarenga Harbour
Travel north for 36 km to Waitiki Landing and turn off SH 1 on to the Te Hapua Road. Te Hapua is 10 km from Waitiki Landing on a slow gravel road. (Access to Parengarenga Harbour is very limited, with the only roads at Te Hapua and Paua.)
Located at the northern end of Great Exhibition Bay and protected by the hills of the Aupouri Peninsula to the north, this is one of New Zealand's biggest harbours. Largely tidal and shallow, huge volumes of water shift through the sandy entrance each day, creating a landscape of deep channels, vast sandbanks, long tidal creeks and scrub-covered headlands. The outstanding feature is the vivid white silica sand, especially noticeable on the Kokota sandspit, which protects the harbour from the open sea.

The tidal nature of the harbour and the extensive mangrove forests make Parengarenga an important habitat for shore birds. Migratory waders in their tens of thousands arrive each summer to feed on the rich seabed pickings. The harbour is the first landfall on the southward migration of the godwits, and in autumn enormous flocks gather before flying north to Siberia and Alaska.

5 Spirits Bay/Kapowairua
From Waitiki Landing on SH 1, turn into Te Hapua Road and then into Spirits Landing Road. The distance is 16 km and the roads are gravel.
A wide 10-km sweep of pinkish sand beach and sparkling clear waters, Spirits Bay is flanked to the east by North Cape and the Surville Cliffs. Low vegetation covers the dunes behind the beach and protects the extensive wetlands, which are home to the elusive fernbird. Shore birds are common along the length of the beach and include Caspian terns, oystercatchers, New Zealand dotterels and godwits in the summer months. There is a camping ground at Pandora at the western end.

6 Te Paki Sand Dunes
Turn off Cape Reinga Road (SH 1) at Te Paki, 5 km north of Waitiki Landing, and on to Te Paki Stream Road.
It is here, at its northern end, that the sand dunes of Ninety Mile Beach are at their most extensive and most impressive. Covering an area of approximately 7 sq km and rising to a height of 150 metres, the sandhills are a gentle golden colour, with the occasional native grasses, spinifex and sand pimelea threading across the bare sand. The area is home to one of New Zealand's rarest plants, Bartlett's rata (only discovered in 1975), and to the endangered flax snail.

The most accessible point is via the Te Paki Stream, a shallow creek winding through the dunes. Unfortunately, this is

Te Paki Stream and sand dunes.

also the favourite access for tour buses and four-wheel-drive vehicles that travel fast along the stream and are not so considerate of those on foot. It is also popular as a place to sand-surf.

7 Tapotupotu Bay

The bay can be reached either on foot from the car park by the lighthouse (one hour, one way) or via a steep road just before Cape Reinga.
In contrast to the more exposed Te Werahi Beach to the west, Tapotupotu is a small northerly-facing bay just below the cape. In addition to a beautiful sandy beach, the bay has a popular camping ground. However, care needs to be taken when swimming as occasionally the bay is subject to heavy northeasterly swells.

8 Cape Reinga

Cape Reinga is at the very end of SH 1, 15 km from Te Paki. The last 18 km of the road is gravel and hilly, although there are plans to seal it in the near future.
Wild and wonderful, the cape is the tumultuous meeting of the Pacific Ocean and the Tasman Sea, an area of swift currents, battering waves and howling winds. While Cape Reinga is often

Mangroves
Although mangroves grow as far south as Ohiwa Harbour near Opotiki on the east coast and Kawhia on the west, it is here in the warm north that they attain their maximum height of around 10 metres. Northland has some of the most impressive mangrove forest in the country, particularly in large harbours at Parengarenga, Hokianga, Kaipara and Whangapoua, as well as along the numerous tidal rivers in the north.

described as the most northerly point of the North Island, Surville Cliffs to the east is in fact further north, but is part of a scientific reserve and inaccessible. Part of the Aupouri Peninsula, these volcanic hills rise to over 300 metres and were once an ancient island. At one time the cape was covered in dense native forest. These days, the bush is slowly regenerating and the surrounding area is well known for its varied flowering forms of manuka and kanuka. A short walk leads down to the lighthouse with marvellous views along the coast, both to the south and to the east.

9 Te Werahi Beach

Accessible by a good track from the Cape Reinga car park.
While the tour buses and tourists flock to the cape, this beach is less than a 45-minute walk away and is often deserted. The walk to Te Werahi skirts massive sea cliffs that are the most impressive in the area. At the far southern end of the beach is Cape Maria van Diemen and just offshore is Motuopao Island, an important breeding ground for white-faced storm petrels, fairy prions and black-winged petrels.

Cape Reinga and lighthouse.

3 Bay of Islands, Whangarei and the Tutukaka Coast

Volcanic peaks • Kauri forests • Poor Knights Islands • Outstanding coastal scenery • Beaches • 195 km

From quiet bays to spectacular volcanic peaks and magical islands, this coastal trip encompasses the stunning Bay of Islands, dramatic Whangarei Heads, delightful sandy coves and unique offshore islands.

INFORMATION

Bay of Islands i-SITE, The Wharf,
Marsden Road, Paihia,
ph (09) 402 7314
Destination Northland, corner
Williams and Selwyn Roads, Paihia,
ph (09) 402 7683
Department of Conservation,
Bay of Islands Maritime and
Historic Park Visitor Centre,
The Strand, Russell,
ph (09) 403 7685
Whangarei i-SITE, Tarewa Park,
92 Otaika Road (SH 1),
Whangarei,
ph (09) 438 1079

Getting there

The main route begins at Whangarei, Northland's largest centre, and finishes at Paihia with side trips from both locations. The roads throughout are sealed and in excellent condition.

Best time to visit

The Northland climate is pretty equable all year round, although inland Northland can get frosty at times in winter and the coast is open to wet, cool easterly weather even in summer. However, when the weather is right, Northland is just stunning. The peak of the tourist season is January and February when things can get hectic, but even then it's not too hard to get away from the crowds.

Facilities

Whangarei has plenty of accommodation, extensive shopping, good cafés and facilities that would be expected of a city of around 74,000 people. Paihia is one of New Zealand's most popular tourist destinations and as such has a wide range of accommodation, places to eat,

banks and shopping. Nearby Kerikeri also offers a good choice of places to stay or eat, though is less frenetic than touristy Paihia. Both Whangarei Heads and the Tutukaka Coast have limited accommodation that is often booked out through mid-December to early February.

1 Mt Manaia

From Whangarei take Riverside Drive out towards the Whangarei Heads; Mt Manaia is 30 km from the city.
Easily recognised by the numerous volcanic outcrops that define the peak, Mt Manaia rises on part of a massive volcano that erupted around 20 million years ago. Other remaining sections of this ancient volcano are Bream Head, Mt Lion and the Hen and Chicken Islands.

At 420 metres the views in all directions are spectacular and the bush cloaking the mountain is home to kaka that have established themselves from Little Barrier Island to the east. The track to the top is a steady rather than steep climb and takes around two hours return.

2 Whangarei Heads/Bream Head

Bream Head is 10 km from Mt Manaia.
Whangarei Heads is the general name given to the steep hills from Busby Head to Bream Head at the entrance to Whangarei Harbour. An area of outstanding coastal beauty with sand beaches and dense bush, the rugged peaks rise to 476 metres at Bream Head. The Bream Head Scenic Reserve is the

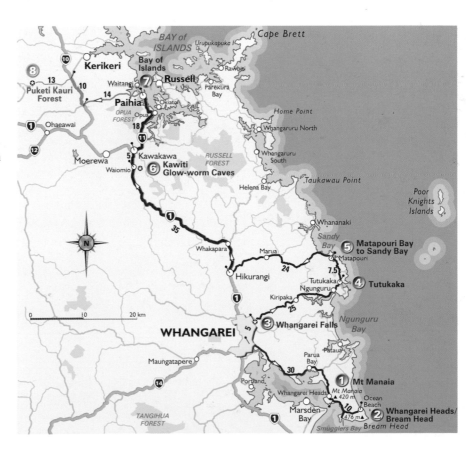

largest remaining area of coastal forest in Northland and contains rare flora and fauna including kiwi, Northern kaka and red-crowned kakariki.

On the eastern side of the heads is Smugglers Bay, a beautiful white sandy cove, overhung with pohutukawa and just a 20-minute walk from Urquharts Bay. A track from Smugglers Bay follows the ridge over Mt Lion, down to Peach Cove and then over the rocky peak of Bream Head, down to the magnificent sweep of Ocean Beach. While this track is quite demanding, shorter tracks lead directly to Peach Cove and Bream Head. On a good day, the coastal views from the top of Bream Head are nothing short of extraordinary.

3 Whangarei Falls
Accessed from Kiripaka Road, Tikipunga, 5 km from the city centre on the road to Ngunguru.
An impressive waterfall by any standard, few cities big or small can boast such an attractive natural feature within the city boundaries. Here at the Whangarei Falls the Hatea River drops 25 metres into an attractive bush-lined valley, and the pools above and below the falls are ideal for swimming. There is also an extensive picnic ground at the top of the falls.

4 Tutukaka
Tutukaka is 25 km from the Whangarei Falls via Ngunguru.
A small sheltered harbour, Tutukaka is the main centre for trips to the Poor Knights Islands, 30 km to the north. The remnants of old volcanoes, these islands lie in an area where warm subtropical currents converge with cooler water giving rising to some extraordinary sea life. Numerous operators based in Tutukaka offer trips catering for both the amateur snorkeller and the experienced diver.

5 Matapouri Bay to Sandy Bay
Matapouri is 7 km north of Tutukaka and Sandy Bay is 4.5 km north of Matapouri.
A number of beautiful sandy bays, beginning with the sheltered Matapouri Bay, are to be found north of Tutukaka. A wide curve of beach shaped like a horseshoe, Matapouri is protected from the rough swells of the open ocean by rocky headlands. Just 2 km north of

Whale Bay, Tutukaka Coast.

Matapouri, and a 20-minute walk from the road through nikau palms and puriri trees, is the small cove of Whale Bay, north-facing and overhung with old pohutukawa that are covered in vivid red flowers around Christmas time. Just 1 km on is the open stretch of Woolleys Bay, and Sandy Bay another 1.5 km further north. Bisected by a small stream, Sandy Bay is marked by rocky headlands at either end of the beach and has a reputation for good surf in an easterly swell. Matapouri has a small settlement of beach houses and a shop, while the other bays are less developed and only have toilet facilities.

6 Kawiti Glow-worm Caves
From Sandy Bay drive back 24 km to SH 1 at Hikurangi and then north for 35 km to the Kawiti Caves at Waiomio.
Over 200 metres in length, 12 metres wide and up to 20 metres at their highest point, the Kawiti Caves feature delicate stalactites and stalagmites and clusters of glow-worms. Set in a limestone valley, the caves are surrounded by sculptured cliffs, huge boulders, caverns and rock pillars. Entrance to the caves is by guided tour only and includes a short bush walk. (Open daily 9 am to 5 pm, ph (09) 404 0583 or (09) 404 1256; entry fee applies.)

7 Bay of Islands

From Kawiti Caves continue north on SH 1 for 5 km, then turn right on to SH 11 and continue 18 km north to Paihia.

Like much of Northland, the Bay of Islands is volcanic in origin dating back over 2 million years, though the most recent eruptions were less than 2000 years ago. Eroded over time and flooded by a rising sea, the bay today is dotted with over 140 islands, mostly small and uninhabited, and protected as the Bay of Islands Maritime and Historic Park. The deep sheltered waters support a flourishing marine life with schools of kahawai, huge marlin, dolphins and blue penguins. The bay is sheltered from the southeast by the long Cape Brett Peninsula, at the end of which is the famous Piercy/Motukokako Island with its 'Hole in the Rock' large enough for small vessels to pass through. For the more energetic there is the Cape Brett Walkway, a 16-km track from Rawhiti to the cape. Walks can be guided or independent, and boat transport can be arranged for those just wanting to walk one way (www.capebrettwalks.co.nz).

Urupukapuka is a small island in the heart of the bay with sheltered sandy beaches and easy walking tracks through the bush and just a short ferry ride from Paihia. Just north of the town the Waitangi River forms a wide estuary below the Haruru Falls, and is lined with a dense mangrove forest. A long boardwalk snakes through the old mangroves with their distinctive white and grey bark and tough leathery leaves. Below the boardwalk the mud is thick with the trees' aerial roots providing a perfect hideaway nursery for young fish.

While the Bay of Islands is a popular tourist destination and is now developing a somewhat intrusive 'adventure' industry, it is still a beautiful bay and it is not so hard to get away from the bus tour throngs.

Poor Knights Islands

The Poor Knights Islands, like the nearby Mokohinau and Hen and Chickens Islands, are the remains of ancient rhyolite volcanoes that erupted around 4 million years ago. The islands rise 240 metres from the seabed and feature underwater cliffs that drop 100 metres, arches and sea caves. The group comprises two main islands, Tawhiti Rahi and Aorangi, neither of them large, along with a number of islets and rock stacks. While the original vegetation was largely destroyed during Maori occupation, the Poor Knights were set aside as a reserve in 1922 and have been fully protected since 1975. Since then the flora has significantly recovered and the forest today is made up of pohutukawa, ngaio and karaka. It is also the home of the Poor Knights lily, a plant found only on this island group and on nearby Hen Island, and is noted for its superb red bottlebrush-type flowers and hardy strap-like leaves. In addition, the islands are home to nine species of petrels and are the only breeding ground of the two million Buller's shearwaters. On land, tuatara flourish, along with five species of skink and two species of gecko, including Duvaucel's gecko (*Hoplodactylus duvaucelii*), New Zealand's largest gecko.

However, it is the waters surrounding the islands that make the Poor Knights particularly famous and they were once described by French explorer Jacques Cousteau as being one of the top ten dive sites in the world. Protected as a marine reserve since 1998, the islands lie in the path of the warm East Auckland Current, which attracts unique and diverse marine life not normally found this far south. Stingray, tropical groper, perch, snapper, moray eel, blue maomao, colourful nudibranchs as well as bright corals are all found within reach of an easy dive.

Ohututea Bay, Cape Brett.

GOT TIME? (+37 KM)
8 Puketi Kauri Forest

From Paihia take the Haruru Falls Road 14 km to SH 10. Turn north and travel for 10 km and turn left into Puketi Road. The forest is 13 km down this road, part of which is gravel and narrow.

The Puketi State Forest together with the Omahuta Forest and the Manginangina Scenic Reserve form a 20,000-hectare kauri forest that is home to kiwi, tomtit/miromiro, kaka and Northland's largest population of the rare kokako. While other forests contain bigger trees, Puketi gives the visitor a feel of the great kauri forests of the past. There are a number of tracks that range from all-day treks to the 20-minute Manginangina Kauri Walk. This short boardwalk loops through huge mature trees and allows the visitor to get up close and truly appreciate this iconic New Zealand conifer. The boardwalk is suitable for wheelchairs, and this forest is a good option if a trip to the kauri forests on the opposite coast isn't part of the itinerary.

4 North of Auckland • Auckland to Whangarei

Long empty beaches • Goat Island Marine Reserve • Limestone caves • 220 km

While close to Auckland, this region has many uncrowded beaches, fine areas of native bush, one of the country's best marine reserves and magnificent coastal scenery.

INFORMATION

Warkworth i-SITE, 1 Baxter Street,
Warkworth, ph (09) 425 9081
Whangarei i-SITE, Tarewa Park,
92 Otaika Road (SH 1), Whangarei,
ph (09) 438 1079
Auckland i-SITE, Atrium, SKYCITY
Auckland, corner Victoria and
Federal Streets, Auckland,
ph (09) 363 7182; 137 Quay
Street, Princes Wharf, Downtown
Auckland, ph (09) 307 0612
Orewa i-SITE, 214a Hibiscus Coast
Highway, Orewa, ph (09) 426 0076

Getting there

This trip starts in Auckland and winds around the coast to Whangarei. Most of the roads are good, although from Leigh to Mangawhai Heads some stretches have gravel surfaces and are winding.

Best time to visit

Many of these places are within a comfortable day trip from Auckland so can be enjoyed all year round or combined with a visit to the wine-growing region around Matakana. The summer months from November to April are the best time if you are after a beach trip, though traffic in and out of Auckland on weekends and during the holidays can be a grind. Goat Island is a relatively small yet very popular marine reserve and is best visited during the week to avoid the crowds.

Facilities

Naturally, Auckland has all the facilities befitting a city of one million-plus people, but along with the population comes traffic problems. As an alternative, Warkworth is a pretty town 45 minutes north of Auckland; it possesses plentiful cafés and good accommodation, and lies within easy reach of all the places described. Equally, Whangarei to the north is a good base — accommodation is not as expensive as in Auckland and with a population of some 74,000 it has banks and a good range of shops as well as some excellent eateries.

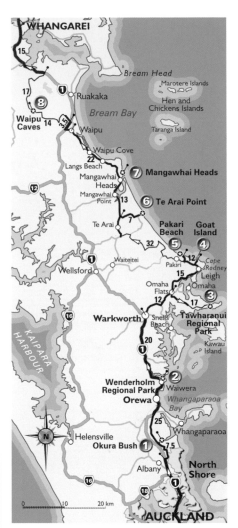

Okura Bush.

1 Okura Bush

Situated 18 km north of Auckland. From the motorway (SH 1) take the Oteha Valley Road exit to East Coast Bays Road and drive north for 7.5 km, then turn right into Haigh Access Road and park at the end of the road where the track begins.

Okura Bush is a mix of fine mature forest that somehow escaped the miller's axe, regenerating kauri and tidal estuary. From the car park a good track passes over a small creek and into a dense stand of mature puriri. This handsome native tree has glossy leaves and a broad spreading habit, though the trunk is usually short and often full of hollows and is host to the native puriri moth. Puriri is unusual in that it flowers and fruits all year round and the attractive small purple-red flowers often carpet the forest floor beneath the tree. Beyond the grove the forest is regenerating, with young kauri along the drier ridges and nikau and kiekie in the damp gullies. The bush borders the small Okura River, and the tidal flats and shell banks are home to numerous wading birds including oystercatchers, stilts and plovers.

2 Wenderholm Regional Park

From Auckland drive north on SH 1 for 46 km. The entrance to the park is 1 km north of Waiwera.

Wenderholm (meaning 'winter home' in Swedish) is a fine stretch of sandy beach at the mouth of the Puhoi River. The beach itself is backed by magnificent old pohutukawa trees and sheltered by a bush-covered headland that overlooks the Waiwera River just to the south. Both rivers are very tidal and their banks are lined with mangroves, home to multitudes of small fish and birds including the rare fernbird and banded rail. The Puhoi River

is particularly popular with kayakers and this is an excellent way to experience the mangrove forest and the diverse life it shelters. On the headland the small but fine stand of native bush is alive with native birds following extensive predator control. A short walk of less than an hour not only offers the chance to see fantail, robin, kereru and tui, but also provides magnificent views out over the islands of the Hauraki Gulf. There is also every chance of seeing — or at least hearing — the raucous kookaburra that have established a small colony in the area.

3 Tawharanui Regional Park

From Wenderholm drive north 20 km on SH 1 to Warkworth and follow the signs to Leigh for 12 km. Turn right at the sign for Tawharanui and from there it is 17 km to the regional park, the last five of which are unsealed, winding and narrow.

This park occupying 600 hectares of the Tawharanui Peninsula largely comprises rolling open farmland and bushy gullies. Now protected by a predator-proof fence, the park is a haven for both bush and shore birds, including the rare New Zealand dotterel which nests in dunes behind

Wenderholm Regional Park.

beautiful Anchor Bay, while offshore the Tawharanui Marine Park protects the sea life below the waves. With easy walking on good tracks, the views of the Hauraki Gulf are magnificent and panoramic, with Little Barrier looming to the north and wooded Kawau Island just to the south. While the flora is mainly regenerating bush, the rare prostrate manuka flourishes at Tokatu Point at the end of the peninsula. The rolling hills make for easy walking — the longest walk will take two hours and shorter walks under one hour — and the beaches are safe for swimming.

Tawharanui Regional Park, looking out to Little Barrier Island.

Goat Island Marine Reserve.

4 Goat Island

From the Tawharanui turnoff head east toward Leigh and then turn left following the signposts to Goat Island, a total distance of 15 km.
Established in 1975, Goat Island was New Zealand's first marine reserve, and the rapid return of abundant sea life led to the establishment of numerous such reserves all around the country. The centre of the reserve is tiny Goat Island and the narrow channel between the island and the beach teems with marine life including huge snapper, giant crayfish and schools of the dramatic blue maomao. The channel and the rocky shores of the island are safe for swimming and snorkelling, although the water can get rough and murky in easterly weather. This is a very popular spot over summer and can get crowded on the weekends. Snorkelling equipment is available for hire locally.

5 Pakiri Beach

From Goat Island continue north for 12 km over a steep range to Pakiri Beach. Although sealed the road is narrow and winding.
Pakiri Beach is a long sweep of golden sand sheltered from the south and west by bush-covered Mt Tamahunga. A tidal estuary winds through wetland at the southern end of the beach, which is the only access point to the 9 km of shoreline stretching north to Te Arai Point. The often deserted beach is popular for surfing and horse riding.

6 Te Arai Point

From Pakiri Beach head north towards Mangawhai Heads. Te Arai Point is 39 km from Pakiri.

From Pakiri Beach to Mangawhai Heads is a long sweep of undeveloped beach broken only at the rocky outcrop of Te Arai Point. This headland attracts shore birds and is now a reserve, with native bush making a slow comeback through the rank grass. From the point there are magnificent views along both beaches, north and south, and out to the islands of the northern reaches of the Hauraki Gulf. A short walk over the headland to the shore passes through a small wetland. Relatively isolated, Te Arai Point attracts few visitors and the roads in the area are gravel and winding though in good condition.

7 Mangawhai Heads

From Te Arai Point continue north for 20 km to Mangawhai Heads.
Forming a broad shallow estuary, the tidal Mangawhai River empties sluggishly into the ocean below a high bluff and is protected from the open sea by a long sandspit. The dunes of the spit are now conservation land — the 245-hectare Mangawhai Wildlife Refuge — and together with the estuary attract numerous shore birds including Caspian and fairy terns, oystercatchers and New Zealand dotterel. The fairy tern, a subspecies of the Australian fairy tern, is one of New Zealand's most endangered birds with fewer than 10 breeding pairs in existence (in 1984 only three pairs remained) and they only breed at Mangawhai, Pakiri, Waipu and Papakanui. The vegetation on the spit consists mainly of spinifex and pingao.

North of the river is the Mangawhai Heads, rising to 167 metres and noted for massive pohutukawa trees and pockets of native bush. A new loop track climbing steadily along the heads affords spectacular coastal views and takes around two and a half hours return.

8 Waipu Caves

Continue north along the coast for 22 km from Mangawhai Heads to Waipu township via Langs Beach and Waipu Cove. From Waipu rejoin SH 1 and drive 3.5 km north and turn left and follow this road for 17 km to the caves. The last 5 km of the road is unsealed and narrow. From the caves it is a further 14 km to rejoin SH 1 and 15 km north to

Whangarei. From Waipu to Whangarei is 35 km via SH 1.
This cave system within a karst/limestone terrain is just a short five-minute walk from the road and features limestone formations, stalactites and stalagmites, and clusters of glow-worms deep within. Karst landscapes are common in New Zealand and are the result of water erosion creating caves, limestone bluffs, arches and sinkholes. A torch is essential as the caves are deep enough to be quite dark and it is necessary to wade through shallow water to see the glow-worms, which are about 100 metres to the left from the entrance.

Blue Maomao
At Goat Island one of the most striking fish to be found in abundance is the blue maomao (*Scorpis aequipinnis*). Growing an average of 30 cm long and living up to 15 years, the fish are easily recognised by their uniform bright blue colour. When gathering in shoals, they make a spectacular sight as they slice through the water in a moving cloud of vivid blue. Found in shallow waters along rocky coast where they feed off plankton, blue maomao are common in the waters around the northern half of the North Island, though are occasionally found as far south as the Cook Strait. They are also common off the eastern coast of Australia, where they are known as the hardbelly. A close relation, *Scorpis violaceous*, is a darker, duller blue colour and is often found in association with blue maomao. Both are commonly referred to as maomao.

5 Waitakere Ranges, West Auckland

Wild surf • Black sand beaches • Lush bush • Gannet colony • Excellent walks • 145 km

The Waitakere Ranges are a natural treasure right on the back doorstep of Auckland. A multitude of tracks laces the dense bush, and raging surf lashes the coast against a magnificent backdrop of black volcanic sand and steep cliffs.

> **INFORMATION**
> Arataki Visitor Centre, Scenic Drive (5 km from Titirangi on the road to Piha), ph (09) 817 0089

Getting there

The Waitakere Ranges are an easy drive from downtown Auckland. This trip starts in the north off SH 16, but most of the places described are easily accessible from various points in West Auckland. The roads are mostly sealed and in good condition, but this is steep and rugged country and many of the routes are slow, winding and narrow. Watch out for speedsters on the road to Piha.

Best time to visit

Any time of the year this area is worth checking out. Summer is a great beach time, but even in winter a stroll along an empty shore with a cool wind blowing and the surf roaring is the perfect tonic. In fact, during stormy weather this coast is at its most dramatic. There are tracks to suit every age and fitness level, though keep in mind that this is wet muddy country even in summer. The landscape is rugged, with deep valleys, dense bush and sudden cliffs and people do get lost walking in here, despite the close proximity to the city.

Facilities

Most people travel to the 'Waitaks' as a day trip so there are surprisingly few facilities in the area. There are camping grounds at Whatipu, Piha and Muriwai, but very little other accommodation, although there are always beach houses to rent. Likewise, there are few cafés and only general stores at Piha and Muriwai. For those interested in learning more about the history of the Waitakere Ranges, the Arataki Visitor Centre on Scenic Drive has excellent displays and information, including up-to-date track details.

1 Muriwai Gannet Colony

The colony is at the end of Motutara Road at Muriwai, 10 km from Waimauku on SH 16.
Related to shags and pelicans, gannets are a very elegant seabird with beautiful white and yellow colouring and a streamlined shape, perfect for diving into water from a height in order to catch fish. Just one species breeds in New Zealand, *Morus serrator*, and the 30 breeding colonies are scattered around the country, mainly on offshore islands.

Early in the twentieth century gannets began establishing nesting sites on Oaia Island and Motutara Island, just off Muriwai Beach. In 1979 they established themselves on Otakamiro Point on the mainland. Now, each year from August to April, more than 1200 pairs nest here, the proximity of the nesting birds giving the public easy and close access. The view point, just a short walk from the car park above the beach, is directly above the colony and is a perfect spot to watch the birds land or launch themselves from the sheer cliff. The best time to see the chicks is November and December.

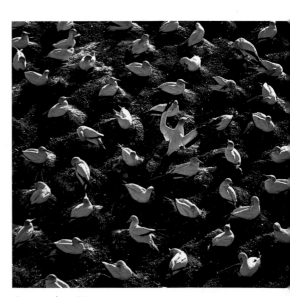

Gannet colony, Muriwai.

2 Lake Waimanu

From Muriwai return to Waimauku and head south on SH 16 to Kumeu for 6 km, turning right into Waitakere Road. Continue for 8.5 km to Waitakere and then turn right into Bethells Beach (Te Henga) Road for a further 12 km. The track to the lake is just over the bridge 1 km before the beach.

The Waimanu Stream has been blocked by massive dunes from sand driven up from Bethells Beach by the relentless westerly winds. Behind the dunes, which are completely devoid of vegetation, is a small but deep lake that is an ideal swimming spot. The eastern edge of the dunes is being constantly eroded by the Waimanu Stream creating steep sandhills up to 30 metres high. Children and the young at heart will have great fun sliding down the steep dunes along this stream.

3 Cascade Kauri Park — City of Auckland Walk

From Bethells Beach return up Te Henga Road for 6 km. Turn right into Falls Road and head through the golf course to the car park.

At Cascade Kauri Park the Waitakere Stream flows gently through jungle-like vegetation, thick with ferns and nikau palms. On the ridges above the stream are flourishing stands of kauri including two giant specimens that somehow survived early milling of the area. Keep an eye out for sulphur-crested cockatoos that have established a colony high on the ridge opposite the car park, although you are likely to hear these raucous birds before you see them.

The loop track follows the stream and winds past the large kauri trees and takes less than an hour. The Cascade waterfall is hidden from view in a rock cleft and is disappointing. Cascade Kauri is part of the Waitakere Regional Park, a huge conservation area covering 16,000 hectares of West Auckland's Waitakere Ranges.

4 Fairy Falls

From Cascade Kauri return to Te Henga Road and turn right and continue 1.5 km to Scenic Drive. At Scenic Drive turn right and drive 6 km to the Fairy Falls on your left. The car parking is on the right opposite the beginning of the track.

Set in very attractive bush with large kauri and rimu along the way, these falls are particularly pleasing. The falls themselves begin as a series of cascades before a final 15-metre drop into the pool below. Stoney Creek, which feeds the falls, is a dense jungle of kiekie, supplejack and nikau.

The track to the top of the falls is excellent, but to reach the bottom is a bit of a scramble down steep steps, uneven ground and wet rocks, and good footwear is necessary.

5 Piha

From Fairy Falls drive 5 km to the intersection of Scenic Drive and the Piha Road and turn right (this is a tight intersection so take care). Continue directly along the 19.5 km to Piha.

Piha is a wild stretch of black sand constantly pounded by rolling surf off the Tasman Sea. Behind the beach the land climbs steeply with deep bush-clad valleys and vegetation shaped by strong salt-laden westerly winds. Dividing the beach is the iconic Lion Rock with tough flax and coprosma clinging tenuously to its crumbling cliffs. The area is noted for its attractive bush and coastal walks including Kitekite Falls (one hour return), Tasman Lookout (30 minutes return), and Nikau Grove (20 minutes return). To the north of Piha and reached only by foot is rugged Whites Beach (45 minutes one way) and north of that again is lonely Anawhata Beach.

6 Te Ahua Point

From Piha return back to the top of the hill (2 km) and turn right into Te Ahuahu/Log Race Road and park at the very end.

Situated between Karekare and Piha Beaches, Te Ahua Point is a superb lookout atop volcanic cliffs that drop hundreds of metres into a turbulent sea. The view south along the coast is to the dangerous bar that marks the entrance to the Manukau Harbour. Jutting out to sea even farther to the south is

Muriwai Beach, looking north.

Mt Kariori near Raglan, while to the north is Piha Beach and the Muriwai coast.

The track across the point is well formed and well marked, though this area is exposed to strong westerly winds. For those wanting a longer walk the track continues downhill to Karekare Beach.

7 Karekare Beach

From Te Ahuahu Road drive 2.5 km back along the Piha Road and then turn right into Karekare Road and continue 3 km to Karekare Beach. This road is sealed but very steep and narrow so take extreme care.

Karekare is more wild and dramatic than Piha and considerably less developed with just a handful of holiday houses huddling from the westerly wind in the bush. Featured as a setting for the film *The Piano*, steep cliffs drop into the sea at the northern end of the beach while to the south black sand stretches all the way to Whatipu on the Manukau Harbour. A grove of old pohutukawa trees in a hollow in the dunes behind the beach is an ideal picnic spot. A track links Karekare to Te Ahua Point to the north (one hour one way) and another track follows the cliffs south to Whatipu (three hours one way).

8 Whatipu

Return along the Piha Road back to Scenic Drive and continue 10 km to Titirangi. At the Titirangi roundabout turn right into Huia Road and continue 18 km to Huia. Beyond Huia skirt the shore and take the Whatipu Road to the very end. This last section is 10 km of winding, narrow, gravel road.

Windswept and wild and pummelled by the thundering seas of the Manukau Bar, Whatipu on the south head of the Manukau Harbour is a wonderful coastal landscape of dune and rock. Over the past century the shoreline has changed dramatically with powerful westerly storms and savage tides moving huge amounts of sand from season to season. Even on a moderately good day, surf pounds the shoreline (swimming is not recommended!), and salt-laden winds whip up the black sand along this exposed section of coast.

A short walk along the base of the cliffs leads to several large sea caves and a small camping area. Shaped by years of wave action, the caves are now some distance from the sea as the marshy area beneath

Lion Rock at Piha.

the cliffs has built up since 1940. The wetland between the caves and the beach is now an important habitat for water birds. Do not try to cross the wetlands — aside from disturbing the birds, the vegetation is surprisingly dense and the water deeper than it looks, so return to the car park to get down to the beach.

Overlooking the bar are two islets, Ninepin Rock (the rock with the lighthouse) and Paratutae, the much larger island at the entrance to the harbour. Below Paratutae lie a few weathered beams, all that remains of the wharf from where kauri was formerly shipped in vast quantities to Onehunga. A tramline once ran from the wharf to Pararaha Valley to the north, though very little of the track now remains.

Nikau

The nikau (*Rhopalostylis sapida*) is New Zealand's only member of the palm family and the most southerly growing palm in the world. On the east coast nikau will grow as far south as Banks Peninsula and on the west to Greymouth. Growing to a height of over 12 metres, the palm is easily recognised by its upright fronds and distinctive trunk marked by scars from old fronds. Young nikau fronds have a more weeping habit than the mature tree. The heart of the palm at the base of the fronds is edible, and was known as the 'millionaire's

salad' as acquiring this food meant the destruction of the entire tree (not recommended!). The variations of nikau that occur on the Kermadec Islands and Little Barrier Island have longer and more weeping fronds. In suitable locations, nikau form dense groves and give the New Zealand bush a distinctly subtropical feel.

6 Hauraki Gulf Islands

Rangitoto • Little Barrier • Tiritiri Matangi • Great Barrier

The Hauraki Gulf is a broad stretch of water on the front porch of New Zealand's largest city and contains numerous islands varying in size from Great Barrier in the outer gulf through to tiny rocky outcrops. Many of the islands are close to the mainland and accessible, and several are havens for rare fauna and flora.

Takahe on Tiritiri Matangi Island.

1 Tiritiri Matangi

Getting there
360 Discovery runs ferries to the island from Auckland and Gulf Harbour. Sailings are such that you will need to plan to spend the best part of a day on the island. Winter and summer sailings may vary (ph 0800 360 3472, www.360discovery.co.nz).

Facilities
Bunkhouse accommodation is available on Tiritiri Matangi and bookings are through the Department of Conservation (ph (09) 425 7812, www.doc.govt.nz/tiritiribunkhouse). There is no food available on the island, though cold drinks and small gifts are for sale from a shop below the lighthouse. Toilet facilities are available in several places.

Tiritiri Matangi is both an inspirational conservation story and the country's most accessible island bird sanctuary, home to some of New Zealand's rarest species. Stripped of its native bush and farmed from 1850 to 1970, only a few coastal remnants remained on this small, relatively flat island of just 230 hectares. In a bold move, DoC embarked on a programme not only to replant the island, but also to develop it as an open sanctuary with easy public access. Equally importantly, it was decided to involve the public in tree planting, and there is hardly an Auckland schoolchild who wasn't involved in the massive operation to plant over a quarter of a million trees between 1984 and 1994.

The result has been an overwhelming success and led not only to a haven for endangered birds, but also to this island being used as a model for many other such reserves around the country. With predators removed and cover established, recovery of birdlife was spectacular and over 70 species have been sighted on the island of which 11 were relocated here. The birds include takahe, hihi, little spotted kiwi, brown teal, kokako, saddleback, bellbird and kakariki, many of which are very common on the island, especially around the bird-feeding stations. The takahe are so tame they will steal your lunch without hesitation!

The island is criss-crossed by a maze of tracks. The walk from the wharf to the lighthouse will take about 50 minutes return while a walk around the whole island can take up to three hours. The terrain is rolling, and none of the tracks are difficult. Recommended, and costing only a few dollars more, is the short guided walk from the wharf to the historic lighthouse given by the ranger when arriving on the island. Hobbs Bay, a five-minute walk from the wharf, is the best swimming beach.

2 Rangitoto Island

Getting there
Fullers runs a regular ferry to the island (ph (09) 367 9111, www.fullers.co.nz) but don't miss your ferry back, as there is no overnight accommodation and alternative transport to the mainland is expensive. Fullers also operates a limited service to adjacent Motutapu Island in the summer.

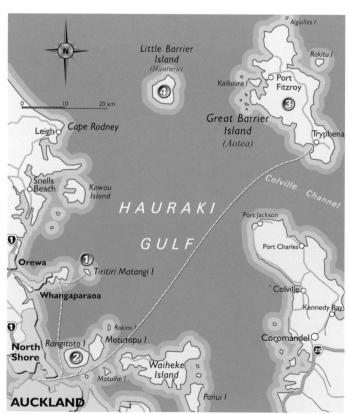

Te Awana Bay, Great Barrier Island.

Facilities

Rangitoto has no accommodation, cafés or shops, though there are toilets, water, information and a large shelter near the wharf. You will need to bring your own food and drink. McKenzie Bay on the western side of the island is a good sandy swimming beach. The tracks are excellent and none are too demanding. There is motorised transport to the top for those who find the walk too difficult.

The largest and youngest of Auckland's volcanoes, Rangitoto erupted from the sea about 600 to 700 years ago, and while opinions differ some scientists believe the volcano was last active as recently as 300 years ago. The island features unusual plant life adapted to the raw lava environment and in recent years has been cleared of exotic pests such as possums and the brush-tailed wallaby. Rangitoto is home to the largest pohutukawa forest in the world, the tough tree thriving on the island's dry and barren lava fields. Another fascinating plant is the kidney fern. Usually glossy, wet and extremely fragile-looking, this fern shrivels up like a dry leaf in very hot weather, returning to normal size

only when there is sufficient moisture. Rangitoto's rocky shore is a perfect habitat for the little blue penguin, the world's smallest penguin, and special viewing boxes enable visitors to take a close look at these aquatic birds. Colonies of black-backed gulls inhabit the shore near the wharf.

The crater and summit (259 metres) are actually covered in reasonably large trees as the original volcanic eruptions that created the cone occurred at very early stages of the island's formation and the last eruptions were much further down the western slope where plants are only slowly colonising these big scoria fields. It will take around an hour and a half of steady climbing to reach the top but the magnificent view over Auckland and the Hauraki Gulf is ample reward. A side track just below the summit (20 minutes return) leads to extensive lava caves. It is possible to scramble through the caves and a torch is useful.

Motutapu Island is in direct contrast to its near neighbour Rangitoto, from which it is separated by a mere few metres and connected by a man-made bridge. While Rangitoto is less than 700 years old and volcanic in origin, Motutapu is comprised of sedimentary rock dating back millions

of years. Currently the 1500-hectare island is undergoing intensive replanting and predator removal.

3 Great Barrier Island

> **INFORMATION**
> Information Centre,
> 67 Hector Sanderson Road, Claris,
> ph (09) 429 0767

Getting there

A number of airlines operate flights to the island (Great Barrier Airlines, ph (09) 275 9120, www.greatbarrierairlines.co.nz; Mountain Air, ph (09) 256 7026, www.mountainair.co.nz; and Island Air, ph 0800 54 55 55, www.islandair.co.nz) while ferries are operated by Fullers (ph (09) 367 9111, www.fullers.co.nz) and Sealink (ph (09) 300 5900, 0800 732 546, www.sealink.co.nz). Fullers operate passenger ferries that take two and a half hours one way and Sealink services are a combination of freight and passengers and take four and a half hours one way. Rental cars are available on the island, though the roads are mainly gravel and winding.

Facilities

The main settlement is Tryphena in the south of the island where the ferry terminal is located, and while there is no public transport, getting around is easily arranged with taxis and minibuses. The airport is at Claris in the middle of the island. The other main centre is Port Fitzroy, a deep harbour in the north, popular with visiting boaties. Accommodation is limited and bookings are essential over the key holiday period from mid-December to mid-January and on weekends. Likewise, there are few cafés and only general stores at each of the main centres.

The largest and most distant island of the gulf, Great Barrier, or Aotea, is believed to be the original landing point of the first Polynesian explorers, who named the new land Aotearoa, or land of the long white cloud, as from sea the first indication of land is long low cloud formations. Today the island is considered remote, but in early times when travel was by sea it was readily accessible, and it has a long history of both Maori and Pakeha occupation. While it is no untouched wilderness, having been ruthlessly stripped of its timber, today 60 per cent of the island is conservation land and fortunately it has never had goats, stoats, deer, hedgehogs or possums. A stronghold of several rare birds including the kaka, brown duck and New Zealand dotterel, Great Barrier is also home to several unique plants including the Great Barrier tea tree and daisy shrub.

On the eastern side of the island are several excellent wide sandy beaches including Medlands, Awana, Kaitoke and Whangapoua, while the west has deep bush-clad harbours. Kaitoke hot springs, a natural spring located in the fork of a stream, is a popular destination for a short walk, while the walk to Windy Canyon and Mt Hobson/Hirakimata takes around four hours return. Mt Hobson, the highest point on the island at 627 metres, is an old volcanic peak dating back 8 to 9 million years and the violent origin of the island is particularly evident from the dramatic outcrops, rocky bluffs and narrow ravine of Windy Canyon. From the summit the view of the gulf is exceptional, though be aware that the peak is often shrouded in mist and cloud. The top of this mountain is, unusually, the nesting ground of a rare seabird, the black petrel.

4 Little Barrier Island/Hauturu

Getting there

Access to Little Barrier is restricted, often booked out well in advance, and landing on the island is strictly by permit only. To apply for a permit to visit Little Barrier, phone the Department of Conservation (DoC) Warkworth Area Office on (09) 425 7812. There is also basic accommodation if you want to stay overnight.

Established as a wildlife reserve in 1895, this island has played a pivotal role in the preservation of some of New Zealand's most endangered species. The island is largely virgin bush, only a small portion of which has ever been cleared, and it is now completely predator free. The forest contains hard beech, a cooler-climate tree that usually occurs much further south, and the nikau palms are a subspecies with broader leaves than their mainland counterparts.

An old volcano, rising to 722 metres altitude, Little Barrier or Hauturu ('resting place of the wind') is home to over 300 plant species, birds extinct or close to extinction on the mainland (including saddleback, stitchbird, kaka, kakariki, kiwi, black petrel, brown teal, and kokako), 14 species of skink, gecko and tuatara, several species of weta, and both species of native bat.

Auckland Volcanoes

Auckland sits on an active volcanic hot spot or plume. Situated 100 km below the city, the temperatures are hot enough to melt rock and create an eruption at the surface. The field covers an area of 350 sq km and around 50 volcanic cones are scattered around the Auckland isthmus.

Geologically young, Auckland's volcanoes began erupting less than 100,000 years ago and 20 have erupted in the last 20,000 years. While most of the volcanic eruptions have been relatively small, Rangitoto Island, the youngest volcano and active just 600 years ago, was also the largest. The eruptions on average lasted only for a short time — anywhere between a few months to a few years. The nature of the volcanic field is such that, while existing volcanoes are unlikely to erupt again, there is every possibility of a new volcano emerging anywhere within the field.

Many of the volcanoes are easily recognisable, such as Mt Eden, One Tree Hill, Mt Victoria and Mt Mangere, while others are less obvious, water-filled craters such as Lake Pupuke, Orakei Basin and Panmure Basin. Lava flows have defined the shape of the city and some of Auckland's best-known streets — such as Karangahape Road, Ponsonby Road and Symonds Street — follow the line of old lava flows. Meola Reef, especially visible at low tide and extending well into the Waitemata Harbour, is an old flow from the eruption of Mt Albert.

Rangitoto.

7 The Firth of Thames and the Hunua Ranges

Godwits • Waterfalls • Coastal vistas • Beaches • 165 km

This largely coastal tour explores the highlights of the Firth of Thames including the world-renowned Miranda Shorebird Centre as well as the fringes of the rugged Hunua Ranges.

> **INFORMATION**
> Miranda Shorebird Centre,
> 283 East Coast Road, Miranda,
> ph (09) 232 2781

Getting there
The trip begins and ends at the southern motorway and skirts the Firth of Thames. The roads are all sealed, though winding and slow in places. Because SH 2 can be very busy on holiday weekends, many travellers use the coast road through Clevedon as an alternative route in to Auckland. The coastal traffic can also be heavy on warm summer weekends.

Best time to visit
If it is a beach experience you're after, then summer is the best time of year to make this trip, and bird life at Miranda is also at a peak during the warm months. However, the bush walks can be undertaken at any season, and if the day is a bit cold and wet, reward yourself with a soak at the Miranda Hot Springs. The climate is mild all year round, though the rainfall within the Hunuas is higher than in urban Auckland.

Facilities
On the fringe of Auckland, cafés, shops and accommodation are never far away. Clevedon has a number of good places to eat and the Kaiaua fish-and-chip shop is particularly famous. For a break, the hot pools at Miranda are a popular stop.

1 Duder Regional Park
From the southern motorway (SH 1) exit at Otara and follow East Tamaki Road, Ormiston Road and Sandstone Road for 11 km to Whitford. From Whitford continue for 12 km to Maraetai and follow the coast south to Umupuia Beach, a distance of 4 km. From the southern end of Umupuia Beach turn right into North Road and the entrance to the park is half a kilometre on the left.

Duder Regional Park occupies the Whakakaiwhara Peninsula and is almost entirely farmed with just a few tiny patches of bush. The main appeal of this park is the wonderful views from the trig over the Firth of Thames, the gulf islands of Waiheke, Ponui, Browns and Rangitoto, and the blue-tinged Coromandel hills to the east. The walk to the trig is not difficult and takes less than an hour.

2 Tawhitokino Bay
From Duder Park continue south for 11 km along North Road to Clevedon and then turn east on to the Clevedon–Kawakawa Bay Road for another 16 km. At Kawakawa Bay follow the coast road for 4 km to Waiti Bay to the car park at the very end. Accessible only at low tide, the track leaves from the rocks at the right of the beach.

This little-known bay is a real gem on the Firth of Thames coast, with a long sandy beach fringed by pohutukawa, kowhai and rewarewa, and can be pleasantly empty even on a hot summer's day. It is good for swimming in all tides and has an uninterrupted view of the Coromandel Peninsula. The track to the beach passes through the equally attractive Tuturau Bay, undulates through regenerating bush and

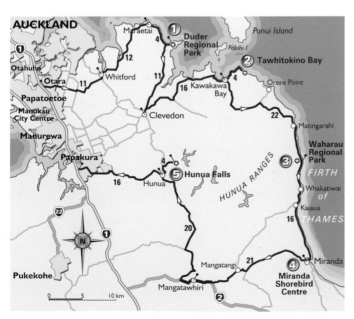

Duder Regional Park.

over rocky headlands, and takes around 45 minutes one way.

3 Waharau Regional Park

From Kawakawa Bay continue south for 22 km along the Kawakawa–Orere Road. Follow the East Coast Road to Waharau Regional Park.

This small, 170-hectare park at the foothills of the Hunua Ranges touches the coast at Waihihi Bay and is linked to the Whakatiwai Regional Park to the south. The park has several pleasant walks, with the longest loop walk (around three hours) leading to a ridge high above the Firth of Thames. The fine forest comprises mainly towai, tawa, kauri, beech, rewarewa and tanekaha. From this high point there are great views over the Firth of Thames, to the Hauraki Plains and the Coromandel and Kaimai Ranges beyond. The extensive tidal flats of Miranda spread out along the coast below.

4 Miranda Shorebird Centre

From Waharau head 16 km south.

Miranda on the coast of the Firth of Thames is recognised by the Ramsar Convention as a wetland of international significance. Each year thousands of birds from the Arctic tundra as well as New Zealand breeding shore birds converge on its rich tidal feeding grounds. These shallow flats are an extension of the broad Hauraki Plains and have been built up by silt from the Piako and Waihou Rivers to the east. At high tide the birds are found on the shell banks and at low tide out feeding on the mud flats.

Over 130 species have been recorded here, including 43 waders, and while there are wading birds all year round the large flocks (7000–10,000) of bar-tailed godwits arrive about September and stay through to March. Other regulars are wrybill, plover, New Zealand dotterel, variable oystercatcher, black-billed gull, pied stilt, curlew and sharp-tailed sandpiper, red-necked stint, eastern curlew, banded dotterel and ruddy turnstone.

A walk begins opposite the visitor centre, traversing salt marsh, shell banks and mangrove creeks, and flanking the huge tidal flats. The best time for bird-watching is two to three hours either side of high tide and a hide is available. Before setting out it is worth perusing the excellent information at the Miranda Shorebird Centre.

Tidal flats, Miranda.

Godwits

The bar-tailed godwit is an extraordinary bird. It makes the longest non-stop flight of any migratory bird, flying the 11,000 km from Alaska to New Zealand in less than a week. Departing in September, the birds time their flight to coincide with strong northerly storm winds and then continue over the open ocean south to these shores to feed during the southern summer. Up to 100,000 birds make the perilous journey, and while they are found all over the country, most favour the rich feeding grounds of the Firth of Thames, Kaipara Harbour, Farewell Spit and the Avon–Heathcote Estuary in Christchurch.

Godwits possess the unusual ability to reduce the size of their body organs by as much as 25 per cent in order to accommodate extra fat (up to 50 per cent of their body mass) in preparation for the flight, most of which is burnt off during the week-long haul. On arrival the birds immediately go to sleep, although a few hours later they begin feeding. In late March/early April they gather to prepare for the return north to breed, though unlike the flight south they take a different route through Australia and east Asia and wisely stop along the way. However, not all the birds leave, with around 10,000, mostly juveniles, wintering over in New Zealand.

5 Hunua Falls

From Miranda head west on the Miranda Road to SH 2, turn right and continue on 21 km to Mangatawhiri. Turn north on to McKenzie, Puparimu and Hunua Roads and drive 20 km to Hunua Village. One km north of Hunua turn right into White Road and after 1 km right again into Falls Road and the car park is a further 2 km. From Hunua it is 16 km back to the southern motorway at Papakura.

Especially impressive after heavy rain, the 28-metre Hunua Falls plunge over hard basalt rock, the rim of an ancient volcano. There is a good picnic ground here and the huge pool at the base of the falls is a popular swimming spot. Two short walks on either side of the pool lead to lookout points above. From the falls an easy three-hour walk leads to the Cossey Reservoir, through the Cossey Gorge passing along the way fine stands of tawa and a small grove of good-size kauri.

Covering 14,000 hectares, the Hunua Ranges are primarily a major water catchment area for Auckland City, but also preserve important native flora and fauna. Rising to a high point of 688 metres at Kohukohunui, the ranges are surprisingly rugged with dense bush, even though the area was milled in earlier times. Over 450 native plants have been recorded here and there are fine stands of rimu, kauri, matai, kahikatea and rata. Hochstetter's frog is found deep in the Hunuas, which are also

Flowering buttercups at Hunua Falls.

home to Auckland's only population of kokako. A 600-hectare area of the ranges has been intensely managed to control predators, and the kokako population has now risen from one pair in 1994 to 10. North Island robin, long extinct in the ranges, have been reintroduced to the kokako management area.

8 Coromandel Peninsula • Thames to Whitianga

Ancient pohutukawa trees • Bush walks • Sandy beaches • Marvellous coastal views • 190 km

Rugged volcanic hills are the backdrop to a beautiful pohutukawa-fringed coastline noted for its exceptional vistas and idyllic sandy beaches.

INFORMATION
Thames i-SITE, 206 Pollen Street, Thames, ph (07) 868 7284
Whitianga i-SITE, Albert Street, Whitianga, ph (07) 866 5555
Coromandel Information Centre, 355 Kapanga Road, Coromandel, ph (07) 866 8598
Kauaeranga Visitor Centre, Kauaeranga Valley, ph (07) 867 9080

Getting there

Thames is located at the base of the Coromandel Peninsula, an hour-and-a-half drive from Auckland City. While the main road is sealed, it is winding and slow, so allow plenty of time. Secondary roads are often gravel and occasionally challenging to negotiate.

Best time to visit

Summer is a magical time on the Coromandel Peninsula with flowering pohutukawa trees, shimmering blue seas and hot sandy beaches. It is a popular destination for both visitors and locals alike, and accommodation can be at a premium from mid-December to early February. The water on the east coast can be quite cool in early summer and the peninsula is exposed to wet and windy easterly storms from the tropics between December and March, and while these storms usually only last a few days they can dump an awful lot of rain precipitating flash flooding. If you're planning to go walking, the bush tracks can be muddy even in summer.

Facilities

Thames is the largest town with a good range of shopping, cafés and accommodation, as well as historic buildings from the gold-mining era, although its coast is very tidal and not especially appealing. Small settlements are scattered along the coastline, many with motels, backpackers, camping grounds and a general store. Whitianga at Buffalo Beach in Mercury Bay on the east coast is a bustling centre of 4000 with plenty of cafés, shops and a wide variety of services. Much of the accommodation is located right on the beach. Coromandel has a population of only 1500, and a reputation for good cafés and trendy shops, but accommodation is lean. There are DoC camping sites at Fletcher Bay, Kauaeranga Valley and Waikawau Bay.

1 Kauaeranga Valley

From just south of the Thames shopping centre turn into Kauaeranga Valley Road. The visitor centre is 14 km down this road, which for the most part is sealed.

Delving deep into the heart of the Coromandel hills behind Thames, the Kaueranga Valley has substantially recovered from intense timber-milling operations from 1871 through to 1928, and today bush has reclaimed much of the land. The old pack tracks and tramlines used to haul out logs now form part of the

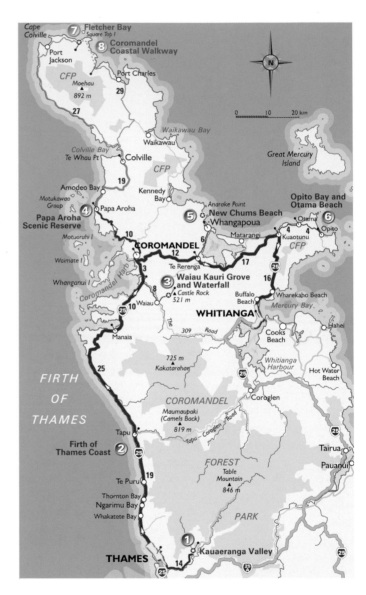

extensive track system. Through the heart of the valley runs the Kauaeranga River — clear, swift and boulder-strewn, it is both attractive and has some great swimming holes. A popular all-day tramp is to The Pinnacles, steep volcanic peaks that dominate the eastern skyline. Other much shorter tracks that take less than an hour fan out from the road, and the new visitor centre has information and photographs of both the natural and human history

View from the summit of The Pinnacles, Coromandel Ranges.

of the valley. Hoffman's Pool is a very appealing swimming hole and there are excellent views from Edward's Lookout (45 minutes return). There are also several attractive camping areas situated alongside the river.

2 Firth of Thames Coast

From Thames head north on SH 25 for 55 km to Coromandel township.

The road north from Thames hugs the coast for a distance of 45 km and is particularly famous for its gnarly old pohutukawa trees. Flourishing in the coastal climate, these ancient trees overhang the road and the water and in early summer the landscape is awash with broad swathes of bright crimson as they flower. The Firth of Thames coast is very shallow and most of the beaches along this stretch are tidal and not especially attractive. Also, the road is narrow and very slow in places, but plans to widen it have been fiercely opposed by locals who would rather save these magnificent trees than travel a bit faster.

3 Waiau Kauri Grove and Waterfall

Approximately 3 km south of Coromandel town turn into the 309 Road and the kauri grove is on the left 8 km from the turnoff. The road is narrow, winding and unsealed.

A small grove of massive old kauri which luckily escaped the miller's axe, this rare patch of mature forest is now accessible by an excellent short track. The boardwalk at one point entirely surrounds the trunk of a kauri so it is possible to touch and feel the texture of the bark. A short loop walk leads to an unusual double-trunk tree, which began life as two seedlings that eventually grew together and fused at the base. A short distance down the road is the diminutive but pretty Waiau Falls with a small pool and no more than a two-minute walk from the road.

4 Papa Aroha Scenic Reserve

Papa Aroha is 10 km north of Coromandel on the Colville Road. The entrance to the reserve is right by the entrance to the Papa Aroha camping ground.

Papa Aroha is a fine reserve of coastal bush especially noted for its pohutukawa, but also containing kohekohe and puriri. A short track leads down to a small beach overhung with trees and presenting great views across to Auckland and the Gulf.

5 New Chums Beach

From Coromandel continue east for 12 km on SH 25 over the ranges to Te Rerenga and then turn north and drive 6 km to Whangapoua.

New Chums Beach or Wainuiototo Bay is a long stretch of white sandy beach lapped by clear water and just a 20-minute walk from the northern end of Whangapoua. The beach is backed by handsome native bush including fine stands of nikau palm and is overhung with old pohutukawa trees providing plenty of shade.

6 Opito Bay and Otama Beach

From Whangapoua return to SH 25 and drive east 17 km to Kuaotunu. At Kuaotunu take the Black Jack Road 4 km to Otama Beach and a further 3 km to Opito Bay — the road is narrow, unsealed and winding.

For many people these two beaches epitomise what the Coromandel experience is all about. The first, Otama, is a long stretch of white sand with only a few houses at the southern end and backed by sand dunes that are now a nature reserve protecting the whole length of the beach from further development. The beach looks out over the Mercury Islands and the best access is from the northern end at the bottom of the Black Jack Hill.

Opito Bay is more developed but the access along the beach is easier, with several good picnic spots and toilet facilities. Neither beach has any shops or accommodation, though there is a very basic camping ground at Otama (water but no toilets).

GOT TIME? (+61 KM NORTH OF COROMANDEL TOWN VIA COLVILLE)
7 Fletcher Bay

Fletcher Bay is as far the road goes on the western side of the Coromandel Peninsula and the bay itself faces directly north to Great Barrier Island just across the Colville Channel. The road hugs the coast all the way and is lined with fine old pohutukawa overhanging boulder beaches and with fantastic coastal views over the Hauraki Gulf, Little Barrier and Great Barrier Islands. The views are particularly spectacular from the hilltop just before Port Jackson.

Dominating the skyline is the brooding peak of Moehau rising to a height of 892 metres, the highest point on the Coromandel Peninsula. Bush-clad and frequently shrouded in mist, Moehau is a stronghold for native fauna such as kiwi, kaka and two native frogs including the rare Archey's frog, notable in that its young hatch from eggs and do not go through a tadpole stage. A possum-proof fence has been erected to protect the northern part of the peninsula from these destructive animals. The mountain is also the haunt of the mythical 'Moehau Monster', a large hairy creature similar to the equally legendary yeti.

Fletcher Bay itself is a broad, sandy, crescent-shaped beach facing Great Barrier Island and with a large DoC camping site. The 21 km of road beyond Colville is unsealed and slow.

Pohutukawa

Perhaps New Zealand's most iconic tree and now found all over the country, the natural range of the pohutukawa (*Metrosideros excelsa*) is north of a line from Poverty Bay through to Urenui in Taranaki. Closely related to the rata, pohutukawa belong to the myrtle family that includes eucalyptus, bottlebrush, manuka, kanuka, guava and ramarama. There are two native pohutukawa, mainland and Kermadec, the latter of which is smaller and has a much longer flowering period.

The tree's leaves are small and leathery and the trunk and roots gnarled and twisted, enabling it to grow in the harshest of environments including salt-laden spray and fierce winds. The wood is dark red and very heavy which is why both rata and pohutukawa are also known as 'ironwood'. Most specimens are spreading and not especially tall, but in forest conditions the pohutukawa can grow surprisingly high and straight. However, the tree is best known for its striking flowers that often entirely smother it in bright crimson during December giving rise to the nickname 'the New Zealand Christmas tree'. The Coromandel Peninsula hosts an annual Pohutukawa Festival in late November and early December, to celebrate this exceptional tree (www.pohutukawafestival.co.nz).

8 Coromandel Coastal Walkway

(+27 km from Colville or +29 km from Stony Bay)

This one-way track can be accessed either from Fletcher Bay, 27 km from Colville, or from Stony Bay, 29 km north of Colville via Port Charles. Well formed and of medium to easy grade, the track winds and dips through regenerating bush over headlands and past small bays. The coastal views are constant out to Great Barrier Island, Mercury and Cuvier Islands. This track links the end points of the roads up both the east and west coasts and although only three hours one way on foot, the trip by road is around 120 km (with camping grounds at each end). So you either have to walk back the way you came or have someone take a car around to meet you. Coromandel Discovery provide transport to the beginning of the track from Coromandel town and pick you up at the other end (freephone 0800 668 175, www.coromandeldiscovery.co.nz). An alternative is to do a short walk from Stony Bay to Poley Bay and return.

9 Coromandel Peninsula • Whitianga to Waihi Beach

Untouched beaches • Stunning coastal scenery • Hot Water Beach • Waterfalls • 185 km

In direct contrast to the more sheltered west coast of the Coromandel Peninsula, this area directly faces the rolling swells of the Pacific Ocean and is renowned for its beautiful white sandy beaches and lush bush.

Getting there

Whitianga is a popular base on the eastern side of the Coromandel and a good halfway point on any trip around the peninsula. The main roads are sealed, but winding and slow in parts as they climb over steep ranges. Secondary roads are often gravel, narrow and winding, including the legendary 309 Road that crosses the peninsula from Coromandel town to SH 25 just 5 km south of Whitianga.

Best time to visit

The Coromandel is a very popular summer destination for New Zealanders and places like Whangamata swell from a population of 5000 to around 40,000 during the peak holiday period of late December to mid-January. By March and April the crowds have eased off, the schools are back, the water is still warm and the weather is settled. The climate is mild all year round, but the high hills attract considerable rain at any time of the year and localised flooding is not unusual. In summer the area can be hit by tropical cyclones from the Pacific that bring strong easterly winds, heavy rain and large ocean swells, though this weather is usually short-lived.

Facilities

While Thames at the base of the peninsula is the largest centre, the Coromandel has several other large towns, all with accommodation, numerous cafés and a good range of shops. These towns include Coromandel, Whitianga, Tairua, Whangamata, Waihi and Waihi Beach. Virtually every location has a camping ground, although the level of sophistication varies considerably. Accommodation, however, can be at a premium from mid-December to early February, on the weekends, and especially on holiday weekends.

1 Shakespeare Cliff and Lonely Bay, Mercury Bay

Access is either by ferry across from Whitianga and then a 5-km walk or cycle, or by car via Cooks Beach. By road travel south from Whitianga for 26 km on SH 25 to Whenuakite and turn left towards Hahei, Hot Water Beach and Cooks Beach. After 2 km turn left into Purangi Road and continue towards Ferry Landing for 10 km. Shakespeare Cliff and Lonely Bay are on the right.

Wide and sheltered, Mercury Bay is a drowned river valley, linked to the tidal Whitianga Harbour by a narrow swift-flowing channel and the location of the largest town on the eastern coast of the Coromandel, Whitianga. Shakespeare Cliff is a high bluff just south of the harbour entrance from where, in November 1769, Captain James Cook observed the transit of Mercury across the face of the sun and thereby accurately calculated his longitude and latitude (hence the name Mercury Bay).

The high headland has extensive views out over the bay and just below the cliffs is Lonely Bay, one of the Coromandel's loveliest small beaches. Overhung with pohutukawa, the small cove is the perfect spot for swimming. And with foot access only the beach is quiet and relaxed.

2 Cathedral Cove, Hahei

From Whitianga head south on SH 25 for 26 km and then turn left at Whenuakite and continue 10 km to Hahei. The access to Cathedral Cove is 1.5 km at the end of Grange Road. Parking when busy can be tricky.

This beautiful small cove is for many the quintessential Coromandel beach — white sand, ancient pohutukawa, clear water and stunning rock formations. The two parts of the beach are linked by a sea cave (hence the name Cathedral Cove), and the coastline is now protected as part of the Te-Whanganui-A-Hei Marine Reserve. Just before the cove, the track overlooks Stingray Bay where, true to its name, stingrays are often seen gliding through the clear waters. The beach access is along a well-formed track which takes around 45 minutes each way, and there are toilet facilities at the beach itself. Unfortunately, Cathedral Cove is in danger of becoming too popular and is getting a bit crowded in the height of the holiday season so, if you can, try to avoid visiting during January or weekends over summer.

Lonely Bay.

Limestone Arch, Cathedral Cove.

3 Te Pare Historic Reserve, Hahei

The track to the pa site begins at the end of Pa Road in Hahei or leads up from the southern end of the beach.

Stronghold of Ngati Hei, who arrived in the area on the waka *Arawa* in AD 1350, this must be one of the most beautifully situated pa sites in the country. The broad terraces occupying this rocky headland, with the sea on three sides, have the most magnificent outlook over Mercury Bay and Hahei Beach. This is a wonderful place to sit for a while and just enjoy being alive.

4 Hot Water Beach

From Hahei return 2 km to Link Road and turn left. After 3 km turn left again and continue 3.5 km to Hot Water Beach.

At Hot Water Beach water heated by volcanic activity deep underground escapes to the surface via two fissures in the rock to emerge on the sand below the high-tide mark. This water is not heated salt water but water from deep below the ground and contains a wide range of minerals including magnesium, calcium and potassium and is said to be beneficial to the skin. The hot springs are only

Hot Water Beach.

accessible for three hours around low tide so you really need to check the tide times to avoid disappointment (www.mercurybay. co.nz/activities/hotwaterbeach).

If this sounds appealing, that's because it is, and unfortunately this place can be jam-packed in high summer and it is impossible to even put a toe in the hot water let alone lie in it. So, if you're looking for a quiet relaxing soak, then try to time your visit midweek or in the off season.

5 Paku Peak, Tairua
From Hot Water Beach return to SH 25 and continue south 16 km to Tairua. At the shopping centre turn into Manaia Road, and then turn into Paku Drive and follow the road to the car park at the top. If you are staying in Pauanui, catch the ferry to the base of Paku and walk up from there.

Once an island, Paku is an old volcanic peak rising to 178 metres and offering incredible coastal views. A short rocky scramble to the top is rewarded with prospects over Tairua Harbour and the Pauanui and Tairua surf beaches and out to sea to Shoe and Slipper Islands, and beyond those a group of islands known as the Aldermen. Far to the south the distinct shape of Mt Maunganui is just visible. The

area was discovered by Kupe around AD 950, and early Maori settlers were attracted to it by the now extinct moa. The only known artefact linking Aotearoa to Eastern Polynesia, a shell fish-hook, was discovered on Tairua Beach.

If you're feeling fit and have time, Mt Pauanui, just to the south, is over twice the height of Paku at 387 metres and has equally fine views, but it is a tough climb that will take one and a half hours return.

6 Opoutere Beach
Continue south from Tairua on SH 25 for 24 km and then turn left to Opoutere. The beach is 4 km from the turnoff (10 km north of Whangamata).

Opoutere is a wonderful long sweep of white sand at the entrance to the small Wharekawa Harbour and is one of the few major undeveloped beaches left on the Coromandel. From the car park it is a short 10-minute walk to the beach and even in the middle of summer it isn't hard to find a quiet spot. The Wharekawa Harbour Sandspit Wildlife Refuge at the southern end of the beach is an important breeding ground for several endangered birds, including the New Zealand dotterel. The nests are mere scrapings in the sand,

the eggs blending perfectly with the environment, and are easy to miss. The nesting grounds are roped off during the spring and summer and aggressive parent birds will make it very clear that you have strayed into their territory.

There are neither facilities nor shelter at the beach.

7 Wentworth Falls
From the Opoutere turnoff drive for 10 km on SH 25 to Whangamata and to the turnoff at Wentworth Valley Road 2 km south of the township. The track to the falls is 4.5 km at the end of this road.

Tumbling over a rocky bluff into a wide pool, the 50-metre-high Wentworth Falls are an ideal destination on a warm summer's afternoon. The track to the falls is easy and meanders through cool bush, though this was once a thriving gold-mining settlement and a major access way across the Coromandel to the Maratoto Valley. These days, thick native forest has completely reclaimed the land with very little now remaining of early mining activities. There is a viewing platform overlooking the falls, and a tricky narrow track to the swimming hole at the bottom. The track continues beyond the platform to a view point at the top of the waterfall. For the more energetic this track continues across the Coromandel Ranges to Maratoto north of Paeroa, a comfortable walk of around five hours.

8 Waimama Bay, Whiritoa

Continue south on SH 25 for 11 km to Whiritoa Beach.

Flanked by rocks at either end, this small stretch of white sand is shaded by large spreading pohutukawa trees, ideal for lounging beneath on a hot day. The beach drops steeply into the water here and the surf can be surprisingly powerful so take extra care swimming. At the southern end at low tide are bath-sized rock pools ideal for cooling off while the waves crash against the rocks below. The track to the beach is from the northern end of Whiritoa Beach and takes about 20 minutes one way.

9 Orokawa Bay, Waihi Beach

Whiritoa to Waihi town is 17 km on SH 25. At Waihi turn south on SH 2 and drive 2.5 km and then turn left towards Waihi Beach, about another 7 km. At the beach, park near the surf club at the very northern end where the track to Orokawa Bay begins. You will get your feet wet getting to the track right on high tide.

Climbing along the coast from Waihi Beach, an easy track (45 minutes one way) winds its way through regenerating bush to a magical bay that is as close to perfect as you can get. Crystal-clear water rushes onto a wide sweep of sand fringed with ancient pohutukawa trees, providing ideal shade from the searing summer sun. A short distance from the beach is the 28-metre-high William Wright Falls (30 minutes return). For the fit the track leads north to another sandy beach, Homunga Bay, although this is a further two hours return from Orokawa and the track is not so well formed. The surf at times can be rough here so take care when swimming, and there are occasional stingrays in the shallow waters.

10 Bowentown Heads, Waihi Beach

From the northern end of Waihi Beach follow the road (Wilson Road, then Seaforth Road) south along the beach 8 km to the heads.

An extinct volcano, Bowentown Heads at the north entrance of Tauranga Harbour is, from a distance, deceptive. What looks like one small hill is in fact two, and in between is the pretty beach of Anzac Bay, a safe place to swim. Both hills are topped by ancient pa sites and from the summit of each are excellent views over Waihi Beach, the bush-clad Kaimai Ranges, Tauranga Harbour, Mayor/Tuhua Island and, looming large to the south, Mt Maunganui.

Enclosed within the tidal Tauranga Harbour is the long sandbar of Matakana Island, now planted in pine trees. From the car park a short steep path drops to the harbour entrance and Cave Bay, a beautiful small beach overhung with pohutukawa, but take care when swimming here as the tidal flow can be fierce.

Cave Bay, Bowentown Heads.

Stingrays

New Zealand has three common stingrays, the short-tailed ray, the long-tailed ray and the eagle ray. The eagle ray (see image) is the smallest, growing up to 2 metres and living in shallow waters and feeding on crabs, molluscs and shellfish which it cracks with its powerful teeth. The largest stingray, and in fact the largest in the world, is the short-tailed stingray also known as the smooth stingray. These massive creatures can grow over 4 metres in length and weigh up to 350 kg. Feeding on fish, these rays are common in warmer waters and not found around the South Island. The long-tailed stingray grows up to 4 metres, with a maximum weight of around 200 kg.

Rays ripple the edges of their wings to propel themselves forward in a beautiful fluid motion similar to flying. Their predators are sharks and (at least in New Zealand waters) orca. However, despite their fierce reputation stingrays are gentle creatures and not at all aggressive, only defending themselves with their razor-sharp barbs when startled or attacked. In New Zealand there has only been one recorded death when a young woman accidentally fell onto a stingray and was stabbed through the heart in 1938. Stingrays are common in the shallow waters around the coast and are often seen in sandy bays and harbours.

10 Waikato • Mercer to Te Awamutu

Kahikatea forest • Coastal vistas • Extinct volcanoes • Waikato River • 280 km

Winding through the fertile farmland of the Waikato basin, this tour touches a surprising variety of landscapes, ranging from bush-clad mountains to wetlands and dramatic coastline, as well as New Zealand's longest river.

> **INFORMATION**
> **Hamilton i-SITE, corner Bryce and Anglesea Streets, Hamilton, ph (07) 839 3580**
> **Raglan Visitor Centre, Wallis Street, Raglan, ph (07) 825 0556**
> **Te Awamutu i-SITE, 1 Gorst Avenue, Te Awamutu, ph (07) 871 3259**
> **Kawhia Harbour Visitor Information, Kawhia Museum, Kawhia, ph (07) 871 0161**

Getting there

The starting point is on SH 1 south of Auckland. From there the tour winds and twists through a variety of landscapes to Te Awamutu. The roads are good and sealed, except for the road from Raglan to Mt Karioi, which is narrow, winding and gravel.

Best time to visit

This trip can be undertaken at any time of the year, though in winter the beach section might not be so appealing. Inland Waikato is generally sheltered from strong winds and can be hot and humid in summer and cool and frosty in winter. The coastal sections around Raglan and Kawhia can be windy but not particularly cold. Rainfall is usually evenly spread throughout the year, with winter understandably being wetter.

Hamilton is host to two very popular events, the V8 Supercars in April and the National Agricultural Fieldays in June, and during this time you won't find a bed for love nor money within 50 km of the city. On the other hand, over Christmas and New Year the good folk of Waikato are off to the beach so accommodation in Hamilton and other inland towns is a breeze to find.

Facilities

Only two hours' drive from Auckland, Hamilton, with a population of over 120,000, has plenty of everything: places to stay, good places to eat, plenty of shops. The smaller towns of Huntly, Ngaruawahia and Te Awamutu also have camping grounds, motels and a good range of shops, with Te Awamutu being the pick of the three. Over Christmas and New Year through to mid-January, Raglan is most likely to be booked out, but other than that it is a quiet coastal town with a reputation for good cafés. Kawhia is much smaller than Raglan, but is an appealing coastal settlement with a couple of motels, camping grounds, a pub and half a dozen stores.

1 Whangamarino Wetland

Travel south on SH 1 from Mercer for 4 km to Island Block Road, which cuts through the heart of the wetland, a distance of 15 km.

Covering over 7000 hectares, the Whangamarino Wetland is the second-largest swamp in the North Island and is one of six internationally recognised wetlands in the country. Part of a much larger flood plain for the Waikato River, this wetland once linked the shallow lakes around Huntly, although much of this area has now been drained for farmland. Floodgates control the water level within the wetland, which is a stronghold for a number of threatened

Whangamarino Wetland.

New Zealand birds including the bittern, spotless crake and the fernbird. While important, the wetland has no easy access or walks and the best view point is from Island Block Road.

2 Hakarimata Scenic Reserve

From Island Block Road continue south on SH 1 for 32 km to Huntly. Cross the Waikato River and turn south, travelling 6 km alongside the river to Parker Road. The access to the reserve is 500 metres along this road.

Near the southern limit of their natural growing area, the magnificent specimens of kauri in this reserve loom tall above the surrounding bush. The largest tree is estimated to be over 600 years old, and while the marvellous kauri are a destination in themselves, it is worth continuing up the hill to the lookout, which affords magnificent views. The walk to the kauri takes 40 minutes and it is one hour to the lookout.

3 Taupiri Mountain and the Waikato River

Return to SH 1 at Huntly. Turn south again, this time travelling on the eastern side of the river, to Taupiri, a distance of 6 km.

Taupiri is sacred to the Tainui people and it is the principal burial ground for the iwi (tribe). It is also the point where the Waikato River cuts through the Taupiri Gorge on its path north to the sea. The Waikato is New Zealand's longest river at 425 km and begins at Lake Taupo in the centre of the North Island. Originally, the Waikato River emptied into the ocean at the Firth of Thames and the old bed of the river is very clear at Hinuera, east of Cambridge. It is believed the river broke through the hills at Taupiri in the second century AD, when the huge Taupo eruption sent a wall of water surging down the watercourse.

A steep track to the summit (288 m) is to the right of the burial grounds and marked by a wooden arch. From the top the views are incredible on a good day when even snow-capped Ruapehu is clearly visible far to the south. The mountain is tapu (sacred) and should be treated with respect.

4 Bryant Memorial Scenic Reserve

Travel 14 km south from Taupiri to Ngaruawahia, turn right and follow SH 39 for 17 km to Whatawhata. Turn right on to SH 23 and drive 32 km to Raglan, and from there take the Wainui Road to the reserve 6 km on the right. Parking can be tricky.

A short walk downhill through bush ends at a great lookout point over Ngarunui Beach, the entrance to Raglan Harbour, and further north along the Waikato coast. Raglan Harbour is an old drowned river valley that extends 12 km inland. There are two major rivers entering the harbour, Waitetuna to the south and Waingaro to the north. From the viewing platform a track continues down and through the bush to the sand dunes and the beach.

5 Mt Karioi

From Bryant Memorial Scenic Reserve continue around the coast for 8 km (Wainui Road changes its name to Whaanga Road). Beyond Manu Bay the road becomes gravel, narrow and winding as it climbs along the coast. The car park is on the right, 1 km past the sign that reads 'Te Toto Gorge Scenic Reserve'.

Like nearby Mt Pirongia, Mt Karioi is an extinct basaltic volcano that experienced a series of five major eruptions between 2 and 3 million years ago. Now substantially eroded, the summit rises to 756 metres and is still partially covered by native bush, but since it juts out to sea the vistas from the top are stunning, with views as far south as Taranaki and to Mt Te Aroha to the east. The vegetation up here is montane and in direct contrast to the lusher bush on the lower slopes. On the seaward side stunted, almost prostrate, manuka are testament to the fierce westerly winds that sweep the mountain. The track to the summit is a slog and takes around three hours, though a slightly lower lookout takes just over two.

6 Bridal Veil Falls

Return to Raglan and travel 7 km back towards Hamilton on SH 23. Turn right into Te Mata Road and continue for 13 km to the falls, 3 km beyond Te Mata settlement. The car park is notorious for vehicle theft so be extra vigilant here, even if there are plenty of other cars and people about.

Testament to the area's volcanic past, the beautiful Bridal Veil Falls drops 55 metres over a hard layer of volcanic basalt into a pool fringed by moisture-loving plants. Constantly damp from the spray from the falls, parataniwha flourishes here. An attractive native with wide nettle-like leaves, this plant is only found in the North Island and thrives in damp shady areas. The colour of the leaves varies from green through to shades of light pink and deep red, although what exactly causes this variation in colour has yet to be discovered.

The flat, five-minute walk from the car park follows a stream to two viewing platforms at the top of the falls, though the view from the bottom is more spectacular.

7 Mt Pirongia

Return to SH 23 and proceed to Whatawhata. Turn right into Kakaramea Road/SH 39 and travel south 21 km to Te Pahu Road. Turn right into Te Pahu Road and continue for 6 km. Turn into Corcoran Road and continue to the car park 5 km up this road.

The bush-covered volcanic cone of Mt Pirongia (959 m) dominates the Waikato skyline. The first eruptions occurred nearly 3 million years ago and the last around 1.5 million (the same as Mt Karioi to the west), with lava flows reaching as far as Kawhia. This mountain is surprisingly rugged and the original bush is an unusual mixture of cooler- and warmer-climate plants. The track to the summit is demanding and will take around four to five hours.

A good alternative is the much easier walk along the same track to the Ruapane Lookout, a prominent outcrop at 723 metres. This walk takes two hours and passes through very fine tawa forest. The canopy of these trees is relatively light, allowing sunlight to filter through to the forest floor and creating an open feel to the usually densely shaded bush.

In the Kaniwhaniwha Reserve on the Limeworks Loop Road near Te Pahu, a track leads to New Zealand's tallest native tree, a kahikatea that towers above its surrounds at 66.5 metres.

8 Yarndley's Bush, Te Awamutu

From Mt Pirongia return to SH 39, turn right and head south for 4 km to Pirongia village. Turn left into Pirongia Road and drive 10.5 km to Te Awamutu. Just after entering the town turn left into Paterangi Road and drive north for 2.5 km to Ngaroto Road. Turn right and the reserve is 1.5 km along on the right.

Consisting almost entirely of kahikatea trees, this 14-hectare reserve is the largest remaining lowland kahikatea forest in the Waikato. The immediate impression is not of native bush, but of a pine forest, and it is easy to see why kahikatea was dubbed 'white pine' by early European settlers. The trunks are straight and clean, topped by conifer-like foliage, with only the buttress-shaped roots a telltale sign that kahikatea are actually denizens of the swamp. Drainage of nearby farmland has led to a drop in the water table, exposing the distinctive root systems of the trees.

GOT TIME? (+48.5 KM)
9 Kawhia Harbour

From Te Awamutu return to Pirongia village. Turn left on to SH 39 and drive south for 10 km.

Turn right into Ngutunui Road, which after 6.5 km joins the Kawhia Road/SH 31. From here Kawhia is a 32-km drive.

Kawhia Harbour covers over 6000 hectares and is a complicated body of water, with long arms and estuaries twisting and snaking deep into the surrounding limestone countryside. Half the harbour is exposed at low tide, creating an ideal feeding ground for wading birds. Black swans are common, feeding on the sea grass *Zostera* that covers large areas of the tidal flats.

A group of schoolchildren discovered the fossilised bones of a penguin on the mud flats here belonging to an extinct species that once stood 1.5 metres high, weighed over 100 kg and lived 40 million years ago. Not only is it the most complete fossil of any giant penguin ever found in New Zealand, but it is also one of the largest penguin fossils in the world.

Between the harbour and the ocean are extensive sand dunes that have become 'stabilised' with pine forest. The beach is a wide and somewhat windswept stretch of black sand with high iron content. Very hot to walk on during sunny summer's days, the sand is mined for the iron at Taharoa on the harbour's southern head.

Accessible for two hours either side of low tide are the Te Puia hot water springs, situated directly out from the main track to the beach from the car park. This beach is exposed to the westerly wind so bring a substantial digging tool to make a protective wall around your very own hot pool in the sand.

Kahikatea

Dense kahikatea forest once covered the wetter lowlands of New Zealand, and while there are 370 fragments remaining in the Waikato, the largest of these, Yarndley's Bush near Te Awamutu, is a mere 14 hectares. Kahikatea is New Zealand's tallest tree, with some colonial sources recording specimens up to 90 metres. Currently, one tree on the Kaniwhaniwha Caves track on Mt Pirongia is 66.5 metres tall, making it New Zealand's tallest living native tree, 15 metres taller than the giant kauri Tane Mahuta.

Also known as white pine, kahikatea (*Dacrycarpus dacrydioides*) belongs to the conifer family, and while pure stands of kahikatea forest are now rare, it is in this small forest that the conifer's features are most apparent. The tree is tapering toward the top, the leaves are small and narrow, and the bark is rough and flaky. Despite its height, the tree is relatively slender and seldom more than a metre in diameter, though it does have broad spreading buttresses at the base, providing it support in damp soils.

Kahikatea has separate male and female trees, with males producing pollen-bearing cones and the females producing the seeds — the latter being a favourite food of keruru and kaka. The timber is not particularly durable, but is fine-grained and odourless. In early times it was used for cheese crates and butter boxes.

11 Waikato • Hamilton to Te Aroha

Bush walks • Dramatic waterfalls • Mountain vistas • Hot pools • 145 km

This tour runs east of Hamilton and links the leafy native bush of Maungatautari Ecological Island with the stunning headwaters of the Waihou River and the impressive Wairere Falls. It ends at the hot pools at the foot of Mt Te Aroha.

INFORMATION
Hamilton i-SITE, corner Bryce and Anglesea Streets, Hamilton, ph (07) 839 3580
Cambridge i-SITE, corner Queen and Victoria Streets, Cambridge, ph (07) 823 3456
Te Aroha i-SITE, 102B Whitaker Street (The Domain), Te Aroha, ph (07) 884 8052

Getting there
Starting at Hamilton City, this trip makes for a pleasant day's drive on good sealed roads through the rolling farmland of the Waikato basin.

Facilities
Spoiled for choice, there is a wide range of accommodation, shopping and cafés in Hamilton, a city of over 120,000 people. Equally, smaller towns along the way such as Cambridge, Matamata and Te Aroha all have good places to stop over, eat and shop.

Best time to visit
This is a good trip for any time of the year. The Waikato has a mild climate, though temperatures can reach the 30°C mark in summer and frosts are common in the middle of winter. Rainfall is usually evenly spread throughout the year. If you are planning a bush walk, be prepared for a bit of mud in winter or summer.

1 Jubilee Park
Boundary Road, Hamilton
This tiny patch of bush in urban Hamilton is a poignant reminder of how little remains of the vast lowland forest that once blanketed the Waikato basin, which was subsequently cleared and turned into some of the most productive farmland in the world. The dominant tree in the reserve is kahikatea, New Zealand's tallest native, which thrives in damp swampy soils. Known locally as 'Claudelands Bush', a raised boardwalk through the trees protects the fragile roots exposed by a soil drier than in the past. In addition to kahikatea, the small bush fragment also contains mature tawa, mahoe and pukatea.

2 Maungatautari Ecological Island
From Hamilton take SH 1 to Cambridge, a distance of 25 km. In Cambridge take Victoria Street (the main street) over the Waikato River and follow Cook Street, Shakespeare Street and Browning Street to Maungatautari Road. Once on Maungatautari Road drive for 14 km and turn right into Hicks Road. Access to Maungatautari is at the end of Hicks Road.

An extinct volcano, rising to 797 metres and lying just south of Cambridge, bush-covered Maungatautari is an inspirational example of a community taking action to restore a local mountain with unrivalled dedication and hard work. While cleared around the fringes, most of the 3360 hectares is still virgin forest — a forest that includes silver beech, a tree usually found much further south.

As in so much New Zealand forest, predators had taken a heavy toll on native birds and fauna, but locals, under the auspices of the Maungatautari Ecological Island Trust, decided enough was enough. Inspired by successes on offshore islands and not content to do things by half, the trust erected the longest predator-proof fence in the country, at over 47 km long. The fence encircles two enclosures, one to the north of the mountain and the other just to the south. Native birds including northern kaka, takahe and kiwi have been reintroduced, and in December 2007 the first kiwi chick hatched at Maungatautari. In 2004 it was discovered that a small colony of the rare Hochstetter's frog had also survived on the mountain.

A walk to and through the northern enclosure will take less than an hour; make sure you stop to peek into the 'weta motels' along the way. The track to the summit is moderately difficult and takes less than two hours one way, but the top of the mountain is bush-clad and views are minimal.

Te Waihou River flows from the Blue Springs.

3 Te Waihou Walkway

From Maungatautari return down Hicks Road, turn right at Maungatautari Road and continue for 13 km until you rejoin SH 1. Turn right and continue 20 km on SH 1 and SH 5 towards Rotorua. Turn right into Whytes Road (6 km past Tirau) and after 2.5 km turn left into Leslie Road. The access to the walkway is 4 km down Leslie Road on the right.

The Waihou River begins at the Blue Springs, which produce the most stunningly pure water, filtered down from the Kaimai Ranges after being underground for over 50 years. Crystal-clear and a brilliant blue-green colour, the stream supports an incredible array of aquatic plants that drift languidly in the transparent water while trout, very easy to spot, glide effortlessly in the swift-running current. However, think twice before leaping in as even on a hot day the water emerges from the Blue Springs at an even 11°C all year round.

This easy walk takes one and a half hours one way, and most of it is through farmland, though there is a small section of bush along the short gorge, and replanting of native trees is occurring in several sections. If you don't have transport at either end, or the time or inclination to do the return trip, start at the Leslie Road end as this is the shortest distance to the springs and the gorge, which are the most attractive parts of the walk.

Weta

Found in just about every New Zealand environment from alpine heights to lowland bush, weta are also quite at home in smaller urban gardens and aren't at all shy about coming inside and making themselves comfortable on the heated towel rail either!

Related to crickets, locusts and grasshoppers, weta-type insects are found elsewhere in the southern hemisphere in South Africa, Australia and South America. Ancient creatures, weta are older than the tuatara and have hardly changed in the last 100 million years. New Zealand has over 100 species divided into two distinct families and five main groups: giant, tree, tusked, ground (see image), and cave weta. The giant weta is the heaviest insect in the world, the largest recorded specimen weighing in at a hefty 71 grams — the weight of an average sparrow. The extraordinary alpine weta has specially adapted cells that allow it to freeze in order to survive temperatures as low as –10°C. When the temperature rises above freezing they simply thaw out again.

While widespread and common, many weta species have very limited ranges, including one in the King Country that has adapted to a single patch of gorse. Today, as many as 20 of the 100 species are endangered.

4 Wairere Falls

*Return to SH 5 and turn right, travelling
towards Rotorua. After 1 km turn left into
SH 28/Harwoods Road and drive 16 km to
SH 29. Turn left towards Matamata and after
3.5 km turn right into Old Te Aroha Road.
Continue 15.5 km to Goodwin Road, which
is on your right. The track to the waterfall
begins at the end of this short road.*

The North Island's highest waterfall,
the impressive Wairere Falls tumbles
153 metres in several drops over the
Okauia Fault in the Kaimai Ranges.
The falls can be seen clearly from a long
way off, though during the 45-minute
walk to reach them are not visible at all,
leaving the surprise right until the last
few metres. If the falls aren't enough of
an attraction, the bush walk along the
stream is particularly pretty with mosses,
ferns and overhanging mature native
trees. There is a very steep track to the
top of the falls that will take another
45 minutes, but the views are worth
the effort.

The Kaimai Ranges are the result of
a gradually tilting landmass, with the
Bay of Plenty side of the range relatively
gentle in slope, but the western edge
sharply defined by steep-sided hills.
This is particularly evident on SH 29
to Tauranga, where the road on the
Waikato side is winding and quickly
climbs to the summit over just a few
kilometres, and the descent on the
eastern side to Tauranga gently ambles
over rolling hills.

5 Mt Te Aroha

*From the Wairere Falls, head north on the Te
Aroha–Gordon Road for 25 km to Te Aroha.*

At 952 metres Mt Te Aroha is the highest
point in the Kaimai Ranges. Although it
doesn't look like a volcano, the mountain
was built by a series of eruptions over a
period of 16 million years. The distinct
peak and bush-covered slopes loom over
Te Aroha, once a flourishing spa town,
which with its renovated Edwardian
domain and hot pools makes an
appealing end to this tour. The hot pools
and the unique hot soda-water geyser
(the only such geyser in the world) at the
foot of the mountain are reminders of
Te Aroha's explosive volcanic past.

The climb to the top is hard work

Wairere Falls.

and steep, but the spectacular views over the
Waikato basin to the west and the Bay of
Plenty to the east are ample reward. The top
is distinctly subalpine, and near the summit
the cooler wet climate results in the silver
beech being much diminished in size and

festooned with hanging mosses. If the trip to
the top is too much of a challenge, Bald Spur
Lookout at 350 metres is not too difficult
— and of course you can always reward
yourself with a relaxing soak in the hot
pools afterwards.

12 King Country • Otorohanga to Pureora Forest

Glow-worm Caves • Limestone bluffs • Kokako • Ancient forests • 169 km

The Waitomo Caves are at the heart of this fascinating limestone country that includes amazing natural formations and bush walks, while to the south is Pureora Forest with incredible walking tracks and the Mapara Reserve, a stronghold of the rare native bird, the kokako.

INFORMATION
Te Awamutu i-SITE,
1 Gorst Avenue, Te Awamutu,
ph (07) 871 3259
Otorohanga i-SITE,
21 Maniapoto Street, Otorohanga,
ph (07) 873 8951
Te Kuiti i-SITE, Rora Street, Te Kuiti,
ph (07) 878 8077
Waitomo i-SITE, Waitomo Caves,
ph (07) 878 7640
Pureora Forest Field Centre,
198 Barryville Road, Pureora,
ph (07) 878 1081

Getting there
The King Country is part of the Waikato and SH 3 runs through the heart of this region. The roads are generally good, although within the Pureora Forest the gravel roads are narrow and in some places are little better than rough tracks.

Best time to visit
While this trip can be made any time of year, naturally the summer months will be more pleasant. The King Country can be cold and foggy in the depths of winter during July and August, but apart from those months the climate is generally mild. The bush tracks can be muddy in any season. While Waitomo attracts endless coach-loads of tourists very few people venture much further, so the other places on this tour have relatively few visitors.

Facilities
Te Awamutu, Otorohanga and Te Kuiti are all reasonable-sized towns with a sprinkling of camping grounds, motels and cafés. These urban centres have a good range of banks, supermarkets and general shops. Otorohanga is the closest town (14 km) to the Waitomo Caves, and the latter has accommodation but not much else.

1 Otorohanga Kiwi House Native Bird Park
Alex Telfer Drive, off Kakamutu Street, Otorohanga. Well signposted from SH 3.
Among the earliest and largest breeding programmes for kiwi, this native bird park is one of the best places to view this New Zealand icon. The park prides itself on rotating several pairs of kiwi each day so the birds are not stressed, meaning visitors are guaranteed to see these nocturnal birds on the move. Set in attractive native bush, the park contains a wide range of other native birds including

North Island Brown kiwi at Otorohanga.

kaka and weka, as well as other indigenous creatures such as tuatara and geckos (www.kiwihouse.org.nz; an entry fee applies).

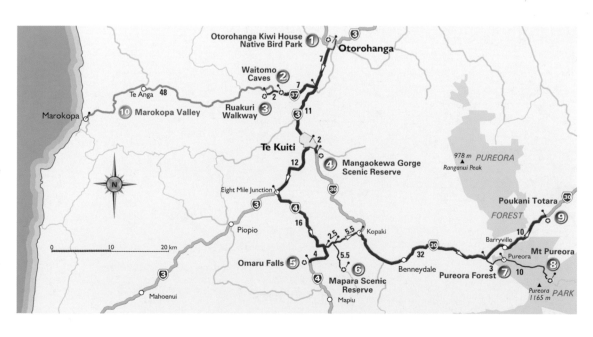

Limestone stalactites and stalagmites, Aranui Cave.

2 Waitomo Caves

From Otorohanga, head south on SH 3 for 7 km and turn right into Waitomo Caves Road. The caves are another 7 km down this road.
Collectively known as the Waitomo Caves, this area has in fact three separate cave systems open to the public: the Glowworm Caves, Aranui, and Ruakuri.

The best known and most spectacular (and the most crowded) underground system is the Glowworm Caves. The tour begins with a walk through a number of limestone formations including the Cathedral, the Banquet Chamber, the Pipe Organ and the Catacombs. However, the highlight of the trip is a silent boat journey through the amazing glow-worm grotto, lit only by thousands of tiny pinpricks of light. The combination of glow-worms in such resplendent numbers and the boat trip in the dark makes Waitomo a special place.

Located 3 km west of the Glowworm Caves is the Aranui Cave. The formations here are more spectacular even though there are no glow-worms. The multi-coloured stalactites are huge, with one at 6 metres long and estimated to weigh 2.5 tonnes. Other formations include the Butcher Shop, Aladdin's Cave, the Temple of Peace and Cathedral Majestic.

Ruakuri ('den of wild dogs') was first discovered by Maori 400–500 years ago. Reopened in 2005, this cave has 1.5 km of twisting limestone passageways, hidden waterfalls and fascinating cave formations.

For the more adventurous, several companies offer exciting options both above and below ground, including black-water rafting, abseiling (above and below ground) and guided caving (www.waitomo.com).

3 Ruakuri Walkway

Ruakuri Walkway is on Tumutumu Road, 2 km from the Waitomo Glowworm Caves and next to the entry to Ruakuri Cave.
This short 30-minute walk along the Waitomo River is crammed with fantastic limestone outcrops, caves, and a huge natural tunnel. The unspoiled bush features luxuriant growth, in particular ferns, mosses and lichens. Easy to miss is the fantastic underground cavern, which is about 5 metres past the natural bridge viewing platform. Initially it appears to be just a hole in the ground, but let your eyes adjust and the short flight of steps quickly becomes apparent. These lead to a lookout point in a huge cavern high above the river as it disappears underground. The area has glow-worms at night, but don't forget your torch. (There is no charge for the walk.)

4 Mangaokewa Gorge Scenic Reserve

Return to SH 3 and head south for 11 km to Te Kuiti. The entrance to the gorge is 2 km south of Te Kuiti on SH 30 (the road to Mangakino).
Set in a deep gorge just south of Te Kuiti, the main feature of this reserve is the

Glow-worms

Glow-worms are common throughout New Zealand and can be found in clusters in caves, on the banks of streams and in almost any damp overhang, though it is usually in caves that they are the most impressive. Found throughout the world, glow-worms are the larvae of a fungus gnat, and New Zealand has just one species, *Arachnocampa luminosa*, that is also found in southeastern Australia (the New Zealand glow-worm is not related to the European glow-worm).

The larval stage is the only time in its life cycle when the insect eats, as during the adult stage the gnat has no mouth. To attract food the glow-worm creates a natural chemical reaction that produces light known as bioluminescence. Attracted by the light, prey is trapped by numerous long viscous threads that the worm reels in once the insect is caught. In a particularly fine evolutionary development, the hungrier the glow-worm, the brighter the light. Most glow-worm clusters are of modest size, but at Waitomo the glow-worms number in the tens of thousands, creating a massed spectacle that is especially impressive.

huge limestone bluffs that tower high above a broad stream. The valley of the gorge supports mature native bush that includes large tawa, rimu and kahikatea. For a pleasant change, native bird life, in particular kereru (wood pigeon), is common in this bush. An easy track through the gorge follows the stream, passes two small waterfalls and gives access to numerous swimming holes, ideal on a hot summer's day.

The Ruakuri River.

5 Omaru Falls

Drive south from Te Kuiti on SH 3 for 12 km, then continue south on SH 4 for another 20 km to Omaru Road. The falls are 500 metres down this road.

The Omaru Falls are created by the Mapiu Stream plunging 50 metres over a hard basalt lip into a rocky pool, particularly spectacular after heavy rain. The walk follows the stream through farmland and regenerating bush with some huge kahikatea to be seen. The viewing platform is high above the falls and gives the visitor an excellent view, though there is no access to the pool below. Despite its handy location just off the main highway south of Te Kuiti and a flat walk all the way, these falls draw very few visitors.

6 Mapara Scenic Reserve

Return to SH 4 and drive north for 4 km. Turn right into Kopaki Road and continue 2.5 km to Mapara Road South. The reserve is 5.5 km on the left down this gravel road.

One of the last strongholds of the rare kokako, this 1400-hectare reserve is the most accessible for those who want to hear or see this elusive bird. Between 1989 and 1995, 257 stoats, 113 weasels and 91 ferrets were trapped in the reserve; while between 1978 and 1995, 8200 goats were removed. The result was that kokako pairs rocketed from a low of five to over 80 in 2007. A one-hour loop walk in the reserve leads through the territories of several birds so the chance of hearing them is pretty high, but you will need to be very patient to see one. The best opportunity is the period two hours after dawn, so you'll just have to get up extra early to sight them, especially in summer.

7 Pureora Forest Park

Return to Kopaki Road and turn right; after 5.5 km this road joins SH 30. Turn right and drive 32 km to Barryville Road and the turnoff to Pureora Forest.

This magnificent forest was saved from the axe by protesters in 1978 who perched themselves on platforms in the trees. Logging was finally halted in the early 1980s, and the area is currently a mixture of forest park and commercial forest, which makes for some interesting contrasts between pristine native bush and clear-felled pine plantation.

The entire forest was destroyed in the Taupo eruption 1800 years ago — not by fire, but by a combination of the impact of the blast flattening the forest and the ash subsequently covering the fallen trees. What makes this forest special is the grandeur of the mature totara, maire, rimu and tawa trees, all of which have flourished in the rich volcanic soil and grown to vast proportions. All the largest totara in the country are to be found in this one forest.

Today there are numerous short walks in the park, though some of them are only accessible from the fringes. The Totara Walk, Buried Forest Walk and Forest Tower Track are all easy walks and are close to the visitor centre.

8 Mt Pureora

From the visitor centre turn right into Link Road. Travel 10 km and look out for a car park on the left-hand side of the road. The Link Track to the top is opposite the car park.

While not a distinct peak, the rounded summit of Mt Pureora, at over 1100 metres, has amazing views over the central North Island, including Lake Taupo. The appeal, however, is not just the views but

Kokako

Related to the saddleback and the extinct huia, the kokako, also known as the blue-wattled crow, is a survivor of an ancient line of birds that may go back as far as the existence of the supercontinent Gondwanaland. Noted for their distinctive organ-like song, the birds are not good fliers and tend to glide and crash through the trees. Unfortunately, the South Island kokako, which had orange rather than blue wattles, was last seen in the 1960s and is now considered extinct. Slow breeders and particularly vulnerable to predators and forest clearance, kokako dropped to perilously low numbers in the 1980s, but good management has seen the bird's population make a rapid recovery. Kokako have distinctive territories, the boundaries of which they define by singing. At the Mapara Reserve in the King Country over 70 pairs have established territories and a loop track cuts through several territories making it the most likely place for the public to hear and see these unique birds. The best time for viewing them is just after dawn or just before dusk.

also the track leading up to the peak, which travels through beautiful forest, much of it moss- and lichen-covered, reminiscent of some hobgoblin grotto. The vegetation close to the summit suddenly turns subalpine and includes tussock. The walk to the top takes around one and a half hours and is a steady rather than a steep climb. In bad weather it gets very windy and cold up here, even in summer.

9 Poukani Totara

Return to SH 30, turn right and drive 10 km east (12 km from Mangakino). The track to Poukani is on the right.

While thousands of visitors flock to Tane Mahuta, this tree, the tallest totara in the country, is hardly known, rarely visited, and yet equally impressive. Poukani is a giant tree, over 42 metres tall and estimated to be 1800 years old. Its rivals, the second and third-largest totara trees, are both located in the nearby Pureora Forest. The walk to the tree is through a handsome grove of wheki (tree fern), with a sprinkling of larger trees, and takes 20 minutes one way.

GOT TIME? (+48 KM)
10 The Marokopa Valley

From Waitomo take the Te Anga Road west, which beyond the junction with the Taiaroa Road becomes known as Marokopa Road. The entire length of the road is 48 km and the only facilities along this stretch are the pub at Te Anga and the camping ground at Marokopa Beach.

First stop is the Mangapohue Natural Bridge, 26 km from Waitomo. Just a short distance from the road are two magnificent natural limestone arches, one on top of the other, created by the waters of the Mangapohue Stream. The walk to the arches is through an attractive gorge lined with ferns and mosses, and which at night features glow-worms (a torch is necessary if a night walk is planned). Beyond the bridges the track continues into open farmland, and returns to the road via large rocky outcrops that contain the fossilised remains of gigantic oysters from a time when the land was submerged beneath the sea.

Five kilometres on are the Piripiri Caves. Not especially deep, they are also known for their fossilised oysters, but you will need a torch and good shoes as the caves can be very wet and muddy. (Free entry too!)

Just 2 km further on are the Marokopa Falls, reached after a 10-minute walk through cool bush. The Marokopa River cascades 30 metres downwards, creating a spectacular waterfall. Parataniwha flourish in the cool wet atmosphere at the base of the falls.

Marokopa Beach is at the end of the road, 15 km from the falls. A typical west coast beach, this wild stretch of black sand is constantly battered by the westerly winds and relentless surf off the Tasman Sea. With just a small cluster of baches by the estuary you are quite likely to have this beach all to yourself.

Mangopohue Natural Bridge.

13 Bay of Plenty • Tauranga to Opotiki

White Island • Surf beaches • Pohutukawa forest • 2000-year-old puriri tree • 160 km

Famous for its sunny climate, the Bay of Plenty boasts long stretches of fine beaches, a volcanic offshore island and, in the eastern bay, some surprisingly rugged bush country.

INFORMATION
Mt Maunganui i-SITE, Salisbury Avenue, Mt Maunganui, ph (07) 575 5099
Tauranga i-SITE, 95 Willow Street, Tauranga, ph (07) 577 6234
Te Puke Visitor Information Centre, 130 Jellicoe Street (SH 2), Te Puke, ph (07) 573 9172
Whakatane Visitor Information Centre, corner Kakahoroa Drive and Quay Street, Whakatane, ph (07) 308 6058
Opotiki i-SITE, corner St John and Elliott Streets, Opotiki, ph (07) 315 3031

Getting there

This tour begins at the beach resort of Mt Maunganui and follows the coast to Opotiki in the eastern Bay of Plenty. All the roads are excellent.

Best time to visit

This is definitely a summer trip. The Bay of Plenty enjoys a sunny climate, with Whakatane in the east regularly topping the charts as the place with the highest number of sunshine hours. March through to May, after the peak of the holiday period, still has warm days, but with cooler nights. If you are planning a boat trip to either White Island or Mayor Island, remember that you will be sailing over the open ocean and will be exposed to heavy swells. Also, build a bit of flexibility into your tour as sailings to both these islands are weather dependent and can be cancelled at the last moment.

Facilities

Tauranga and Mt Maunganui both have plenty of accommodation, though 'The Mount' is more expensive and also more likely to be booked out over the peak holiday times in the summer. Tauranga has a marvellous hospitality strip of nearly 30 restaurants, bars and cafés along the waterfront. Further east, Te Puke, Whakatane, Ohope and Opotiki all offer a good range of accommodation. There are also camping grounds at the numerous attractive beaches, although Ohope Beach accommodation is likely to be booked out over the Christmas/New Year period. These towns have good shopping centres and plenty of places to eat, too.

1 Mt Maunganui/Mauao

Looming over the central Bay of Plenty is Mt Maunganui/Mauao (known as 'The Mount'), rising 232 metres above the entrance to Tauranga Harbour. The mountain is a dormant lava dome dating back over 3 million years, and is one of several such domes in the Tauranga area. Once an island, the mountain is now joined to the mainland by a long sandbar known as a tombolo.

The views from the summit are dramatic: along the coast with views out to Mayor Island, inland to the Kaimai Ranges, with Tauranga, Mt Maunganui town and Matakana Island spread below. There is a good track to the top that is not such a hard climb and there are small patches of regenerating bush along the way. The southern entrance to Tauranga Harbour is at the foot of the mountain with a forceful current on each tide.

Pleasant hot pools at the base of the mountain are a reminder of Mt Maunganui's geothermal past, and the surf beach on the seaward side is considered one of the best in the country.

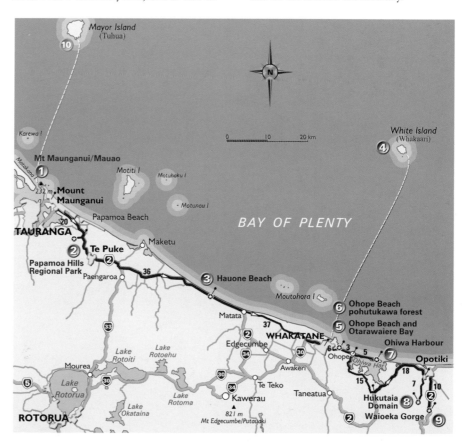

52

2 Papamoa Hills Regional Park, Te Puke

From Mt Maunganui head east on SH 2 for 20 km (5 km before Te Puke) and turn right into Poplar Lane then drive 800 metres to the car park.

The highest point of this small park is 224 metres, crowned by an impressive old pa site, Karangaumu, from where the whole of the Bay of Plenty is laid out before you. Beneath the pines on the uphill climb is an unusually dense understorey of the native plant kawakawa (*Macropiper excelsum*). Found in lowland forest in the North Island and the top half of the South Island, kawakawa is a small tree and easily recognised by its heart-shaped leaves and bamboo-like stems. More often than not the leaves are dotted with small holes formed by a looper caterpillar. Take some time to chew a small piece of a new leaf and enjoy the peppery taste followed by a mild numbness as you experience its anaesthetising effect. Early herbalists alleviated toothache by packing the infected tooth with kawakawa leaf, thereby numbing the pain.

3 Hauone Beach

Return to SH 2 and continue southeast for 36 km.

Beyond Te Puke, SH 2 continues along a particularly attractive stretch of coast. Dunes back a long magnificent reach of sand of which Hauone is just one beach, although there are numerous access points to others along this coast.

Old pohutukawa cling to crumbling cliffs above the road and there are plenty of places to stop for a swim or stroll along an empty shore. The surf can get wild here, and as there are no surf patrols take care when swimming. Just inland is the distinct volcanic cone of Mt Edgecumbe/Putauaki (821 metres), now extinct, rearing high above the Rangitaiki Plains.

Mount Edgecumbe and farmland.

Otarawaraire Bay near Whakatane.

Motuhora/Whale Island seen from Kohi Point, above Piripai Beach.

4 White Island/Whakaari

From Hauone continue east for 37 km to Whakatane from where sea trips to White Island depart.

White Island is one of the world's most accessible marine volcanoes, and a boat tour to the island includes a two-hour walk right inside the crater, where visitors are issued with a hard hat and a gas mask. Eruptions are frequent, the last major one in 2000, although the volcano is unlikely to erupt without warning. No eruptions have occurred while visitors have been on the island (visit www.whiteisland.co.nz for more information). There is also the option of taking a helicopter to Whakaari, either locally or from Rotorua.

5 Ohope Beach and Otarawairere Bay

From Whakatane drive a further 6 km to Ohope Beach. The short track to Otarawairere Bay is at the end of West End Road.

A long sandy stretch running from Kohi Point to Ohiwa Harbour, Ohope Beach is a popular seaside destination. Otarawairere Bay is a secluded beach only accessible by foot from the very western end of Ohope Beach via a good track that will take about 30 minutes one way. From a lookout point Ohope Beach and the eastern Bay of Plenty unfurl in the distance, framed by native bush including old pohutukawa, the home of tui and bellbirds. The beach itself is a small cove of sand and shell, enclosed by rocky headlands and overhung by huge pohutukawa trees, making this the ideal destination on a warm summer's day or for an early-morning walk. In the distance White Island smoulders away quietly.

6 Ohope Beach, pohutukawa forest

On immediately entering Ohope from Whakatane, the forest is to the right. The entrance is marked by an arch.

The usual image of the pohutukawa is of a gnarled old tree fringing a beach or clinging to a cliff face. However, pohutukawa is also a tree of the forest. Here in the Fairbrother Reserve the growth habit of this myrtle is much more upright, less spreading, and drawn up by the other trees of the forest to reach some surprising heights. This forest is dense with tall pohutukawa that range in age from saplings to ancient trees.

7 Ohiwa Harbour Sandspit Wildlife Refuge

From Ohope continue 8 km east along Pohutukawa Drive and Harbour Road to the car park by the golf course.

Ohiwa Harbour is very tidal, with over 70 per cent of the seabed exposed at low tide, making it one of the most important feeding grounds for wading and migratory birds such as the godwit, which flies non-stop from the Arctic each spring, the New Zealand dotterel and the oystercatcher. While there are reserves on both heads of the harbour, this one is on the western (Ohope) side and is the most accessible.

Unfortunately, there is no signage or map at the beginning of the reserve, and the only track is a four-wheel-drive access road through the middle of the dunes, which is not at all helpful if you are here to see the birds. The simplest way to access the spit is to follow the shore along the inner harbour to the entrance. This area is the main bird-watching site, with wading birds favouring the tidal flats and nesting seabirds occupying the sand above high tide. Ohiwa is also famous for its oysters, which can be purchased locally.

8 Hukutaia Domain, Opotiki

Head back along Harbour Road for 5 km and turn left into Wainui Road. Drive 15 km towards Opotiki, at which point the road joins SH 2. From here it is another 18 km to Opotiki. Just before the bridge over the Waioeka River turn right into Woodland Road. Continue 7 km down this road to the Hukutaia Domain.

This small reserve of low rainforest was established in 1918, primarily to protect Taketakerau, an ancient puriri. The tree was used by the local Upokorehe hapu (subtribe) to conceal the bones of notable dead from desecration by enemies, though after it was damaged in a storm the remains were buried elsewhere. Thought to be over 2000 years old, this huge tree is typical of puriri, with multiple short hollow trunks and a wide spreading crown of glossy leaves.

From 1933 to 1970 local amateur botanist Norman Potts travelled throughout New Zealand gathering trees and shrubs to be planted in the domain and created one of the most extensive collections of native flora in the country. His work was continued by Marc Heginbotham from 1970 to 1990.

9 Waioeka Gorge

The Waioeka Gorge begins 10 km south of Opotiki on SH 2. The road from Opotiki to Gisborne is 150 km in total.

New Zealand's longest reserve is the Waioeka Gorge, which follows the Waioeka River and Wairata Valley along the road from Opotiki to Gisborne. Covering 1800 hectares, the reserve protects the landscape on either side of the road for 50 km, creating a wonderful if lengthy drive through native bush and alongside fast rivers. To the east of the gorge is the Waioeka Conservation Area, covering nearly 40,000 hectares and protecting rare birds such as kaka and kiwi.

Some of the land was cleared for farming by returned soldiers after the Second World War, but the farms were not economical units and most were abandoned 20 years later to be reclaimed by bush. The road is sealed, but winding and slow. The historic Tauranga Bridge, 30 km from Opotiki, is a popular picnic spot and it's just a short walk down to the bridge over the Waioeka River. A longer loop walk through the bush will take three hours.

White Island/Whakaari

White Island is New Zealand's only active marine volcano. The island rises 1600 metres from the seabed, of which just 321 metres are above sea level. The volcano is unusual in that the water in the crater is derived from rainwater and condensed steam, as the volcano is sealed from the surrounding sea water, with the vent below sea level. Steam from the crater is sometimes visible from the mainland depending on the level of water in the lake.

A combination of the warm Auckland Current and heat from the volcano and underwater hot springs makes the waters around White Island several degrees warmer than the surrounding ocean. This attracts a wide variety of fish to this location, including subtropical species only found much further north, and they come in huge numbers. With visibility up to 30 metres, diving is exceptional (www.divewhite.co.nz).

Known by Maori as Whakaari ('to be made visible') and named White Island by Captain Cook in 1769, the island was mined for sulphur during the early twentieth century. Bear in mind that White Island is still very active and volatile, and while tour operators take every precaution the volcano can erupt without warning at any time.

GOT TIME? (+35KM)
10 Mayor Island/Tuhua

Lying off the Bay of Plenty coast, this rhyolite volcanic cone has a special appeal of its own. Dormant rather than extinct, Mayor Island/Tuhua has on average erupted every 3000 years over a period of some 130,000 years. Very similar in shape to the more active White Island further east, most of this island comprises a large caldera containing two small lakes appropriately, but unimaginatively, named 'Black' and 'Green'.

In pre-European times the island supported a significant Maori population that traded in obsidian or tuhua (hence its Maori name), a rare volcanic glass with a sharp edge that was a highly valued commodity in a stone-age culture.

Obsidian is still common on the island, and from the sea on the eastern side great veins, dark and glassy, are clearly visible. With the coming of iron tools Tuhua's population fell substantially, and as the terrain was unsuitable for farming it has remained virtually untouched for over 200 years.

Today the crater also contains a superb pohutukawa forest and recent clearance of pests has led to a recovery of native bird life, including bellbirds. A walk around the island will take approximately six hours and there is a good swimming spot in Sou' East Bay, where the boat lands. Blue Ocean Charters runs regular boat trips to Mayor Island from Mt Maunganui and the 35-km journey takes about two hours (ph 0800 224 278, www.blueocean.co.nz).

14 Rotorua

Geysers • Volcanoes • Boiling water and mud • Bush walks • Stunning lakes • 130 km

Based primarily on its geothermal activity, Rotorua has long been one of New Zealand's most popular tourist attractions. In addition to hot pools, bubbling mud and spouting geysers, the area also offers clear lakes, superb bush and mountain vistas.

> **INFORMATION**
> Rotorua i-SITE, 1167 Fenton Street, Rotorua, ph (07) 348 5179

Getting there

Rotorua is a comfortable three-hour drive from Auckland and all the main roads around the region are sealed and well maintained. Regular flights also link Rotorua to the main centres and major car rental companies are based there.

Best time to visit

Rotorua is a good all-year-round destination. The summers can be warm, while in winter the Rotorua basin can experience some bleak and cold days, with mornings often frosty. The cold and wet, however, can create spectacular steamy landscapes — often the best time to take the most impressive photos. In addition, Rotorua offers some excellent indoor attractions for a wet day, including a superb local museum; and, of course, what better excuse than a wet cold day to loll around in a hot pool? While it has great accommodation, bear in mind this does come under some pressure during long holiday weekends.

Facilities

One of New Zealand's most popular tourist towns, Rotorua has the best and most extensive range of accommodation anywhere in New Zealand and it is not usually difficult to find somewhere to stay. Likewise, there are plenty of choices when it comes to eating and the city has an extensive shopping centre. The major geothermal areas and attractions are commercially run businesses and can be expensive, especially by New Zealand standards, so before promising the family too much it would be prudent to check the prices of the individual attractions on their respective websites.

1 Lake Rotorua

Covering over 80 sq km, Lake Rotorua is the North Island's second-largest lake. The last major eruption occurred about 140,000 years ago and the crater has subsequently collapsed and partially filled with water. In fact, the whole Rotorua basin is part of a much larger crater known as the Rotorua caldera, of which the lake is the lowest point. The lake is very shallow, only 45 metres at its deepest, and the area on the southeastern shore where Rotorua City is situated is currently the most geothermally active.

2 Mokoia Island

At the centre of Lake Rotorua, Mokoia Island is a rhyolite dome of volcanic rock and was prized by Maori as a strategic defensive site and a rich fertile area to grow the valuable kumara. During the twentieth century, however, the island became considered too isolated and the last residents left in 1953. Today Mokoia is a bird sanctuary and an excellent place to view rare species such as the saddleback, stitchbird, brown teal and North Island weka, though visits are by organised tour only. Several trip operators are based on the lakeshore (www.mokoia-island.com).

3 Lake Okareka

From Rotorua take SH 30 east towards Whakatane. After 3.5 km turn right into Tarawera Road and continue for 5 km. Turn left into Okareka Loop Road and continue 4 km to Lake Okareka.

The landscape around Lake Okareka is quite different from other Rotorua lakes

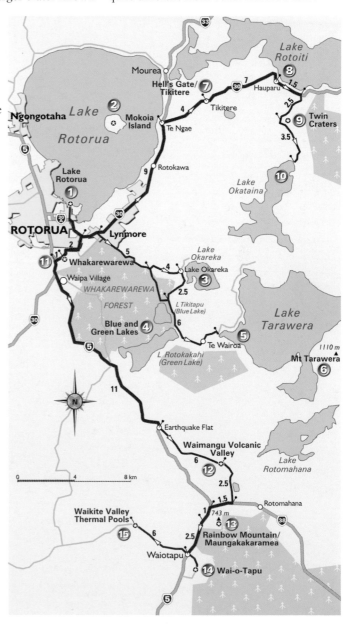

Sunrise over Lake Rotorua.

which are bush- or at least tree-fringed, whereas the land around Okareka is largely farmed. However, on one side of the lake is an extensive wetland area with an excellent track and boardwalks. The track cuts through a marshland of sedges, rushes and raupo, and is home to a wide range of freshwater aquatic birds including black swans, pukeko, shags, ducks and stilts. A hide in the middle of the wetland is an ideal spot for the enthusiastic bird-watcher.

4 Blue and Green Lakes
From Lake Okareka continue on the loop road to the Blue and Green Lakes, a distance of 2.5 km. The Blue Lake is 8 km from the turnoff on SH 30.

These two water-filled volcanic craters are obviously named for their colour and are known respectively in Maori as Tikitapu and Rotokakahi. Surrounded by a mix of native and exotic trees, the Blue Lake has no visible outlet, but drains underground into the Green Lake, 20 metres lower. The water level rises and falls substantially from year to year, meaning that at times the lake is ringed by beautiful small beaches, while for other periods all but two of these beaches disappear. An easy walk circumnavigates the Blue Lake and will take around one and a half hours. The Green Lake is restricted to members of local iwi.

5 Lake Tarawera
Continue along the Tarawera Road from the Blue Lake for 6 km to Lake Tarawera.

This large lake of beautiful clear water lies at the foot of Mt Tarawera and was substantially altered by the 1886 eruption, after which the lake level rose by an incredible 12 metres. The access point to the lake at Tarawera Landing has a small sandy beach and boat ramp. To the right of the car park is a short walk to the Wairua Stream, the outlet for the Green Lake, and to the left another short walk leads to rare Maori rock drawings and a pleasant sandy beach. Hot springs beneath the sand at Hot Water Beach on the northern arm of Tarawera create an area of warm water perfect for a relaxing swim. This beach is only accessible by boat, and charter boats operate from Tarawera Landing. For the more active, the Eastern Okataina Walkway follows the shore of Lake Okataina to Humphries Bay on Lake Tarawera and takes around three hours one way. Several boats offer trips on the lake (www.laketarawera.co.nz).

6 Mt Tarawera
Lying 24 km south of Rotorua, this mountain is a series of rhyolite domes, with two main peaks, Tarawera and Wahanga. At 1110 metres the top of the mountain is definitely subalpine.

In the early hours of 10 June 1886, Rotorua experienced a series of small earthquakes, followed at 1.30 am by an explosion and a large quake. At 2.30 am three peaks had erupted and at 3.30 am Lake Rotomahana blew out, covering a huge area in ash and volcanic debris. Heard as far away as Wellington and Auckland, the eruption was at first mistaken by some to be an attack by Russian warships. The eruption buried several nearby villages including Te Wairoa, destroyed the famous Pink and White Terraces and killed at least 150 people.

Rather than the more familiar circular crater usually associated with volcanoes, the crater at Tarawera is a gigantic raw rip extending the whole length of the mountain, and is particularly impressive from the air. Many lakes surrounding the mountain were drastically altered, including Lake Rotomahana, which originally was only one quarter its present size.

The mountain is now private property and access can only be gained through tours operated by Mt Tarawera Ltd (www.mt-tarawera.co.nz).

Lake Tarawera with Mt Tarawera.

7 Hell's Gate/Tikitere

Return to SH 30 and travel east from Rotorua. After 9 km turn right towards Whakatane. Hell's Gate is 4 km on the left.

Considered to be the most active of the Rotorua thermal areas, Hell's Gate is of great importance to the Ngati Rangiteaorere tribe, who have lived in this area for more than 700 years. Hell's Gate boasts a mud volcano that stands nearly 2 metres tall, Kakahi Falls, the largest hot waterfall in the southern hemisphere with an average temperature of 40°C, and the exceptionally hot 'Steaming Cliffs' pool. In addition to the thermal area there are hot mineral pools and a spa complex, which offers a bath of mud from the site said to be good for the skin (www.hellsgate.co.nz).

8 Lake Rotoiti

From Hell's Gate continue east on SH 30 for 7 km to Lake Rotoiti.

Lake Rotoiti is a bush-fringed lake linked to Lake Rotorua by the Ohau Channel and drained by the Kaituna River via Okere Falls at its northeastern corner. Like Lake Rotorua, Rotoiti is a crater lake and is famous for the rustic Manipura Hot Springs that are only accessible by boat.

From the eastern end of the lake Hongi's Track/Hinehopu is a fine one-hour bush walk that links Rotoiti to Lake Rotoehu. One of the highlights is the famous matai tree under where, as a baby, Hinehopu was hidden from enemies by her mother. It was also under this tree that Hinehopu met her husband, Pikiao, and many of the Ngati Pikiao iwi trace their lineage directly back to this ancestral couple.

Jetty at Lake Rotoiti.

Geothermal Rotorua

Rotorua lies at the heart of New Zealand's most active geothermal area, known as the Taupo Volcanic Zone. The zone stretches from the central North Island volcanoes to White Island in the eastern Bay of Plenty. Here the earth's crust is at its thinnest, with molten rock not far from the surface, allowing ground water to heat up and rise to the surface as hot water and steam. Major volcanic eruptions are most likely to occur within this zone. Common features of a geothermal zone are geysers, mud pools, hot springs and steaming ground, all of which are routinely found around Rotorua.

The main geyser activity is centred at Whakarewarewa, just a few kilometres from the centre of town. The largest geyser, Pohutu, can erupt as high as 30 metres, though 10 metres is more typical. In the early years of the twentieth century the Wairoa geyser at Whakarewarewa regularly erupted as high as 60 metres, but today it is dormant. However, beginning early in 1901, the largest recorded geyser in the world erupted at Waimangu and ended just as abruptly and inexplicably in November 1904. This extraordinary geyser regularly expelled a mix of water, sand and rocks to the height of 150 metres, and on one occasion an eruption reached 460 metres! (Auckland's Sky Tower is 330 metres.) Naturally, the Waimangu geyser became a great tourist attraction, until four people were killed in 1903 when the geyser erupted without warning.

The geothermal activity around Rotorua is unpredictable, with new hot pools appearing suddenly, frequent small earthquakes, and steam billowing out of the stormwater drains around the city.

Before you go — walking in geothermal areas

When geologists talk of the earth's crust as 'thin' in geothermal zones, they are talking literally not figuratively. The ground here is actually a thin layer over some extremely hot subterranean water and can collapse without warning. Thus, when walking in these areas, the warnings to stay on the paths are to be taken seriously as even the smallest steam vents are hot enough to inflict a painful burn.

Lake Okataina.

9 Twin Craters

Turn off SH 30 at Lake Rotoiti into Okataina Road and the track to the Twin Craters is 4 km on the left, opposite the turnoff to the Okataina Education Centre.

A crater formed over 3000 years ago now holds two small lakes, Rotongata and Rotoatua, a haven for water birds. An easy 40-minute walk begins through a grove of spectacular large totara, though most of the trees along the track are tawa, their light foliage giving the forest a soft filtered ambience. The steady climb leads to a high ridge overlooking Lake Rotongata and then follows the ridge to a lookout over Lake Rotoatua.

10 Lake Okataina

From the Twin Craters continue 3.5 km down the same road to Lake Okataina.

Okataina is a beautiful small lake surrounded entirely by bush, dominated by high rocky bluffs, and with no visible inlets or outlets, although water does seep through the rocks at Otangimoana Bay into Lake Tarawera, which is 20 metres lower. Over the years the lake level has varied by as much as 5 metres.

The Okataina Walkway on the eastern shore of the lake is an easy bush walk of three hours one way to the shores

of Lake Tarawera, with a swimming beach and views across the lake to the mountain. A shorter option is a 40-minute walk to Te Koutu pa, located on a small peninsula jutting out into the lake.

11 Whakarewarewa

From central Rotorua take SH 30 towards Taupo; Whakarewarewa is 3 km on the left.

Whakarewarewa is the best known of Rotorua's geothermal areas and, in particular, is famous for the most active and impressive geyser in the country, Pohutu. In addition to the geyser, silica terraces, boiling mud and scalding hot water also feature throughout the thermal valley.

The valley is divided between two tourist operators. Te Puia (www.tepuia. com) has the most thermal activity, and the Maori Arts and Crafts Institute offers fine examples of carved houses and gateways, while Whakarewarewa Thermal Village (www.whakarewarewa.com) is an actual Maori community with a geothermal background and presents a unique opportunity to observe daily life, albeit with a strong tourist bent.

12 Waimangu Volcanic Valley

From Rotorua travel 11 km south on SH 5, then turn left into Waimangu Road. The valley is 6 km along this road.

A direct result of the 1886 Tarawera eruption, the Waimangu Volcanic Valley is the newest geothermal system in the world. Lake Rotomahana exploded to 20

Pohutu Geyser, Whakarewarewa Thermal Reserve.

times its original size and seven craters erupted in the area that now makes up this valley, in which prior to 1886 there was no geothermal activity.

The valley is extensive and features several walks downhill through native bush linking the various thermal activities, and finally leading down to Lake Rotomahana. There is an option of a lake cruise and a bus to return to the visitor centre. This valley is also the site of the world's largest recorded geyser, which was active between 1901 and 1904; and in 1917 a huge explosion created the Frying Pan Lake, the world's largest hot-water spring.

Waimangu Valley is also a scenic reserve and wildlife refuge and has won a number of New Zealand ecotourism awards (www. waimangu.com).

13 Rainbow Mountain/ Maungakakaramea

From Waimangu continue on the loop road for 2.5 km to SH 38. Turn right and continue back to SH 5 for 1.5 km. Turn left into SH 5 and Rainbow Mountain is 1 km on the left.
Maungakakaramea, or Rainbow Mountain, lies about 25 km south of Rotorua. The mountain is scarred and torn by a series of volcanic eruptions going back thousands of years, the last of which is believed to have occurred around 1000 years ago. Today the mountain still steams and boils, and the geothermally active lake (an old crater) near the beginning of the track up the mountain presents the rare sight of ducks swimming unperturbed at one end, while at the other the water furiously boils.

Above the lake tower raw cliffs of red, orange and brown multi-hued volcanic rock that have been discoloured by continual exposure to steam, lending this mountain its European name. Many of the plants found on its slopes are peculiar in that they have specifically adapted to these harsh geothermal conditions.

14 Wai-o-Tapu

From Rainbow Mountain turn left back on to SH 5 and then into Waiotapu Road, 2.5 km on the left.
Wai-o-Tapu has been active for over 150,000 years and has the most surface geothermal activity in the area. As well as hot mud pools and boiling springs, the

Devil's Home Crater, Wai-o-Tapu Thermal Reserve.

park contains several unique features. As you enter there is a series of very deep craters (some up to 20 metres deep), at the bottom of which is ferociously boiling water that gives an extremely vivid impression of a look deep into the raw material of the planet.

The huge Primrose Terrace is a 1.5-hectare sinter terrace that has developed slowly over the past 700 years and is the largest such terrace in New Zealand. Stealing the show, however, are the coloured pools (these vary considerably with the conditions), including the multi-coloured Artist's Palette, the Champagne Pool, and the amazingly bright-green Devil's Bath. The Lady Knox Geyser (named after Lady Constance Knox, the daughter of Lord Ranfurly, New Zealand's fifteenth Governor) erupts to a height of up to 20 metres each day at 10.15 am (with

a bit of assistance), but is not in the main part of the park so allow 20 minutes' travel from the ticket office. The nearby huge Mud Pool is well worth the short detour and is free to enter (www.geyserland.co.nz).

15 Waikite Valley Thermal Pools

Return to SH 5 and directly opposite is Waikite Valley Road. The valley is 6 km down this road.
Tucked away in a quiet side valley, this mineral pool consists of a large family pool, a small soaking pool and private spas, and is fed by the impressive hot spring Te Manaroa. Accessed by a short walkway from the pool complex, this large spring is fringed by mosses and ferns and pulses scalding-hot water down a steaming narrow river past the pools. The hot river is particularly impressive on a cold winter's night when the whole valley fills with steam (www.hotpools.co.nz).

15 Central North Island • Orakei Korako to Mt Ruapehu

Huka Falls • Silica terraces • Tongariro Crossing • Lake Taupo • 200 km

The area around Lake Taupo, New Zealand's largest lake, is a geothermally diverse region that combines steaming hot pools and boiling mud with active volcanoes and alpine experiences second to none.

Getting there

Orakei Korako is 41 km south of Rotorua on SH 5. From SH 1 it is 55 km from Tokoroa. The roads are sealed and good, although snow occasionally causes problems in the middle of winter on SH 1 south of Turangi, on what is known as the Desert Road. If you intend to ski in winter then you will need snow chains if you're going up beyond the Department of Conservation Visitor Centre.

Best time to visit

The central North Island is a popular summer as well as winter destination. In summer the activity focuses on Lake Taupo, though it is also the preferred season for tramping in Tongariro National Park. Winter brings the snow-sport enthusiasts as Mt Ruapehu has ski fields on the northern slopes at Whakapapa, and on the southern slopes at Turoa via Ohakune. The mountains, isolated within the central North Island, can be exposed to high winds, snow and ice at any time of the year. School holiday periods in the winter can be very busy with skiing trips.

Taupo also hosts a number of very large sporting events and during these times the town is absolutely packed. If you haven't organised accommodation the only options might be sleeping in the car or moving on. Check www.laketauponz.com for details and remember that Rotorua is only an hour's drive away if you are stuck for a bed.

Facilities

Both Rotorua and Taupo have extensive accommodation, places to eat and shopping, so there is generally not too much problem finding what you need. There is a scattering of motels and camping grounds on Lake Taupo's southeastern shores, but almost nothing elsewhere as access to the northern and western shores of the lake is very limited. Turangi and National Park townships are considerably smaller centres, but they are closer to the mountain and have limited accommodation proving popular with skiers.

1 Orakei Karako Cave and Thermal Park

From Rotorua head towards Taupo on SH 5 for 41 km and then turn right into Tutukau Road. Continue along this road for 16 km then turn right into Orakei Korako Road and drive 5 km.

This active and unpredictable thermal area consists of three large broad silica terraces containing geysers, boiling springs and mud pools. The terraces, formed by an earthquake in AD 131, are covered with brightly coloured hot-water algae and multi-hued silica deposits created by aeons of hot water cascading over the rocky base. Above the terraces is the Ruatapu Cave, at the bottom of which is the warm Waiwhakaata Pool ('Pool of Mirrors'), where visitors can make a wish that will come true provided they have their left hand in the water and tell no one what they have wished for.

With the fewest visitors of all the thermal areas, this one is the least crowded and feels the most natural. Accessed by a short boat trip across the Waikato River, the area is relatively compact, with 2.5 km of good tracks and boardwalks easily managed by most people.

2 Craters of the Moon

Return to SH 5 and turn right towards Taupo. Craters of the Moon is 30 km on the right, 3 km after SH 5 joins SH 1.

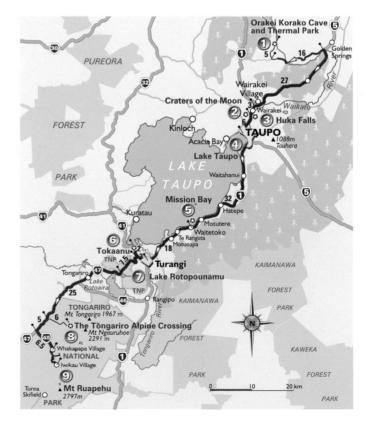

The Craters of the Moon is one of the most recent and most active thermal fields in the area and is constantly changing. Over the years the thermal area has expanded considerably and the activity is unpredictable; sometimes mass columns of steam rise from the entire field, while at others it is disappointingly quiet. The most common thermal activity is in the form of steam vents, though there is one major crater with furiously boiling mud or water depending on the water levels. The area is open and populated with intriguing low-growing plants that have adapted to the inhospitable environment (www.cratersofthemoon.co.nz; entry fee applies).

3 Huka Falls

The road to Huka Falls is opposite Craters of the Moon. The falls are 5 km along this road.
Although modest in size with a final drop of only 10 metres, the sheer volume of beautiful bright clear water that gushes through this narrow gap is spectacular. Above the falls the Waikato River is about 100 metres wide, but at the falls more than 200,000 litres per second is forced through a granite gap 15 metres wide with a fury that is truly impressive.

Rather than drive to the waterfall, the easy walkway from Spa Road in Taupo is a very appealing way to get there. The walk takes an hour one way and passes a small ho-water stream that joins the river, creating a popular swimming hole where hot water mingles with the cooler water of the Waikato River. As it leaves Lake Taupo the river is stunning, with clean and clear waters that are a beautiful iridescent blue-green.

4 Lake Taupo

Return to SH 1 and drive 6 km to Taupo.
Fed by melting snow from the mountains to the south and covering an area of 616 sq km, Lake Taupo is New Zealand's largest lake and is 186 metres at its deepest point. The whole basin is in fact an old caldera created by a series of 30 eruptions over the last 27,000 years. While the last eruption — known as the Hatepe eruption — took place over 1800 years ago, the area around the lake is still geothermally active, particularly around Wairakei, to the northeast, and Tokaanu in the southwest.

Huka Falls.

That eruption, however, is believed to be the largest in recorded history and was seen in both Rome and China in the form of particularly vivid sunsets. Situated on the western side of the lake, this explosion ejected 100 cubic km of volcanic material and devastated much of the surrounding region. The buried forest at Pureora, 70 km distant, is an area of flattened forest knocked over by the incredible force of the blast. A towering wall of water was sent thundering down the Waikato, breaking through the hills at Taupiri and permanently changing the course of the river. Huge kauri felled by the flood have been uncovered in swamps near Huntly.

Lake Taupo.

Tussockland before Mt Ngauruhoe.

while elsewhere hissing steam escapes from fissures in the ground. A short 20-minute loop track through the thermal area begins right beside the entrance to the public hot pools (an entry fee applies to the pools).

7 Lake Rotopounamu
Return 2 km along SH 41 to SH 47/Ponanga Saddle Road and turn right. Continue on SH 47 for 7.5 km.

Rotopounamu means 'greenstone lake', and refers to the colour of the water, although no greenstone is found here and the water is not always green. Despite its circular shape and the nearby volcanic activity, the lake is not actually a crater but was formed thousands of years ago by a giant landslide. With no visible outlet it is believed that water seeps out through cracks in the lake bed.

The track around the lake is largely flat, following the edges of the water through a mature forest of red beech, kahikatea, rimu and matai. On the eastern shore is Long Beach, an ideal picnic spot and a good place for a swim on a hot summer's day.

8 Tongariro Alpine Crossing
From Rotopounamu continue for 25 km on SH 47 to Mangatepopo Road. The crossing is 6 km on, at the end of a winding gravel stretch.

Universally described as one of 'the best one-day walks in the world', the Tongariro Alpine Crossing traverses the most dramatic volcanic landscape in New Zealand. The vistas are superb, and the atmosphere is like returning to the beginning of time. It will come as no surprise that parts of *The Lord of the Rings* movies were filmed here.

The trip usually starts at the Mangatepopo end with a steady climb up the steep Mangatepopo Bluff on to the South Crater. If a side trip up Ngauruhoe is planned the track begins from the South Crater, and while the scree slope is solid climbing going up, it is a quick trip down and the view from the summit is simply magnificent.

From the South Crater the climb is up and over the rim of the active Red Crater, the highest point on the track at 1886 metres. From here an easy side trip of around two hours return can be made to the summit of Tongariro (1968 metres). From the Red Crater the track skirts two

5 Mission Bay
Continue around the lake on SH 1 to Mission Bay, 32 km from Taupo township.

While Taupo itself is pretty touristy, much of the lake's shoreline is reasonably free of ugly development. Mission Bay, backed by bush-covered bluffs, is a particularly pretty spot. It is on the eastern side of the lake with small pumice beaches, pleasant picnic spots and excellent views across the water to the snow-capped peaks to the south.

6 Tokaanu
From Mission Bay continue for 18 km on SH 1 to Turangi. Turn right on to SH 41 and drive 5 km to Tokaanu.

Once used by local Maori for bathing and cooking, this active thermal area provides a pleasant diversion. Pools of crystal-clear water bubble up from deep in the earth, while in other places brilliant green-blue pools steam gently among the manuka. Small pots of boiling mud plop steadily,

Red Crater and Ngauruhoe, Tongariro Alpine Crossing.

small lakes and follows the rim of the central crater and then is a long downhill trek via the Ketetahi Hut. This hut is usually packed in summer, so if you're planning a two-day trip a good alternative route is the much less populated Waihonunu Track which runs from the north side of the Red Crater and down the raw and rugged lava valley. Along this track you can stay overnight in either the Oturere or Waihonunu Huts, exiting the park on to SH 1.

Transport can be arranged from Taupo, Turangi and National Park. The weather is notoriously fickle, and even in the height of summer the mountaintop can be very exposed to freezing rain and wind. People die on this mountain and you need to be prepared. At a minimum you require good boots, a pair of thick socks, long waterproof trousers, warm clothing, a good wind- and waterproof jacket, gloves, a warm hat plus food and drink.

9 Mt Ruapehu

From Mangatepopo Road continue west on SH 47 for 5 km to the Whakapapa turnoff. Drive 6.5 km to the Department of Conservation Visitor Centre at Whakapapa Village. From here it is 7 km on a sealed road to the Top o' the Bruce at the end of the road.

Ruapehu began its volcanic life some 120,000 years ago. Standing at 2798 metres, it is New Zealand's highest volcano and the highest mountain in the North Island. The last major eruptions were in 1945/46 and 1995/96, although between this period a further 60 smaller eruptions occurred. Ruapehu is the source of four major rivers and has eight glaciers — the only glaciers in the North Island.

The crater contains a small lake that varies considerably in size and disappeared completely during the 1995 eruptions. It was a lahar from this crater-lake that swept down the Whangaehu River on Christmas Eve 1953, washing away the rail bridge at Tangiwai and resulting in the overnight express train crashing into the river, killing 151 people. A similar lahar in 2007 was successfully monitored and damage was minimal. The landscape around the mountain is a mixture of raw lava, tussock, herbfields and small pockets of beech forest. The summit, which is permanently snow-capped, is a demanding but manageable day hike.

Around Whakapapa are several excellent short walks, including Taranaki Falls (one and a half hours return) and

the Tawhai Falls (20 minutes return). The Mounds on the right near the Whakapapa turnoff are geologically fascinating if not exactly riveting viewing. These hillocks were formed by a landslide of volcanic material on the northern slopes of Mt Ruapehu so massive that the debris created a wave pattern resulting in a series of small mounds spread over a distance of many kilometres. There is a viewing platform on one of the higher mounds where you can get some sense of the scale of this huge landslide.

The Tongariro National Park Visitor Centre at Whakapapa has excellent natural history displays and provides up-to-date information on tracks and weather.

Tongariro National Park
Gifted to the people of New Zealand in 1887 by paramount chief Te Heuheu Tukino IV on behalf of the people of Tuwharetoa, Tongariro was New Zealand's first national park and the fourth such park in the world. The three volcanic peaks of Ruapehu (2797 m), Ngauruhoe (2290 m) and Tongariro (1968 m) are within the park. Ruapehu and Ngauruhoe are active volcanoes that erupt periodically; the last major event was the eruption of Ruapehu in 1995/96.

Covering nearly 80,000 hectares, Tongariro is more than just mountains. Interwoven with the stark volcanic landscape of lava and ash are vast expanses of golden tussock and flax, pristine streams, herbfields and untouched rainforest, providing a stark visual contrast of natural elements. The mainly beech forest has survived in pockets and in sheltered valleys protected from both the Taupo eruption and recent, more localised, volcanic activity. There are numerous tracks and walks throughout the park, many based around or near Whakapapa Village on the northern slopes of the mountain. The park is also home to two ski fields, Turoa and Whakapapa.

16 The East Cape and Poverty Bay

Secluded beaches • Feeding stingrays • Pohutukawa • East Cape • 428 km

Even by New Zealand standards the East Cape and Poverty Bay are remote, but therein lies the region's greatest appeal: uncrowded beaches and an unhurried atmosphere, all in an unrivalled climate.

INFORMATION
Gisborne i-SITE, 209 Grey St,
Gisborne, ph (06) 868 6139
Opotiki i-SITE, cnr St John and
Elliott Streets, Opotiki,
ph (07) 315 3031

Getting there

The trip can begin from Opotiki, a good five to six-hour drive from Auckland, or Gisborne if you are coming from the south, an even longer drive from Wellington and a three- to four-hour drive from Napier. SH 35 around the cape is a good sealed road and, while not fast, is easy travelling.

Side roads are almost all gravel, but none are especially long or arduous.

Best time to visit

The popular visitor season is strangely short in this region. New Zealanders pack out the East Cape and Gisborne from mid-December through to the end of January, the traditional school holiday period. As the region doesn't attract so many overseas visitors, February and March are a glorious time on the East Cape: the weather is hot and sunny, the sea is warm and inviting, accommodation is easy, and this is the perfect place to relax. Winters can be cold, particularly with weather from the south, but they are usually short.

Facilities

While Gisborne has plenty of services, cafés and places to stay, the cape along SH 35 is another story. Camping is plentiful (there is an especially lovely camping ground at Anaura Bay), but motels and other accommodation are extremely limited. If you have any intention of staying anywhere between Opotiki and Gisborne during the summer then you have to book ahead. (Both Gisborne and Opotiki have good visitor centres and they will be able to help.)

Likewise, the East Cape has little in the way of facilities,

with very few cafés and just the occasional general store. It is best to leave Gisborne or Opotiki with a full tank of petrol as, while the general stores sell petrol, it is much more expensive than in the larger towns.

1 Motu River

SH 35 crosses the Motu River 40 km from Opotiki.

State Highway 35 crosses the Motu at the point where the river ends its tempestuous journey to the sea. Rising in the Raukumara Ranges, this wild river is one of the last untouched waterways in the country, running for almost its entire length through deep gorges and steep, bush-covered hills. One of the last rivers to be explored in New Zealand, in 1919 an expedition party travelled down the Motu and took 10 days, ran out of supplies, and was eventually met by a rescue party. The Motu River is now protected from any further development by a special Act of Parliament, which has created a Wilderness Zone around it. Today it is very popular with experienced kayakers and white-water rafters. Jet-boat trips up the river are available, leaving from the Motu River Bridge on SH 35.

2 Cape Runaway

From the Motu River, continue 73 km along SH 35 to Whangaparaoa Bay, which lies in the lee of Cape Runaway.

Cape Runaway is the most northerly point of the East Cape region and marks the boundary between the eastern Bay of Plenty and the Gisborne side of the cape.

Usually treated as one entity, the East Cape in reality is two distinct regions, both in landscape and climate. From Opotiki to Cape Runaway the road hugs the rugged coast, weaving in and out of sandy bays and small rocky coves. The area, open to moist northerly winds, has high rainfall resulting in fast-flowing rivers and bush-

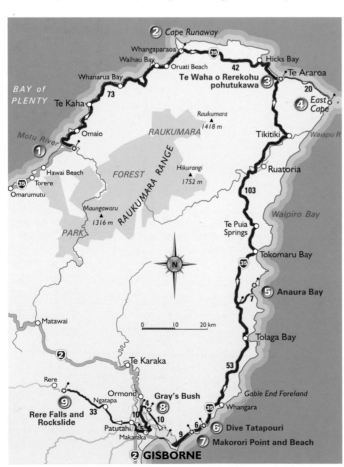

Motu River.

clad hills. In contrast, the eastern side of the cape is much drier, and the bush, cleared in the nineteenth century, has struggled to return.

The road is mostly inland, touching the coast occasionally, but on this coast the beaches are wider and more sheltered.

3 Te Waha o Rerekohu Pohutukawa, Te Araroa

Te Araroa is 42 km from Cape Runaway, just off SH 35.

Reputedly the largest pohutukawa in the world, this massive tree, known as Te Waha o Rerekohu, is almost at the southern natural limit of the species. Spreading over a wide area on the beach at Te Araroa, the tree is 20 metres high and 40 metres at its widest point and estimated to be over 600 years old. Te Waha o Rerekohu is tapu (sacred) so do not climb it.

4 East Cape

The cape is 20 km east of Te Araroa via a winding gravel road.

The East Cape, together with the small offshore East Island, is the most easterly

Te Waha o Rerekohu, possibly the world's largest pohutukawa.

Anaura Bay with Motuoroi Island off the coast.

point of the North Island of New Zealand (the Chatham Islands are in fact the country's most easterly territory, and are sometimes described as 'the last place on earth'). A lighthouse built in 1922 on a 150-metre hill has great views over the surrounding coast.

5 Anaura Bay
SH 35 continues south for 103 km to the Anaura Bay Road turnoff, from where it is 7 km down to the beach.

Anaura Bay is a stunning crescent of white sand, with the tiny Motuoroi Island standing just offshore. The bay is widely regarded as having one of the finest unspoilt beaches on the East Cape. Behind the bay is Anaura Bay Scenic Reserve, 225 hectares of rare native forest, including fine stands of mature puriri, kahikatea and titoki. A loop walk through the bush will take around two hours and from a lookout there are fine views over the bay.

6 Wild Stingray Feeding, Dive Tatapouri
Return to SH 35 and continue south for 53 km to Tatapouri.

Lying just 100 metres off Tatapouri Beach is a reef that becomes exposed at low tide, and it is here that Dive Tatapouri has developed a unique attraction.

The area is home to stingrays that live in the deep channels of the reef to avoid predators and, attracted by regular feeding, will come right up to people and feed from their hands. Mainly eagle and short-tailed rays, the largest of the regular ray visitors is Brutus, who is estimated to weigh around 200 kg. The regular food also attracts other sea creatures such as the shy conger eel, kahawai, kingfish and the very occasional orca (which have an appetite for stingray!).

The trip to the reef is tide and weather dependent (ph (06) 868 5153, www.divetatapouri.com).

7 Makorori Point and Beach

Makorori Beach is 2 km south of Tatapouri.
North of Gisborne is a string of beautiful sandy beaches best known for their lively surf. Most are developed to some degree, apart from Makorori just north of Wainui Beach, though in reality there is plenty of space along this coast for everyone, even at the height of summer.

Between Makorori and Wainui Beaches is Makorori Point, where a short walk to a lookout has spectacular coastal views to the south, beyond Young Nicks Head to the Mahia Peninsula and to the north over Makorori Beach.

On the other side of SH 35 from the point is Okitu Bush Scenic Reserve, a small coastal forest remnant. It takes around 20 minutes to walk the loop track to a lookout.

8 Gray's Bush

Drive from Makorori to Gisborne, 9 km on SH 35. From Gisborne take Back Ormond Road for 10 km to Gray's Bush.
The only remaining lowland bush on the Poverty Bay plain, Gray's Bush is a subtropical forest with an understorey of nikau palms and massive kahikatea and puriri. The combination of the latter trees is unusual in that the puriri tends to favour well-drained soils, while kahikatea thrives in wet conditions. Early recognition of that unique forest combination saved this bush from the axe. Furthermore, the height of the kahikatea has resulted in the puriri growing much taller and straighter than their usual spreading habit.

9 Rere Falls and Rockslide

From Gray's Bush continue on Back Ormond Road for 4 km to the intersection of SH 2, turn left and drive 10 km to Makaraka. At Makaraka turn right and continue on SH 2 for 5 km. At the Waipaoa Bridge roundabout turn right again and follow the Wharekopae Road for 33 km to Rere Falls.
No more than 6 metres high, the Rere Falls make up for a lack of height by being particularly picturesque. Here the Wharekopae River tumbles down an escarpment to form a broad waterfall, made extra appealing because behind the tumbling veil is a cave hollowed out over aeons by the constant action of the water. The swimming hole is a particularly welcoming spot in summer and the falls area has a large grassed picnic area.

Just upstream is the Rere Rockslide, a 60-metre cascade of water and very popular as a natural water slide. A boogie board, wetsuit or something robust to slide on is essential.

Manuka and Kanuka

Widespread throughout New Zealand, manuka (*Leptospermum scoparium*) and its close relative kanuka (*Leptospermum ericoides*) are two of the most common native trees in New Zealand and have for a long time been regarded as little more than weedy scrub. The cousins have flourished as colonising plants on rough ground following the clearance of larger trees and can handle almost any condition from very wet through to extremely dry.

The differences between the trees are subtle. Kanuka is taller, growing up to 15 metres, and has softer, more rounded leaves and smaller flowers. Manuka (see image) is more likely to have a variety of colours to the flowers, ranging from white through to red, and specially bred varieties are now widely planted as ornamental shrubs. The wood is very hard and valued as firewood. The tree is closely related to the Australian tea tree and to similar plants in New Caledonia and Malaysia, and a separate species is found only on Great Barrier Island.

The common name 'tea tree' is said to have been first used by Captain James Cook who boiled the plant for tea to prevent scurvy. Today, manuka is recognised for the valuable role it plays as a nursery plant, stabilising previously cleared ground and providing cover for the saplings of more substantial natives. However, it also makes for a handsome tree in its own right, with attractive flaky bark and a light open canopy. Manuka oil and manuka honey are both highly regarded for their antibacterial and antifungal properties.

17 Te Urewera and Environs • Te Urewera National Park

Untouched wilderness • Waterfalls • Whirinaki Forest • 250 km

Well off the beaten track, Te Urewera is without a doubt one of the best-preserved wilderness areas in New Zealand, and with that comes prolific bird life and virgin forest offering a glimpse into the Aotearoa of the past.

INFORMATION
Aniwaniwa Visitor Centre and Museum, Lake Waikaremoana,
ph (06) 837 3803
Wairoa i-SITE, cnr SH 2 and Queen Street, Wairoa, ph (06) 838 7440
Gisborne i-SITE, 209 Grey Street, Gisborne, ph (06) 868 6139

Getting there

Quite simply, there is the short way or the long way. This trip begins in Rotorua and takes in the Whirinaki Forest. Beyond Murupara the road is narrow, winding and, for most of its 100 km, gravel. While it does traverse some magnificent country, the route is slow driving and if car sickness is a problem don't even think about it.

The alternative is to approach the park from the Hawke's Bay side, a distance of just 65 km from Wairoa to the Aniwaniwa Visitor Centre on a road sealed all the way. Most of the walks and the more spectacular part of the lakeshore are within 20 km of the visitor centre. The last section of the tour is from Frasertown to Gisborne via Tiniroto. The road is not fast, but is sealed and this is an attractive alternative to SH 2 from Wairoa to Gisborne if you're looking for a change of scenery. However, this part of the trip can be easily substituted with the SH 2 option from Wairoa to Gisborne via Nuhaka, a distance of 95 km (see Hawke's Bay entry for details).

Best time to visit

Te Urewera is cold and wet during winter and snow is not uncommon, so this is definitely a trip for the warmer months. The Waikaremoana Great Walk is popular, especially during the school holidays as the trip is suitable for younger people, but its popularity means you definitely have to book ahead.

Facilities

Apart from camping grounds, facilities are pretty thin on the ground through Te Urewera. You will need to make sure you have filled up with petrol in either Murupara or Wairoa and, other than the little shopping centres at these towns, there is only the occasional small general store along this road. There is a good range of accommodation at Wairoa, and a large camping ground on the shores of Lake Waikaremoana with cabins and camping sites.

1 Whirinaki Forest Park

From Rotorua take SH 5 south for 23 km, then turn left into SH 38 and travel 37 km to Murupara and then a further 21 km on Route 38 to Te Whaiti; this road is sealed but winding. Turn right into Minginui Road and travel 10 km to the forest park.

Famed for huge trees, rare bird life and pristine waterways, the 55,000-hectare Whirinaki Forest lies between the wild and mysterious Te Urewera National Park and the pine trees of Kaingaroa, the largest planted forest in the world.

In the 1980s Whirinaki, like Pureora further north, was a major conservation battleground, with the forest finally saved from the axe, but leaving side by side the oddly contrasting landscapes of untouched native bush and commercial pine plantation. Matai, kahikatea, miro, totara and rimu grow to a magnificent size in this forest, and support bird life such as kaka, kakariki, kereru and the endangered whio, or blue duck.

There are a number of short walks near Minginui including Forest Sanctuary, Arahaki Lagoon and Te Whaiti Nui-a-Toi Canyon walks and, for the more determined tramper, the four-day Whirinaki Circuit.

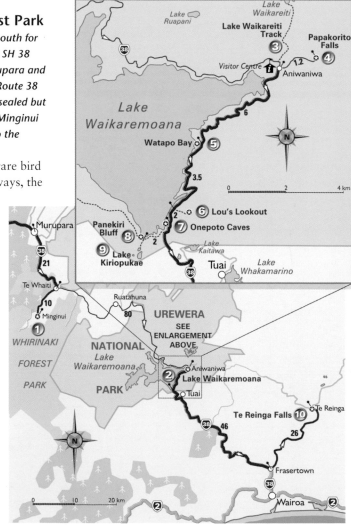

Te Whaiti Nui-a-Toi Canyon, Whirinaki Forest Park.

2 Lake Waikaremoana

Return to Route 38 and turn right and drive 80 km to the park headquarters at Waikaremoana. This road is winding, gravel and rough.

This large lake, formed only 2000 years ago by a massive landslide across the Waikaretaheke River, lies at the centre of the rugged Te Urewera National Park. The lake is over 240 metres deep and has deep bays that extend far into the rugged bush-covered terrain.

The Lake Waikaremoana Great Walk follows the shore for most of its 46 km. It is by no means flat, but is within the reach of a moderately fit tramper who is prepared for a three to four-day trip. In addition to the continual lake views, the bird life is prolific and the virgin bush is magnificent. The weather in the area is very changeable and can be cold and wet even in summer, while snow is common during winter.

Due to the popularity of the tramp, it is necessary to book huts and campsites well ahead in the busy season. However, as an alternative, a water taxi is available for those who wish to shorten their journey or even do sections of the walk as a day trip (www.lakewaikaremoana.co.nz).

WAIKAREMOANA SHORT WALKS (entries 3–9)

If the Great Lakes Walk is not an option there are several excellent short walks, all within 20 km of the Aniwaniwa Visitor Centre and Museum. This visitor centre is a destination in its own right with up-to-date information on weather and tracks and excellent natural history displays. Housed within the centre is a small museum, home to the famous Colin McCahon *Urewera Mural*, a huge triptych painting that was stolen from this location in 1997 and returned 15 months later.

3 Lake Waikareiti Track

The track begins 200 metres from the visitor centre and takes one hour one way to the lake through red and silver beech trees. Lake Waikareiti is free from introduced aquatic plants and is renowned for its remarkable clarity and pristine surrounding bush.

4 Papakorito Falls

Just 1.2 km from the Aniwaniwa Visitor Centre down Aniwaniwa Road and only a few minutes' walk from the car park, Papakorito is a very picturesque waterfall that drops over a wide bluff and fans out over a rocky outcrop into a broad pool.

Mokau Stream drains into Lake Waikaremoana, Te Urewera National Park.

Te Urewera National Park

Established in 1954, at over 212,000 hectares Te Urewera National Park is the largest native forest in the North Island. Located at its very heart is Lake Waikaremoana, New Zealand's second-largest lake. Over 600 native plants have been recorded in the area and all the North Island native birds can be found here, with the exception of weka. The northern part of the park is home to the largest remaining population of the North Island kokako.

Te Urewera has always been isolated country — rugged and bush-covered, this is a land of steep hills, deep valleys and a tough climate. It is also the home of the Tuhoe, known as the 'Children of the Mist', the last iwi (tribe) to be influenced by Europeans and regarded as a fiercely independent people. As in the past, even today much of the park is remote and not easily accessible — a condition that has contributed to the protection of its flora and fauna.

7 Onepoto Caves

Onepoto Caves are a further 1 km south of Lou's Lookout. The return trip takes around two hours. The caves are an intricate system of tunnels and cavities under and between the massive jumble of limestone rocks deposited by the landside that formed the lake. Subsequently shaped by water and overgrown by trees, this is a fantastic landscape of hidden recesses.

The caves, not surprisingly, were used by early Maori as a refuge from enemies. You will need a torch and keep a lookout for cave weta as they are common.

8 Panekiri Bluff

Panekiri Bluff is 1 km south of the entrance to the Onepoto Caves. The bluff dominates the southern end of the lake, rising to over 1100 metres at the summit, which is known as Puketapu. The first trig can be reached after a steady uphill walk of one hour and there are magnificent views across the lake. The track begins at the far end of the flat grassed area that was the old Armed Constabulary parade ground.

9 Lake Kiriopukae

Lake Kiriopukae is located on the same track as that to the Panekiri Bluff and is a small wetland that expands and shrinks considerably with the season. Surrounded by delicate limestone outcrops and weather-sculpted boulders, the lake has the tranquil feel of a natural Japanese garden.

10 Te Reinga Falls

From the lake travel 46 km towards Wairoa to Frasertown. Turn left into Tiniroto Road and drive 26 km to Te Reinga Falls (that are clearly signposted). From the falls it is a further 80 km to Gisborne.

Here the waters of the Ruakituri River are forced through a narrow limestone gorge and over the 35-metre Te Reinga Falls. Over time, the exposure of the limestone has revealed numerous fossils of long-extinct penguins, whales, seals and dolphins. Fossilised shellfish are reminders that over 3 million years ago this terrain was once a seabed.

While the view of the falls from the short track is not particularly satisfactory, the back road from Wairoa to Gisborne, once the main coach road, is sealed, pleasant driving and a good alternative to SH 2 further east.

5 Whatapo Bay

Situated 5.5 km south of the Aniwaniwa Visitor Centre is a pleasant sandy beach backed by bush with views out over the lake and south to Panekiri Bluff. It's also a good swimming spot if you're game enough to brave Waikaremoana's cool waters. In the car park is an enclosure containing kaka beak, an attractive native flowering shrub that is now rare in the wild owing to introduced pests such as the possum.

6 Lou's Lookout

Lou's Lookout is 3 km south of Whatapo Bay and is a short uphill walk through massive limestone boulders that are a startling indication of the size of the enormous landslip that occurred over 2000 years ago, blocking the Waikaretaheke River and creating Lake Waikaremoana. The boulders now form arches, caves and overhangs along this track. At the top the reward is a fantastic lake view that includes the dramatic Panekiri Bluff to the south.

18 Hawke's Bay • Napier to Gisborne

Gannets • Lonely beaches • Wetlands • Mineral hot springs • 270 km

Traversing some particularly rugged hill country, the northern Hawke's Bay is a region of surprising natural gems, mostly undiscovered by New Zealanders and international visitors alike.

INFORMATION
Napier i-SITE, 100 Marine Parade,
Napier, ph (06) 834 1911
Hastings i-SITE, cnr Russell and
Heretaunga Streets, Hastings, ph
(06) 873 5526 or 0800 429 537
Wairoa i-SITE, cnr SH 2 and Queen
Street, Wairoa, ph (06) 838 7440
Gisborne i-SITE, 209 Grey St,
Gisborne, ph (06) 868 6139

Getting there

The tour starts in Napier and finishes far to the north, in Gisborne. While the main highway is sealed, it winds through steep hill country, so it isn't a fast road by any means. The side roads are mainly gravel, but are not difficult.

Best time to visit

The Hawke's Bay is well known for its hot dry summers and from November through to May is a good time to visit. The region is exposed to southerly weather and can be surprisingly cold in the middle of winter, though not particularly wet. During January and February, the Bay hosts a number of very popular events including Harvest Hawke's Bay, the Mission Estate Winery Concert and Art Deco Weekend. Be warned that during this time casual accommodation is nigh on impossible to find. If your travels include a weekend in the Hawke's Bay any time between Christmas and Easter, it will pay to book well ahead.

Facilities

Both Napier and Hastings have a wide range of accommodation, good places to eat, and all the shopping and services you'll require. Napier, with its extensive art deco architecture, tends to attract more visitors. Hawke's Bay is famous for its

excellent wines, and in addition vineyards throughout the Bay run top-rated restaurants and smart cafés, and many offer boutique accommodation as well.

To the north, Wairoa has a hotel, motel, camping accommodation and shopping. The local Osler's Bakery is famous for its award-winning pies and cakes. While not New Zealand's smartest town, Wairoa is a good halfway point, especially if you plan a side trip to Te Urewera National Park.

1 Ahuriri Lagoon

From Napier follow SH 2 north for 6 km to Westshore and the Ahuriri Lagoon is on the left. The Ahuriri Lagoon, once the estuary for both the Tutaekuri and Waiohinganga (Esk) Rivers, was a vast tidal wetland until the Napier earthquake of 1931. Raising the ground level by over 2 metres, the quake created nearly 4000 hectares of dry land, reducing the wetland to a fraction of its original size. Rorookuri Hill, at the northern end of the lagoon, was once

an island. Subsequent draining and infill reduced the lagoon even further, and today Ahuriri is a small but vital wetland for both migratory and wading birds.

2 Waipatiki Reserve and Beach

Continue north on SH 2 for 18 km and turn right into Tangoio Settlement Road. After 6 km turn right again, into Waipatiki Road. The reserve is 4 km on the left and Waipatiki Beach is 2 km beyond that.

So little native lowland forest remains in the Hawke's Bay that it's hard to believe that the region was once densely covered with lush bush like that at Waipatiki. Thick with mosses, ferns and nikau palms, the 64-hectare reserve is a dramatic contrast to the pine forest and bare tawny hills surrounding the area. The striking subtropical nature of the reserve is such that even locals claim this bush is 'unusual'. However, it is also a sad reminder of the irreplaceable forest that has been lost due to logging. While the reserve contains dense

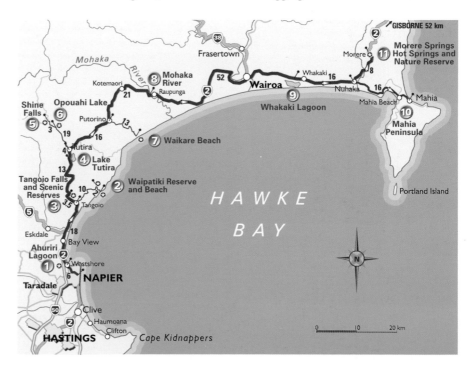

nikau groves and some 400-year-old trees, enormous tree stumps are the telltale signs of former forest giants.

Waipatiki Beach, just down the road from the reserve, is a sandy beach, providing contrast to the numerous pebble beaches of the Hawke's Bay.

3 Tangoio Falls Scenic Reserve

Return the way you came to SH 2 and turn right. The falls are 3.5 km on the right.
The 550-hectare Tangoio Scenic Reserve has two short walks along the Kareaara Stream to a pair of small but attractive waterfalls. The Te Ana Falls plunge out of a narrow gap in a rock face and arch into a small swimming hole. The Tangoio Falls are a much gentler affair, spreading gracefully over a wide rock face in a fern- and moss-clad basin. The walk to the Te Ana Falls is easy, while the side track to the Tangoio Falls is a bit rougher and muddier.

4 Lake Tutira

From Tangoio continue 13 km north on SH 2 to Lake Tutira.
This popular swimming and picnic spot was originally part of the Tutira Station, owned by farmer and author Herbert Guthrie-Smith. Recognising very early on the need for conservation of native plants and birds, in 1921 Guthrie-Smith published his massive tome *Tutira: The Story of a New Zealand Sheep Station*, based on years of painstaking observation and note-taking.

The lake is alive with water birds including ducks, pukeko, swans, herons and teal, and the early fertility of the land is attested to by numerous pa sites around its environs. There are two short walks on the eastern side of the lake and a short 30-minute walk around tiny Lake Waikapiro, which adjoins Lake Tutira.

5 Shine Falls

From Lake Tutira continue north on SH 2 for 4 km to the Tutira Store. Turn left into Matahorua Road and after 10 km, at the junction with Pohokura Road, veer to the right; this is still Matahorua Road. After 5 km, veer to the left into Heays Access Road. The access to Shine Falls is on the left, 7 km down this road. Most of the road from SH 2 is winding, gravel and slow.

Gannets

These handsome seabirds are part of the booby family and are related to pelicans and shags. The three subspecies are the North Atlantic gannet, the Cape gannet and the Australasian gannet, with the latter found only in New Zealand, and Victoria and Tasmania in Australia. Most large gannet colonies are on offshore islands, including Great Barrier, Three Kings, White, Colville, Gannet, the Poor Knights and Colville Islands. Cape Kidnappers and Muriwai are the only mainland colonies in the country. Naturalist Henry Hill recorded a small colony of 50 pairs at Cape Kidnappers in 1870, which today has expanded over a wide area and is estimated at well over 6000 pairs.

Gannets are elegant birds and particularly impressive when diving for small fish. From heights of up to 30 metres the gannet transforms itself into a streamlined bullet, hitting the water at speeds of 145 km/h and diving as deep as 45 metres. The front of the bird's skull is especially strong to withstand the impact and air sacs help cushion the shock. While gannets do not mate for life, they do form bonds over several seasons and engage in intricate rituals which involve the birds entwining their necks and tapping bills. The chicks are raised during the spring and early summer. Amazingly, the young birds launch off the tops of cliffs for their first flight without the benefit of a practice run!

The birds arrive at the beginning of August and leave by the end of April, and the best time to see chicks is in December and January. The walk to the colony is around five to six hours return and is along the coast all the way from Clifton. However, at high tide parts of the track are impassable and it is essential to check tide times before you set out. If walking isn't an option, there are several tour operators running vehicular trips to the cape (www.hawkesbaynz.com).

Waipataiki Beach.

Waikokopu Beach, Mahia Peninsula.

At 58 metres Shine Falls is the highest waterfall in the Hawke's Bay, and certainly one of the most attractive in the North Island, with two streams breaking into a myriad of rivulets fanning out over a broad rock face into a wide and deep pool. The falls are located in an 800-hectare 'mainland island', an area where predators are intensely managed resulting in an obvious recovery of both plant and bird life in the reserve, including the reintroduction of kokako and kiwi.

While it's a bit of a journey to get there, the 45-minute walk to the falls is not hard and the track meanders through a handsome limestone gorge with rocky bluffs towering above the stream amid cool, deep-green native bush.

6 Opouahi Lake

From Shine Falls head back down Pohokura Road. The lake is 3 km on the left but is not well signposted so is easy to miss.

Opouahi is one of the few intact wetlands in the Hawke's Bay, and supports a wide range of both bush and aquatic bird life, including the rare spotless crake and the brown kiwi. Formed by a massive landslip in times long past, the lake is surprisingly deep at 24 metres and is encircled by attractive bush, including some fine old kowhai trees leaning out over the water. An easy loop track around this pretty little lake takes about 40 minutes.

7 Waikare Beach

Return to SH 2 and from the Tutira Store head north again on SH 2 to Putorino, a distance of 16 km. From Putorino turn right into Waikare Road and follow this gravel road 13 km to the very end. The beach is a 10-minute walk from the end of the road.

Waikare Beach is a long sweep of sand piled with mounds of driftwood, backed by huge cliffs and attracting just a few fisher folk. Once the main highway down the coast — both in pre-European times for Maori, and for Pakeha prior to the road further inland being built — the beach has an untamed beauty all of its own and is an ideal place to just slow down and do nothing much at all. Clearly visible to the south is the massive Moeangiangi Slip, created when a 3-km section of the high crumbling cliffs collapsed during the 1931 Napier earthquake.

8 Mohaka River

Return to Putorino and continue north on SH 2 for 21 km to the Mohaka River.

With its headwaters in the Kaweka Ranges, the Mohaka is a dramatic river and best known for the deep gorges that feature along almost its entire course. Closer to the sea, the river has carved through ancient mudstone, creating a series of wide terraces and steep white cliffs.

New Zealand's highest railway viaduct, at 97 metres, crosses the Mohaka just above the road bridge; and it was in a tributary of this river that amateur palaeontologist Joan Wiffen discovered a small bone from a land-dwelling dinosaur, thus dispelling the prevalent theory that New Zealand only had marine dinosaurs.

Morere Springs River, Morere Springs Scenic Reserve.

9 Whakaki Lagoon

The Whakaki Lagoon is 52 km north of Mohaka Bridge on SH 2.

Stretching from the mouth of the Wairoa River almost to Nuhaka is a series of shallow lagoons and salt marshes, the largest of which is the Whakaki Lagoon. There is scientific evidence that the nature of Whakaki was radically altered from freshwater lake to brackish lagoon about 8000 years ago by a sudden event such as a tsunami.

Whakaki is an important refuge for aquatic birds, and today over 600 hectares are managed by the Whakaki Lake Trust with the aim to preserve and restore this significant wetland.

10 Mahia Peninsula

From Whakaki Lagoon continue north for 16 km and at the roundabout at Nuhaka turn right and drive a further 16 km to Mahia.

Jutting far out into the Pacific, the wild and barren Mahia Peninsula separates Poverty Bay from Hawke Bay. The sandbar that connects the peninsula to the mainland is the largest tombolo in New Zealand. The north side of the peninsula is characterised by small rocky coves and is protected from the worst of the southerly weather by high hills (403 metres is the highest point). On the southern side is the wide sandy sweep of Opoutama Beach.

The Maungawhio Lagoon at the base of the peninsula is today protected as an important wetland reserve. Most of the native forest has long gone, but the small Mahia Peninsula Scenic Reserve preserves lush nikau, tawa and kohekohe bush that is home to native birds such as kereru.

11 Morere Hot Springs and Nature Reserve

From Mahia return to Nuhaka and turn north on to SH 2. It is 8 km to Morere and 57 km from Morere through to Gisborne.

These hot springs are set in the 364-hectare Morere Springs Scenic Reserve, which is particularly famous for the luxuriant growth of its nikau palms. The bush also includes mature rimu, totara, matai, tawa, kohekohe and pukatea, with a dense understorey of ferns, mosses and vines, but it is the thick groves of nikau with their huge fronds that give this reserve an unexpected tropical feel. Within the reserve are a number of tracks ranging from a walking time of 30 minutes to three hours.

The springs, producing 250,000 litres of water a day, are unusual in that they tap into hot mineral water that is actually ancient sea water which has been trapped underground for centuries, even though Morere is situated 15 km inland from the ocean. There are a number of pools, indoor and out, suitable both for families and for those wanting a more relaxed soak. Particularly attractive are the small soaking pools located in dense bush and reached by a short walk. (There is an entrance fee to the pools.)

19 Taranaki

Mt Taranaki volcano • Alpine rainforest • Wild surf beaches • Pristine rivers • 321 km

Taranaki encompasses a monumental mountain and a windswept coastline that is exposed to the wild Tasman Sea. Geographically isolated, the ancient though not extinct volcanic cone of Mt Taranaki is the lodestone of this tour, which offers both a unique mountain experience and a bush environment shaped by a mild climate and abundant rainfall.

INFORMATION
New Plymouth i-SITE, foyer of Puke Ariki Museum, St Aubyn Street, ph (06) 759 6060
South Taranaki i-SITE, 55 High Street, Hawera, ph (06) 278 8599
Stratford i-SITE, Prospero Place, Broadway, Stratford, ph (06) 765 6708
Egmont National Park Visitor Centre, 2879 Egmont Road, North Egmont, ph (06) 756 0990
Dawson Falls Visitor Centre, Manaia Road, Kaponga, ph (06) 756 0990

Getting there

This tour starts 11 km south of Te Kuiti in the King Country, where SH 3 intersects with SH 4, and ends at Hawera, also on SH 3. However, a significant portion of the tour is on SH 45 following the coast around the mountain. The roads are all sealed except for the detour to Mt Damper Falls, although the section through the Awakino Gorge and from Mokau to Urenui is hilly and travel is often slow.

Best time to visit

Taranaki has an equable climate throughout the year, with very few extremes, though it can rain very heavily any time, even in summer, and the southern coast is exposed to the prevailing westerly winds. If you intend to climb the mountain, December through to April has the most reliable weather. New Plymouth hosts a number of popular festivals through the summer months, such as WOMAD (World of Music, Arts & Dance), so if your visit coincides with one of these events, accommodation can be tight.

Facilities

While New Plymouth is the major centre and has the best range of accommodation, places to eat out and shopping, the more significant towns of Waitara, Stratford and Hawera, and to a lesser extent Opunake and Eltham, also provide a good range of services and are less expensive than the city. There is limited accommodation around Awakino and Mokau, mid-December to early February and over weekends.

Before you go — mountain weather

The exposed nature of Mt Taranaki gives rise to very changeable weather at any time of the year and any attempt to climb the mountain should not be undertaken lightly. It is a solid uphill slog requiring a good level of fitness, and proper alpine equipment is vital, even in summer. The most popular route is from North Egmont, though there are routes from the east as well as from Dawson Falls on the southern side of the mountain. It would be wise to check conditions with the visitor centres at either North Egmont or Dawson Falls before setting out. There are also a number of very good local guides who can be contacted through either the i-SITEs or the visitor centres.

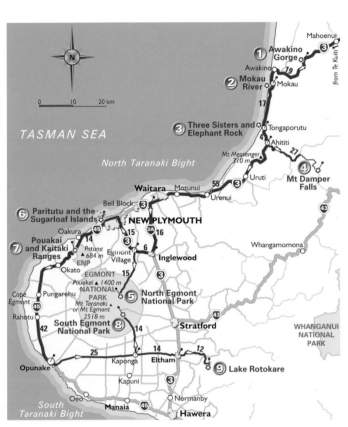

1 Awakino Gorge

The Awakino Gorge is 46 km from the junction of SH 3 and SH 4, which is 11 km south of Te Kuiti.

The Awakino River drains a wide area of the western King Country. Towards the sea it forms the Awakino Gorge as the river is forced through the steep coastal hills. The road travels 12 km through rugged hillsides cloaked in fine lowland forest, protected within the Arorangi Scenic Reserve that straddles both sides of the river.

Fast-flowing along a gravel bed in the gorge, the river quickly broadens near the coast and this tidal section is well known as a prime spot for whitebaiting.

Whitebait are the young of the two species of the smelt family that migrate from the sea up coastal rivers in huge numbers in spring.

2 Mokau River

Drive for 7 km from Awakino to Mokau along SH 3.

Like the Awakino River, the Mokau River forms a steep-sided gorge just inland from the sea and the tidal reaches are famous for whitebait. However, the Mokau is only accessible by boat. Huge trees, nikau palms, tree ferns and climbers overhang the river banks, giving a trip up this river a distinctly tropical feel. Two tour operators run trips upriver from Mokau township, including one on the tiny historic riverboat the MV *Cygnet* that in earlier times collected cans from inland farms and transported the cream to the factory that has long since closed, but still stands just below Mokau village.

3 Three Sisters and Elephant Rock, Tongaporutu

Drive 17 km from Mokau to the Tongaporutu River along SH 3.

In addition to the tall rock remnants just offshore known as the Three Sisters, the views from this wave- and wind-lashed coast are magnificent. High cliffs, sea caves and arches, and a marvellous view of the mountain to the south make this short walk along the Tongaporutu River well worth the stop. One of the 'sisters' is now just a few metres high, leading the locals — in comparing her with her 25-metre-high siblings — to nickname the formation 'the two and a half sisters'. A century ago there was in fact a fourth sister, which eventually succumbed to the elements.

There are several easily accessible sea caves here, as well as Elephant Rock that, not surprisingly, looks like an elephant. The walk to the rocks is only 30 minutes return, though the beach is only accessible close to low tide (best on an outgoing tide) and even then you will get your feet wet and muddy.

Just to the south is the Tongaporutu Coastal Walkway that follows the high cliffs above the sea. It takes three hours to walk one way.

The Three Sisters rock stacks.

Rock formation on Tongaporutu Beach.

4 Mt Damper Falls

From Tongaporutu, head south for 4 km on SH 3 and take the Mt Damper turnoff. The falls are 27 km from the turnoff. At least half of the road is narrow, winding and gravel, with one steep uphill climb that will be a special challenge to larger vehicles.

Plunging 74 metres over a smooth papa rock face, Mt Damper Falls is the highest single-drop waterfall in the North Island. There is an excellent view of the falls from a lookout platform, but no access to the pool or the falls themselves. The walk from the road takes about 45 minutes return and is mainly through farmland, though there is a short bush section near the falls. The

Taranaki/Mt Egmont

Taranaki first erupted nearly 2 million years ago and has blown its stack on a regular basis ever since, with the last eruption occurring just over 300 years ago, making this mountain dormant and not extinct. Rising to 2518 metres, the almost perfect cone of Taranaki is in fact geologically the youngest part of the mountain, with the Pouakai Ranges near New Plymouth the oldest of the four main centres of volcanic eruptions.

Wind-lashed and snow-covered in winter, the mountain juts far out to sea and is exposed to very wild weather, even in summer. The northern slope is one of the wettest places in New Zealand, with an annual rainfall of nearly 7 metres. This gives rise to an extraordinary forest, thick with lush ferns, deep moss and lichens of every hue. The alpine region of the mountain is home to a number of plant species endemic to the area, as well as several moths that are only found on Taranaki.

Egmont National Park, formed in 1900, was New Zealand's second national park and has been vital in hosting protected virgin forest which has all but disappeared elsewhere in Taranaki. The traditional name of the mountain is Taranaki, but Captain Cook named it in honour of his patron, the Earl of Egmont, and today the mountain carries both names, though the park remains the Egmont National Park.

track is not difficult but is rough and on the muddy side.

If you continue on rather than drive back the way you came, it is 105 km from Mt Damper to Stratford along the Lost World Highway (SH 43), which is sealed all the way though winding and slow.

5 North Egmont National Park, Mt Taranaki

From the Mt Damper turnoff continue on SH 3 for 55 km, towards New Plymouth. This section of road includes bush-covered Mt Messenger (310 m), which is famed for its narrow road tunnels and hairpin turns. Just past the turnoff to Waitara, turn left on to SH 3A and drive 16 km south to Inglewood. At Inglewood turn right on to SH 3 towards New Plymouth and after 6 km turn left at Egmont Village, following Egmont Road 15 km to the North Egmont Visitor Centre at the end of the road.

North Egmont is the most direct and popular starting point for climbing the summit, but ascending Taranaki is a challenge and should only be undertaken with proper alpine gear and a good level of fitness, even in the summer months. A good alternative is to visit the area around the North Egmont Visitor Centre; at an altitude of 936 metres this is a good base for beginning a number of shorter bush and alpine walks that range from 15 minutes to three hours.

The forest here is goblin-like, with every tree and rock festooned with lichens, mosses and ferns, all flourishing in the cool and very wet climate. The centre track climbs through the forest, which changes quickly to more sparse subalpine vegetation including hebes, tussocks and alpine plants, to lookout points with marvellous views over the coast, and the mountain looming high above. The visitor centre has excellent displays of the natural and human history of the Taranaki region.

6 Paritutu and the Sugarloaf Islands

From Egmont Village drive 12 km to New Plymouth on SH 3 and a further 3 km to Port Taranaki where the access to Paritutu is on Centennial Drive.

Paritutu Rock and the seven small Sugarloaf Islands just offshore from New Plymouth's main port are the remains of old volcanic plugs with the outer cone long since eroded away. Below the sea the terrain is just as intriguing, with reefs, canyons and cliffs creating a unique marine habitat. Established as a marine park in 1991, the islands are home to a wide range of seabirds. Dolphins and whales regularly frequent the area, and one of the islands was once a whaling station.

While landing on the islands is now prohibited, sea and diving excursions are available from several companies at the port. On land there is a track up Paritutu, and while the climb is steep and not for those afraid of heights, the rocky scramble to the top is made easier by numerous steps and wire railings. The views to the south along the coast, southeast to the mountain, and north over the port and the city are spectacular to say the least.

7 Pouakai and Kaitaki Ranges

From New Plymouth port travel 14 km on SH 45 to Lucy's Gully, Oakura.

Lying directly to the south of New Plymouth and protecting the city from the worst of the southerly winds, the Pouakai and Kaitaki Ranges are the remnants of Taranaki's older cones, which erupted over 600,000 years ago. Today the heavily forested ranges are part of the Egmont National Park and are an important lowland bird habitat.

There are a number of popular walking tracks in both the Pouakai and Kaitaki Ranges, which vary from short walks to all-day tramps. Lucy's Gully on SH 45 is an easy point from which to access several short walks within these ranges.

8 South Egmont National Park, Mt Taranaki

From Lucy's Gully, Oakura, follow SH 45 for 42 km to Opunake. Turn left just south of Opunake and continue a further 25 km to Kaponga. At Kaponga turn left and drive 14 km to Dawson Falls.

The main access to the southern section of Egmont National Park is through Dawson Falls, where there is a visitor centre, café and the historic Dawson Falls Hotel, built in 1895. Here the usually perfectly conical shape of Taranaki is broken by another of the mountain's major cones, Fantham's

Lake Rotokare.

Peak. Rising to 1692 metres, the peak has been built up by eruptions within the last 3500 years and is one of the younger cones on the mountain.

A popular tramp for the more fit, the walk to Fantham's Peak takes around four hours return. Somewhat more accessible is Dawson Falls, which will take less than an hour return to visit. The 18-metre falls drop over an ancient lava flow and

throw up a continuous spray which, in combination with the normally high rainfall, results in a lush bushscape thick with ferns and mosses.

9 Lake Rotokare

From Dawson Falls return the 14 km to Kaponga. At the town turn left and travel to Eltham, a distance of a further 14 km. At Eltham turn left on to SH 3 towards Stratford, and just north of the town turn right into Anderson Road. From Anderson Road turn left at Rawhitiroa Road and then right into Sangster Road. The lake is at the end of Sangster Road, a distance of 12 km.

Very little lowland forest has survived in Taranaki, so this bush-fringed lake nestled in hill country east of Eltham comes as somewhat of a surprise. Unlike most other Taranaki lakes which are man-made, Rotokare is naturally formed and spring-fed.

Deep beds of raupo ring this lake with its fiord-like arms, and the surrounding hills are densely covered with forest that includes mature kahikatea, maire and totara, even though the area was milled well into the middle of last century. Native bird life is surprising prolific, despite Rotokare being popular with boaties and water skiers (though use is seasonally limited). The circuit around the lake is flat and will take around one hour.

Dawson Falls on the slopes of Mt Taranaki/Egmont.

20 Wanganui, Manawatu, Rangitikei and Horowhenua

Wetlands • Kapiti Island • Wild beaches • Rangitikei River • Manawatu Gorge • 412 km

Open to the Tasman Sea and bounded by the Ruahine and Tararua Ranges to the east, this region combines unspoilt beaches and internationally recognised wetlands with some appealing river valleys and impressive bushscapes.

INFORMATION

Rangitikei Information Centre,
Hautapu Street, Taihape,
ph (06) 388 0604
Wanganui i-SITE, 101 Guyton
Street, Wanganui, ph (06) 349 0508
Feilding and District Information
Centre, 10 Manchester Street,
Feilding, ph (06) 323 3318
Palmerston North i-SITE,
The Square, Palmerston North,
ph (06) 350 1922
Bulls Information Centre,
113 Bridge Street, Bulls,
ph (06) 322 0055
Levin i-SITE, 93 Oxford Street,
Levin, ph (06) 367 8440
Otaki i-SITE, Centennial Park,
SH 1, Otaki, ph (06) 364 7620
Paraparaumu Visitor Information
Centre, Coastlands Parade, SH 1,
Paraparaumu, ph (04) 298 8195

Getting there

Although this tour starts in Wellington it is easily accessible from any part of the region and Palmerston North is a good central point. The roads in this area are sealed and very good, making for extremely enjoyable driving.

Best time to visit

Summer is generally warm and dry in this region, while winters, although not especially cold, can be unpleasantly windy (the wind farms are located here for a very good reason!). Even on a warm day the exposed beaches are often subject to a cool breeze, although the shallow water means that the sea temperatures are usually pleasant in summer.

The area is not a major tourist destination in its own right, so finding a place to stay at any time of the year is not usually a problem. Traffic into Wellington along SH 1 south of Otaki is often bumper to bumper on holiday weekends and on a summer's Sunday afternoon as Wellingtonians head home from a weekend away or a day out at the beach.

Facilities

With two good-sized cities, Palmerston North and Wanganui, and several sizeable towns, Feilding, Bulls, Taihape, Foxton, Levin, Otaki, Waikanae and Paraparaumu, along the route there are always plenty of places to stay, eat and shop in this region. Palmerston North is a student city with plenty of motels and inexpensive eating places, while Wanganui possesses the historic charm of an old river-port town. The areas from Paekakariki to Waikanae are almost considered suburbs of Wellington and have a regular train service into the city.

1 Pauatahanui Wildlife Reserve

From Wellington drive north on SH 1 for 29 km to the junction with SH 58, and turn right towards the Hutt Valley. The reserve is 4.5 km on the right at Pauatahanui.

The largest unmodified estuarine salt marsh in the southern half of the North Island, the Pauatahanui Wildlife Reserve is a haven for wading and migratory birds. Five hides all within easy walking distance provide plenty of opportunity for keen bird-watchers to observe the wildlife that includes New Zealand birds such as grey teal, shoveler, paradise duck and pukeko, as well as Arctic visitors such as godwits and knots during the summer months.

Since 1984, the local Forest and Bird

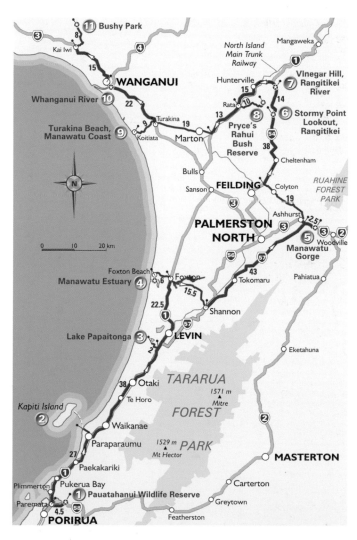

Kapiti Island from the mainland.

Protection Society has worked not only to restore the wetland environment, but also to provide excellent access with paths, boardwalks and information boards.

2 Kapiti Island

Boats to Kapiti Island leave from Paraparaumu Beach, 27 km north of the junction of SH 1 and SH 58.

Kapiti Island, 5 km off the coast, is one of New Zealand's most important bird sanctuaries. It has an area of 1965 hectares and its highest point, Tuteremoana, is 520 metres. In 1987 the management of the island was handed over to the Department of Conservation, which set about removing sheep and possums. In an operation thought impossible at the time, rats were also entirely eradicated in 1998. Today, Kapiti is an important nature sanctuary and home to a wide range of

Manawatu Gorge.

native birds including many rare species such as the little spotted kiwi (extinct on the mainland), weka, kaka, kakariki, tieke (saddleback) and hihi (stitchbird).

The island is reasonably accessible, with two companies operating a ferry service (weather dependent). However, visitor numbers are regulated and you must obtain a permit from the Department of Conservation before going. It is also possible to stay overnight at the Nature Lodge in the north of the island (email kapiti.island@doc.govt.nz).

3 Lake Papaitonga

From Paraparaumu, drive 38 km north on SH 1 towards Levin. Turn left into Buller Road and the lake is 2 km down this road.

This little-known gem is surrounded by the finest lowland bush remnant between Wanganui and Wellington, dominated by titoki, kahikatea, nikau, karaka and kiekie. Now just 122 hectares, including the lake, it is hard to believe that this whole coast was once covered in such dense and luxuriant bush and that so little has survived.

Within the lake are two small islands, Motukiwi and Motungarara, both old pa sites of the local Muaupoko iwi (tribe). In 1897 the land was acquired by the noted naturalist Sir Walter Buller, who recognised its value and preserved this small piece of bush for future generations. Today the wetland is home to the elusive bittern and the spotless crake.

4 Manawatu Estuary

Return to SH 1 and travel north for 22.5 km to Foxton. From Foxton take Foxton Beach Road for 6 km to the estuary.

Covering over 200 hectares, the wetland at the mouth of the Manawatu River is considered one of the most important wading bird habitats on the west coast of the North Island. The estuary is the largest in the lower North Island and over 90 bird species have been recorded here, including a wide range of arctic breeding birds such as bar-tailed godwits, red knots, sandpipers, golden plovers and curlews. Important birds that breed at the estuary are the royal spoonbill, fairy tern and the wrybill, an unusual bird with a beak that curves sideways. Fernbirds, bitterns and marsh crakes are all protected by the

Kowhai

While New Zealand doesn't have an 'official' national flower, the distinctive bright-yellow kowhai flower is certainly recognised as its unofficial representative. In all, there are eight species of kowhai in the country, the most common of which are *Sophora microphylla* and *Sophora tetraptera*. Worldwide there are 30 species of *Sophora* and, despite the considerable distance, one in Hawaii closely resembles the New Zealand species. A member of the legume family (beans, peas, gorse, broom), the family resemblance is most noticeable in the seedpod, which looks very much like a bean. The seeds of the tree are extremely poisonous to humans.

Kowhai is unusual for a New Zealand tree in that most species are semi-deciduous, losing most of their leaves either before or after flowering. Bright flowering plants are not common in our native landscape, so the kowhai tree, when covered in sulphur-yellow flowers in spring, makes for a spectacular sight. Kowhai are common near water and often overhang streams and lakeshores and grow from sea level up to 450 metres. The nectar is a favourite food source for tui and bellbirds, which often shred the flower in the hunt for food. The native kowhai caterpillar moth feeds on the leaves of young trees and, in some cases, can cause considerable damage.

extensive and inaccessible salt marshes.

A public path follows the north bank of the river just before the beach and is a good place for bird-spotting.

5 Manawatu Gorge

After returning to SH 1 at Foxton, take the Foxton–Shannon Road 15.5 km east to Shannon. At Shannon turn left and follow SH 57 north for 43 km, turning right on to SH 3 (Napier Road). Drive 2.5 km to the gorge.

Unlike most river gorges that are created by a river cutting through hill country, the Manawatu Gorge was formed in reverse. The river was actually there first and as the Ruahine Ranges rose along the Wellington Faultline over the last million or so years, the river stayed put, in the process creating the 6-km-long gorge. On the summit of Saddle Road north of the gorge are marine sediments indicating that this land once lay beneath the sea.

The steep greywacke cliffs, largely devoid of significant vegetation, are prone to slips in heavy rain and road closures are not uncommon. A popular track crosses the gorge on the southern side and takes three to four hours one way.

6 Stormy Point Lookout, Rangitikei

Return 4 km to Ashhurst and turn right into the town. Turn left into Colyton Road. Follow Colyton Road for 17.5 km to Feilding and turn right on to SH 54. Follow SH 54 north for 23 km, turning left at Cheltenham, to Stormy Point.

While there are a number of good view points overlooking the Rangitikei River, by far the most spectacular prospect is from Stormy Point. Here the series of broad river terraces are clearly laid out in a panorama stretching all the way north to Mount Ruapehu. Considered to be one of the best-preserved sequences of river terraces in the world, each terrace was formed during a period of climatic cooling, the oldest of which is 350,000 years.

7 Vinegar Hill, Rangitikei River

Continue north for 14 km on SH 54 to Vinegar Hill.

The most notable features of the Rangitikei River are steep papa cliffs and the striking broad river terraces dating back thousands of years. Draining the eastern Kaimanawa and western Ruahine Ranges southwest of Lake Taupo, the Rangitikei is confined to steep gorges for most of its 185 km and only broadens significantly along the last 30 km south of Marton.

The stretch of river along the Vinegar Hill Reserve (Putae Ngahere) is typical. Here the water is fast-flowing over a stony riverbed with a narrow flat river terrace on one side and steep, partially bush-clad cliffs on the other. The leafy camping ground is particularly popular in summer, though only toilet facilities are available.

8 Pryce's Rahui Reserve

From Vinegar Hill continue 1 km on SH 54 to SH 1. Turn left and drive south for 15 km via Hunterville to Rata. At Rata turn left into Putorino Road and drive 10 km to the reserve.
Located on an old river terrace of the Rangitikei River, Pryce's Rahui Reserve contains impressive huge trees including kahikatea, tawa, matai and totara. Of particular note is one massive kowhai standing well over 10 metres high, which could easily be the country's largest specimen, as well as a giant matai.

There are a number of tracks, marked in different colours, none of them particularly long. Although the tracks are a bit overgrown, the reserve is quite small and you can't get lost. The aforementioned kowhai is on the red track and the matai is on the yellow track.

Although just a short distance off SH 1,

this magnificent bush reserve attracts few visitors and you are quite likely to have the place to yourself.

9 Turakina Beach, Manawatu Coast

Return to SH 1 at Rata and turn south, drive 13 km on SH 1 and turn right to Marton. From Marton take Wanganui Road for 19 km to SH 3 at Turakina. At SH 3 turn right and after 500 metres turn left into Turakina Beach Road. Travel 8.5 km down Turakina Beach Road to Koitiata.
From Wanganui all the way down the coast to Paekakariki is a long stretch of continuous sandy beach, broken only by numerous river and stream estuaries. Backed by high dunes, the relentless and cool westerly winds have naturally restricted coastal development and most beach settlements are little more than small bach communities, though to the south around Paraparaumu the housing is considerably more extensive and sophisticated.

There is good access to the shore all along this coast and Turakina Beach, at the mouth of the small Turakina River, is typical of its type. Shy and secretive, the katipo, New Zealand's only spider with a dangerous bite, makes its home in the dunes and under driftwood in the dune country along this coastline.

10 Whanganui River

Back at SH 1, turn north and drive 22 km on SH 3 to Wanganui City, where several major bridges cross the Whanganui River.
At 290 km long, the Whanganui River drains a huge catchment area reaching from the hills in eastern Taranaki near Stratford through to the slopes of Mt Ngauruhoe in the west. Flowing south through Taumarunui, the river cuts through spectacularly rugged hill country, densely covered in native bush, part of which is now protected as the Whanganui National Park. Along much of its length the river banks are steep crumbling cliffs of sandstone and mudstone known as 'papa'. Major tributaries are the Ongarue, Tangarakau and Ohura Rivers. Near the mouth the river widens and is tidal, with dangerous sandbars that have hampered the development of a major port.

Today the river is popular for kayak and rafting trips that usually take several days. An historic paddle steamer, MV *Waimarie*, offers short and more leisurely trips from the centre of Wanganui. In case you are wondering about the differing spelling of the names for the city and the river, the river, park and region are usually spelt with an 'h' and the city without.

11 Bushy Park

From Wanganui head west for 15 km on SH 3 to Kai Iwi and then follow Rangitatau East Road for 8 km to Bushy Park.
Owned and administered by the Forest and Bird Protection Society, Bushy Park is a 90-hectare bush remnant bequeathed to the society in 1962 by Frank Moore whose family had farmed the area since the 1860s. The bush is now surrounded by a predator-proof fence built in 2004 in an effort to protect and restore native bird life to the park, and entry is via automated gates.

A network of tracks, all fairly easy to follow, together with a host of informative labels and panels, make Bushy Park a great place to improve your knowledge of native trees and shrubs. One highlight among the many large trees is an old rata, possibly a thousand years old and the largest surviving example of the northern species — standing at a height of over 40 metres it's hard to miss. The fine old Edwardian homestead houses a café and there is a small charge to enter the park.

Tamatea's Cave, Whanganui River.

Rimutaka Ranges.

Putangirua Pinnacles.

4 Putangirua Pinnacles

Continue for 10 km on SH 2 to Featherston, turn right on to SH 53, and drive 17 km to Martinborough. From Martinborough head south on Pirinoa Road for 32 km to Whangaimoana Road. Turn left on to this road and continue for 12 km on the Whangaimoana and Whatarangi Roads to the Pinnacles.

Over thousands of years the Putangirua Stream has eroded the soft coastal soils in this area to create an unusual 'badlands' landscape of deep gullies with tall pillar-like formations known as hoodoos. Hoodoos are formed when rock protects the soil from rain and prevents the soft gravels from eroding, resulting in high fluted formations.

While quite common along the coast, at Putangirua the concentration of hoodoos in one small valley is little short of spectacular, made even more so by the fact that the walk takes you right into the heart of the valley. As the river is subject to frequent seasonal flooding there is no official track as such, but from the picnic area and camping ground follow the riverbed up to the wide valley that leads off to the left. The walk takes about an hour and a half return.

5 Cape Palliser Lighthouse and Seal Colony

From the Pinnacles drive along the coast for 19 km to Ngawi. The road to Ngawi is excellent, sealed and mainly straight, with just one or two rough patches through unstable terrain. Continue a further 5 km on a gravel road beyond Ngawi to Cape Palliser.

About halfway between Ngawi and the Cape Palliser lighthouse is a large fur seal colony on the rocks right below the road. Once common along this coast, the impact first of Maori and then Pakeha was disastrous for the animals, but now protected by law the seal population is making a rapid comeback. Take care if you plan a closer look as many seals rest right beside the road and are not easy to spot until you're almost on top of them.

At Cape Palliser 258 steps lead straight up to the striking historic lighthouse situated 78 metres above the sea. The lighthouse was put in place to assist ships navigating the perilous Cape Palliser, a coastline that combines rocky headlands and shoals with the fiercest weather blasting straight out of the Southern Ocean. The views from the top along the coast are worth the trudge up the rocky bluff, where succulents and coprosma thrive in crevices on the raw hillside.

6 Ruakokopatuna Caves

From Cape Palliser return towards Martinborough, then at Dryeville turn right on to Dry River Road. After 9 km turn into Blue Back Road. The caves are 3 km down this gravel road.

This cave system has been carved out of limestone rock by an underground stream and has a modest sprinkling of glow-worms. You will get your feet wet wading through here and a torch is essential. This a good first cave experience for the very young. (The caves are on private land and a donation for entry is appreciated.)

7 Mt Holdsworth

Drive back to Martinborough and take Ponatahi Road and Moreton Road 27 km to SH 2, just south of Carterton. Head north on SH 2 for 10 km and turn left on to Norfolk Road. Travel a further 16 km to the parking area for Mt Holdsworth.

Tucked into the foothills of the Tararua Ranges alongside the Atiwhakatu Stream,

Mt Holdsworth reserve at the entrance to the Tararua Forest Park is the starting point for numerous walks ranging from five minutes to five hours, and for casual visitors this is one of the more accessible points in the ranges.

The beech forest here is particularly handsome and the area contains some real botanical plant gems including the very rare native mistletoe, and huge swathes of the delicate kidney fern which adapts to the hot dry Wairarapa climate by shrivelling until its texture is that of old crumpled paper in order to conserve moisture until the next replenishing rainfall. The camping area, set in a glade beside the river, is particularly attractive.

8 Pukaha/Mt Bruce National Wildlife Centre

Return to SH 2 and continue north through Masterton for about 42 km to Mt Bruce.
Pukaha/Mt Bruce is a huge 1000-hectare reserve and includes a substantial remnant of the dense forest known as the Seventy Mile Bush that once covered this area, and which was almost totally cleared at the end of the nineteenth century. Now an important bird sanctuary and home to endangered birds such as kokako, hihi, kiwi, kaka and the Campbell Island teal, the National Wildlife Centre also maintains significant breeding programmes for these threatened species.

Currently the public can only access a small area by the Bruce Stream along well-formed, wheelchair-friendly paths that link a number of aviaries containing rare native birds and a nocturnal kiwi house. This is a great opportunity to see the rare kokako up close. The bush is especially handsome, the trees are well labelled and the walk takes around one hour. A viewing deck off the café overlooks the takahe enclosure and it is worth trying to time a visit to the eel feeding at 1.30 pm and the kaka feeding at 3 pm (www.mtbruce.org.nz).

GOT TIME? (+67.5 KM)
9 Castle Point

Just before entering the centre of Masterton from the north and crossing the Waipoua River bridge, turn left into Te Ore Ore Road, which after 1.5 km becomes Castlepoint Road. Continue 66 km to Castlepoint. (Note that the town's name is spelt Castle Point, but the name of the promontory is spelt Castle Point.)
At Castle Point, a small promontory on the Wairarapa east coast, the seascape is spectacular. Huge waves, arriving directly off the Southern Ocean, hammer the cliffs below the historic lighthouse and thunder and crash over the rocky reef that protects the lagoon. Occasionally cut off by the high tide, a raised boardwalk crosses a sandspit to the rocky bluff on which the lighthouse is situated. In a southerly swell, the full fury of the ocean strikes against the rocks below offering scant hope of return if you tumble into the sea.

View of Castlepoint from Castle Rock.

22 Wellington

Striking natural harbour • Rare wildlife • Dramatic seacoast • Sheltered bush valleys • 80 km

Between the highrise and the urban sprawl, Wellington has a magnificent harbour, a wild sea coast and an extreme landscape that, coupled with a unique climate, adds to the natural drama of New Zealand's capital city. The region boasts over 500 sq km of reserves and parks.

INFORMATION
Wellington i-SITE,
cnr Wakefield and Victoria
Streets, Wellington,
ph (04) 802 4860
Lower Hutt i-SITE, The Pavilion,
25 Laings Road, Lower Hutt,
ph (04) 560 4715
Department of Conservation
Wellington Visitor Centre,
18 Manners Street, Wellington,
ph (04) 384 7770

Getting there
Wellington is well serviced by road, sea and air and is the terminal for the Cook Strait ferries. The roads around the city are all sealed, but the Wellington terrain is hilly and many of the roads are narrow and winding.

Best time to visit
Wellington is a good destination at any time of the year. As well as outdoor activities, if the weather is really bad the city is well endowed with museums, art galleries, cafés and entertainment. While the climate has a reputation for wind (and it *is* often windy), the temperatures do not vary widely from summer to winter, and on a fine day when the weather has cleared from the south, the city is nothing short of magnificent.

Cook Strait has an equally fearsome reputation and it is not unusual for ferry crossings to be cancelled in very rough weather. If sea sickness is a problem, bear in mind the crossing is worse in southerly weather that can bring both strong winds and a heavy swell. Northerly weather is accompanied by strong blustery winds, but the sea swell is minimal.

Facilities
In terms of accommodation, Wellington's lack of flat land has limited the number of sprawling motels and there are no camping facilities in the city itself. There are numerous hotels and very good backpacker establishments catering for a wide range of budgets. For motels and camping you will need to head out to the Hutt Valley, just 14 km away. Wellington accommodation is often at a premium during the week as people attend to business in the capital, but many hotels offer great special rates from Friday to Sunday nights. But note that most hotels charge extra for parking, which can amount to a considerable sum.

As the capital city, Wellington also hosts a number of major sporting and cultural events resulting in accommodation being booked out well in advance, leaving the casual visitor with a long haul north to find anything available. On the plus side, Wellington is a compact metropolis with a good public transport system, so it is easy to get around by bus and train and a taxi trip is not ruinously expensive.

1 Wellington Harbour
At first glance the geology of Wellington Harbour appears simple, but in fact the water hides a complex seabed. The western side of the harbour runs the length of the Wellington Faultline and is an extension of the Hutt Valley, with a shallow seabed between Petone and the central city. East of Somes/Matiu Island the seabed is a deep valley that continues out to sea through the heads, and Somes and Ward/Makaro Islands and the Miramar Peninsula are the tops of the ridge running parallel to

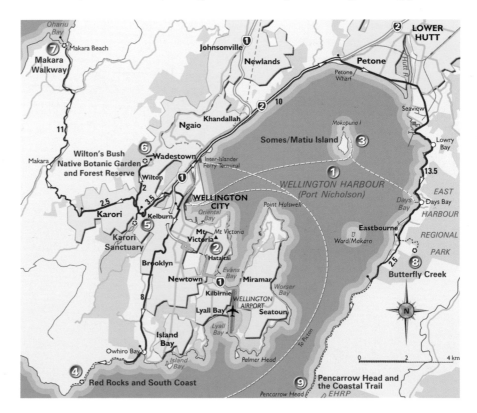

Cook Strait, looking south from Wellington towards the Kaikouras.

a maze of minor faultlines. Small quakes in Wellington are common and Wellington City has been at the forefront of adopting the most up-to-date earthquake-resistant architecture and engineering.

3 Somes/Matiu Island

East By West ferries stop at the island on their Wellington to Eastbourne cross-harbour route (ph (04) 499 1282, www.eastbywest.co.nz). Located in the heart of Wellington Harbour, this 25-hectare island has a long history of human occupation but is now an important nature sanctuary free from predators. The explorer Kupe discovered the harbour around AD 1000 and named the island Matiu after a female relative. While Maori have long occupied the island, it lacked permanent fresh water and was used mostly as a refuge. From 1872, it was used as a quarantine station for people and animals and during both wars it became a detention centre for alien residents.

As an important wildlife sanctuary with extensive replanting by the local Forest and Bird Protection Society, today a surprising proportion of Somes/Matiu has bush cover. In particular, the rare kakariki, a parrot, is common here. Like blackbirds, kakariki forage in the leaf litter on the forest floor and swoop and chatter overhead. However, their ground-feeding habit and lack of shyness made them more vulnerable than most to predators and led to their extinction on the mainland. Other significant inhabitants include 54 Brothers Island tuatara introduced to the island in 1998, and in 2007 the first baby tuatara were hatched here.

the underwater valley. To the east of the harbour is the Orongorongo Range, a southerly extension of the Rimutakas. Rising to a height of over 800 metres, this range is often snow-capped in winter. The Hutt River drains into the harbour to the northeast.

The harbour was significantly altered by the 1855 Wairarapa earthquake, the largest quake recorded in New Zealand since European times. Measuring 8.2 on the Richter scale, this quake along the West Wairarapa Fault to the east of Wellington had a vertical shift of 1.5 metres and a horizontal shift of 12 metres. The uplifted terrace from this earthquake is clearly visible at Pencarrow Head, and the land between Miramar and Kilbirnie, once an area of lagoons and salt marsh, was raised and naturally drained.

2 The Wellington Faultline

From the top of Mt Victoria, Wellington's most popular lookout point, the long line of the Wellington Faultline looks as

clear as if cut by a giant knife. Running along the western side of the Hutt Valley, it follows the motorway along the edge of the harbour and continues along Tinakori Road and then Glenmore Street and through the Karori Sanctuary. A further small fault, the Lambton Fault, follows the line of Lambton Quay and Willis Street, though in reality the Wellington region is

Somes/Matiu Island.

On arrival a good option is to head uphill to the visitors centre and spend a few minutes bringing yourself up to speed with the island's natural and human history. From there continue uphill to the gun emplacements that not only provide a great view over the harbour, but a clear outline of the island's terrain. From that point you can access the circuit track, which is well formed, easy walking and, for the most part, high up on the island with excellent views all the way around.

4 Wellington's South Coast and Red Rocks

From central Wellington head south for 8 km on Brooklyn/Ohiro/Happy Valley Roads to Owhiro Bay. From here the road follows the coast around to the harbour entrance at Seatoun. To get to Red Rocks from Owhiro Bay, follow the Owhiro Bay Parade west to the car park at the end.

Wellington's south coast faces directly into the formidable Southern Ocean. With nothing between the city and Antarctica this coastline takes the full brunt of the wind and sea. In a storm huge seas will pound the rocky shores, which have been stripped of any substantial vegetation, and waves often surge over the road. This coast is home to blue penguins, which cross the road at dusk to roost in the bushy cliffs or under houses — not making them terribly popular with homeowners kept awake at night by their noisy nocturnal squawks!

Red Rocks is a striking formation of red pillow lava, formed underwater over 200 million years ago. A four-wheel-drive track (45 minutes one way) follows the wild exposed coast where bull kelp swirls in the brutal tides, oystercatchers scuttle along the stony beaches, and huge shingle fans, reminiscent of the South Island high country, sweep down the barren cliffs.

5 Karori Sanctuary

From the central city drive towards Karori for 3.5 km via Glenmore Street. Just after the Karori Tunnel turn left off Chaytor Street into Waiapu Road.

Only 2 km from the city, this 250-hectare forest was originally Wellington City's water reservoir catchment and had been closed to the public for over 120 years. In the early 1990s Forest and Bird Protection Society members developed a plan to create an urban sanctuary for native flora and fauna, from which emerged the Karori Sanctuary, a charitable trust. A key element to the success of the sanctuary has been the installation of 8.6 km of predator-proof fencing (a world first), followed by eradication of predators within the fenced-off area.

Now open to the public, the park has been a resounding success and is home to numerous native birds including saddleback, weka, brown teal, tomtit, kaka, whitehead and the little spotted kiwi, as well as tuatara (best seen on summer afternoons). However, while the fence keeps the pests out, it doesn't keep the birds in, and many a bird departs never to be seen again.

The tracks and trails are easily accessible and suitable for all levels of fitness, and you can even take a boat trip on the lower lake. For an additional fee experienced guides take two-hour tours, while for something different a night tour is also available (www.sanctuary.org.nz).

6 Otari-Wilton's Bush Native Botanic Garden and Forest Reserve

From the Karori Sanctuary return to Chaytor Street and turn left into Curtis Street/Wilton Road. The reserve is 2 km along, on the left.

Pioneer botanist Dr Leonard Cockayne, who was instrumental in collecting and classifying many native plants, established these gardens in 1926 as the Otari Open-Air Plant Museum. Today, the gardens are still exclusively dedicated to native species.

Beautifully laid out and easily accessible, the dramatic Canopy Walkway links the two cultivated parts of the gardens over a deep gully. To the left of the information centre are the older gardens with impressive collections of hebe, flax, coprosma and various threatened species among others, while the fernery and alpine gardens in the themed area are equally worth visiting.

The entire reserve covers 105 hectares, with several longer walks (up to one hour) beyond the gardens that go into the original bush reserve on the other side of the Kaiwharawhara Stream.

7 Makara Walkway

Return to Chaytor Street, turn right and continue west on Karori Road for 2.5 km to the very end. Turn right into Makara Road and follow this road for 11 km to the beach.

Exposed to both northerly and southerly winds, the sheer wildness of Makara Beach is its essential appeal — although this hasn't always been the case, as several Maori pa sites in the area are testament to the former richness of both sea and forest. In the eighteenth century Captain Cook remarked on the din of the dawn chorus of birdsong from the coastal forest, even though he was almost a kilometre offshore.

Karori Sanctuary.

Tuatara

Unchanged for over 200 million years, the tuatara is not in fact a lizard but the sole survivor of a large family of reptiles, *Sphenodon*, all of which have been extinct for 60 million years. There are two species, the most widespread being the northern tuatara and the other the Brothers Island tuatara, which is confined to just one small island in the Marlborough Sounds with a population of less than 500. Many aspects of this ancient creature are highly unusual. Unlike most reptiles, tuatara prefer cooler climates, ideally under 25°C, and if the weather is too cold they are able to hibernate. They can also go for very long periods without eating and live for over 100 years. Tuatara only breed every three or four years and the temperature of the egg during incubation determines the sex — the lower the temperature, the more females, and the reverse for males. Despite having no ear hole or drum, tuatara are still able to hear, and they have a parietal or third eye in the top of the head. Visible only in the young and covered as an adult, this eye has a lens, cornea and retina, but only limited connection to the brain.

Tuatara share burrows with seabirds, an arrangement often detrimental to both the eggs and the young of the bird, and the reptile will also feed on any small animal, including other tuatara. The introduction of the kiore (Polynesian rat) by Aotearoa's first colonists devastated the tuatara population on the mainland, and today they only survive in the wild on offshore islands.

The walk from the southern end of the beach is a solid uphill climb over farmland, bypassing an ancient Ngati Ira pa, to Fort Opau, a Second World War gun emplacement. From the top the whole of Cook Strait is in clear view, with Mana and Kapiti Islands to the north, the Marlborough Sounds to the west, and the Kaikoura Mountains to the south. Always wear warm clothing here, even in summer!

8 Butterfly Creek, East Harbour Regional Park

Return to central Wellington and take the Hutt Motorway 10 km to Petone. Follow Esplanade/ Waione/Seaview/Marine Roads for 13.5 km to Eastbourne. The two most common entry points for the walk to Butterfly Creek are Kowhai Street and Muritai Park in Eastbourne.

Butterfly Creek is situated in a valley that runs parallel to the coast, sheltered from the worst of both the southerly and northerly winds by a steep low ridge. This deep valley of magnificent rata, beech and rimu forest is a very popular walking area and the highlight is an attractive picnic spot in a beech glade alongside a small swimming hole in the creek.

The track following the valley has several entry points from Eastbourne, and from the ridge there are good views over the harbour, Matiu/Somes Island, Wellington City and the Hutt Valley.

9 Pencarrow Head and the Coastal Trail

From Eastbourne follow Muritai Road along the coast for 2.5 km to the end, which is also known as Burdans Gate.

Pencarrow Head, at the entrance to Wellington Harbour, has been created from gravel washed down to the sea by the Orongorongo and Wainuiomata Rivers and then heaped back on the shore by strong southerly storms.

The broad terraces along the coast present in graphic form a history of land creation as each represents the upward movement of the earth caused by successive earthquakes. The two small lakes just beyond the head were once tidal inlets, but once having been cut off from the sea by the rising land they became freshwater lakes.

This coastal trail, popular with walkers and cyclists alike, encompasses some of Wellington's wildest seascapes as it is wide open to the worst that the southerly weather can bring, but that very wildness is also its greatest attraction.

There are great views of the harbour, and on a clear day you can see right across to the South Island and the Kaikoura Mountains, snow-capped in winter. The views are even better if you take the short but steep climb up to the old lighthouse. The entrance to Wellington Harbour was even more treacherous in the days of sail than it is today and this lighthouse, built in 1858, was New Zealand's first.

The track follows the coast from the road end right round to the Wainuiomata River mouth (three hours one way).

Pencarrow Head.

South Island

23 Marlborough Sounds • Picton to Nelson

Drowned valleys with bush-clad walls • Glorious coastal scenery • 255 km

The Marlborough Sounds is a labyrinth of coves, inlets, islands and waterways intricately combined with beautiful bush and exquisite coastline.

Getting there

This route starts from Picton, the southern terminal of the inter-island ferries and the beginning of SH 1 in the South Island. It traverses rugged country and even the main highways, while in good condition, are often winding and slow; minor roads in this area are truly something else. In early times (and still today), much of the Sounds was primarily reached by boat, and access by land was limited. Off the main roads be sure to pack plenty of patience because you can expect narrow, winding routes and long stretches of gravel. Relax, because you won't be going anywhere in a hurry!

Best time to visit

Summer is a magical time in the Sounds, but as a popular destination for both New Zealanders and overseas visitors alike there is considerable pressure on rather limited facilities, though it is never crowded as such.

So try to avoid mid-December to early February and holiday weekends unless you have bookings for both transport and accommodation.

Facilities

Nelson to the west and Blenheim to the south are both sizeable centres, with plenty of accommodation, cafés and services. Nelson is a popular summer destination and at the peak of the season last-minute accommodation can be difficult to source, especially around the beach area of Tahunanui. Blenheim is a little easier, although accommodation is often full during the peak holiday periods with travellers staying overnight to catch the morning ferry. Picton, at the head of Queen Charlotte Sound and the home of the ferry terminal, is developing into an attractive seaside town and becoming a destination in its own right, but you will need to book ahead if you plan to stay here during summer. The more popular camping grounds through the Sounds are often full at the season's peak, though it is not too hard to find a spot to pitch a tent. Away from the main centres, the only facilities are usually just a small general store.

1 Queen Charlotte Sound

For most people the experience of the Marlborough Sounds is often limited to the inter-island ferry trip through Queen Charlotte Sound. However, the Sounds is an intricate and complex system of drowned valleys, with fingers of bush-clad land and islands reaching well out into Cook Strait and a myriad bays, beaches and coves, many of which are only accessible by water. It is the perfect place for boating, kayaking, tramping and fishing (blue cod is prized in this area), as well as just getting away from it all.

One of the largest sounds, the sheltered waters of Queen Charlotte are also the most accessible with numerous boat charters, sightseeing trips and water taxis operating out of Picton. Steep hills with regenerating bush, small sandy bays and quiet inlets are typical of this sound, and dolphins are common. Around Picton are numerous excellent short walks along the sound including Bob's Bay, Queen Charlotte View, The Snout and Karaka Point; and behind Picton the Tirohanga Hilltop has marvellous views over the entire area.

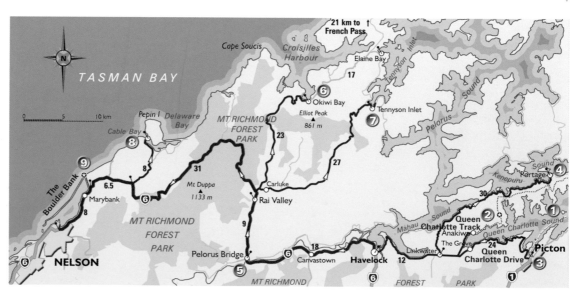

Queen Charlotte Sound.

2 Queen Charlotte Track

The Queen Charlotte Track winds for 71 km along the ridgetops between Queen Charlotte and Kenepuru Sounds. With a moderate grade and endless views along its entire length, the track is popular with all ages. While the full track will take four days, the proximity to the water means that short options are readily available by water taxi from Picton.

3 Queen Charlotte Drive

Queen Charlotte Drive begins at the corner of Dublin and Kent Streets in Picton.
Winding along the coast from Picton to Havelock, this 36-km road is ideal for those travelling on to Nelson. The road initially rises steeply above Queen Charlotte Sound, giving magnificent views over the water, and then follows the Grove Arm of the sound, passing numerous small bays with a backdrop of lush bush.

Nine kilometres beyond Picton is Governors Bay, a picturesque beach with a small crescent of golden sand, reached by a short 10-minute walk. Fourteen kilometres further on is Linkwater, and the road to Portage. Just past Linkwater the road reaches Mahau Sound and 7 km along this road is Cullen's Point Lookout/Mahaki Paoa. Here, a short walk through bush to a lookout point high above Mahau Sound has wonderful views along the sound back to the town of Havelock, famous for the green-lipped mussels farmed in the Sounds' rich waters.

It's just 3 km to Havelock along SH 6 from here.

4 Portage

From Linkwater on Queen Charlotte Drive to Portage is 30 km. Although sealed, the road is narrow and winding, so take your time.
Portage lies on the shores of the sheltered waters of Kenepuru Sound. From here it is a short distance over a sharp ridge to Torea Bay on the Queen Charlotte Sound. The slow, winding 30-km drive along Mahau and Kenepuru Sounds presents endless coastal vistas — yet these are just a fraction of the 4000-km coastline that makes up the Marlborough Sounds.

5 Pelorus Bridge

From Linkwater drive 12 km to Havelock then turn right on to SH 6 and continue 18 km to Pelorus Bridge.
The walks around Pelorus Bridge at the junction of the Pelorus and Rai Rivers give access to some of the best mature lowland forest in the Marlborough region. In addition to black, red, hard and silver beech, there is also miro, tawa, totara and kahikatea, and some of these trees, such as miro, are not found further south. Bird life includes bellbirds, tui and kereru, as well as the occasional kaka and kakariki.

Pelorus has a great café, good swimming spots in the river and four short walks, all easy. They begin from the car park and include the Tawa Walk (25 minutes), Totara Walk (25 minutes), Circle Walk (30 minutes) and Waterfall Walk (two hours).

6 Okiwi Bay and French Pass

From Pelorus Bridge continue west on SH 6 to Rai Valley. Turn right into Opouri Road and then on to Ronga Road and drive 23 km to Okiwi Bay. French Pass is a further 38 km, and while the road is sealed as far as Elaine Bay, 17 km beyond Okiwi Bay, it's often winding and narrow. From Elaine Bay the entire stretch to French Pass is gravel, narrow and winding.
Protected from the open sea by two small islands, Motuanauru and Otuhaereroa, Okiwi is a broad sheltered bay on Croisilles Harbour in the outer Sounds. From the top of the Ronga Saddle there are fine coastal views, while at the bay is a good camping ground, though the beach itself is shingle. French Pass is the narrow passage between the mainland and D'Urville Island famed for its wild and dangerous eddies and violent tidal currents.

7 Tennyson Inlet

From the same turnoff at Rai Valley turn into Opouri Road and continue for 27 km to Tennyson Inlet. The road is sealed, but the final 10 km crosses a high range and is winding and slow.
Tennyson Inlet is a serene and beautiful harbour with trees coming right down to the water's edge. The steep surrounding hills are clad in dense bush that includes mature rata, beech and rimu. With just a few scattered holiday houses, this is a place of solitude. At Duncan Bay there is a lovely sheltered picnic spot by the shore and at Harvey Bay a simple DoC camping ground. Just beyond Duncan Bay, a short bush walk along the shore leads to Pipi Beach, a shingle beach suitable for swimming and with views down the inlet.

8 Cable Bay

Return to SH 6 and turn right towards Nelson. Continue 31 km and turn right into Cable Bay Road. Cable Bay is 8 km from this point.
The Cable Bay Walkway runs from the left of Cable Bay beach up through farmland, bush remnants and pine forest to The Glen. The entire walk takes two and a half hours one way, but a short slog to the top of the hill at Cable Bay will take about 40 minutes and is rewarded with terrific views over Tasman Bay, the Boulder Bank and the Northwest Nelson Mountains. The beach is shingle and not especially good for swimming.

9 The Boulder Bank

From Cable Bay return to SH 6 and turn right to Nelson. After 6.5 km turn right into Boulder Bank Road. From here to Nelson is 8 km.
The Boulder Bank is a fascinating natural phenomenon, although at first glance it is hard to believe that such a prominent and clearly defined breakwater wasn't engineered by human design. Over 13 km in length, the bank has been formed from large granodiorite boulders moved southwest from McKay Bluff during northerly storms. Whether shifted by wind, water or tide to form such an extraordinarily precise line for such a length, it is not surprising that this boulder bank is one of the very few examples of its type in the world.

The bank originally extended to Haulashore Island near Tahunanui Beach, but in 1906 a substantial gap was cut near its western end for better access to the harbour. While it might be tempting to walk the length of the bank, be warned it is made up of loose stones and negotiating your way along it is seriously hard work.

Governors Bay.

24 Golden Bay • Motueka to Farewell Spit

Stunning springs • Farewell Spit • Golden-sand beaches • Unique geology • 260 km

With Golden Bay at its centre, this northwestern corner of the South Island has some of the most memorable landscapes, flora and fauna of anywhere in New Zealand. The natural beauty of the area is enhanced by the surrounding Abel Tasman and Kahurangi National Parks.

Getting there

Starting at Motueka, 50 km west of Nelson, the route includes the formidable Takaka Hill, Abel Tasman National Park and remote Farewell Spit. Most of the roads on this trip are sealed and are comfortable driving, although the narrow, winding, gravel road into Totaranui will take some care, especially in a camper van.

Best time to visit

This corner of the country has glorious summer weather which, combined with great beaches and a stunning landscape, makes it hard to go past Golden Bay as the ultimate natural New Zealand experience. As always, however, there is a downside, and in this region it's the crowds. In January the main street of Takaka is as busy as downtown Wellington, while at Totaranui the holidaymakers number in their thousands and the traffic over Takaka Hill is a steady procession of camper vans. Casual accommodation is almost impossible and the famed coastal walk in Abel Tasman is not only expensive but booked out well in advance. If you want to experience Golden Bay at its best then book early or try mid-March to June.

Facilities

The permanent population of the Golden Bay area is a few thousand, so facilities in general are pretty lean. Motueka is a good-sized town with a respectable range of accommodation, places to eat, shops and services. Places to stay at the beachside towns such as Kaiteriteri and Pohara are booked out well in advance and this includes the camping grounds. The same goes for the huge camping ground at Totaranui in the heart of Abel Tasman National Park. Collingwood and Takaka are little more than villages, and again, if you plan to stay here during the peak of summer it pays to book ahead. But if all this sounds a bit gloomy and not worth the effort, it's only because this particular neck of the woods is so beautiful. Plan ahead and make the trip.

1 Kaiteriteri

Travel north from Motueka on SH 60 and after 7.5 km turn right into Kaiteriteri Road. Drive 5 km to the beach.
Kaiteriteri is a small crescent-shaped bay with deep golden sand and has long been one of the most popular beaches in the Nelson region. Tree-topped headlands shield the bay from most winds and frame stunning views that stretch across Tasman Bay.

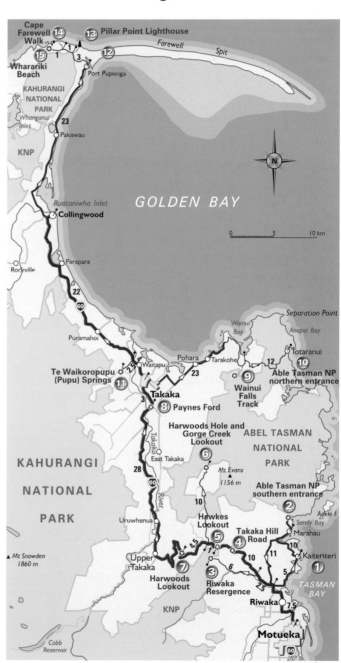

2 Abel Tasman National Park, southern entrance

From Kaiteriteri head north for 10 km on Sandy Bay Road to Marahau. Park by the café at the northern end of Marahau township.

Granite rock headland, Kaiteriteri Beach.

At just over 22,000 hectares, Abel Tasman National Park is New Zealand's smallest national park, and in 1993 the area around Tonga Island was created a marine reserve. In recent years it has gained a reputation as being one of the most crowded from December through to February. At the same time, the combination of lush bush, spectacular coastline, clear water and stunning sandy beaches make this park hard to resist. The DoC Great Walk is a 51-km-long coastal track of mainly easy walking, linking a series of stunningly beautiful beaches with some of the best coastal scenery in the land. Unfortunately, it is also one of the most popular (and most expensive) tracks, and by New Zealand standards extremely crowded in the busy summer months. If crowds bother you, don't be put off walking in this area, just plan a trip outside the mid-December to mid-March period — although be mindful that at no time of the year are you likely to have the track entirely to yourself.

The two main access points are at Marahau at the southern end, and Totaranui (via Takaka) at the heart of the park, but all of the track is easily accessible by water taxi so you can create your own short walk from any point you like. Most water taxis are based at Marahau and Kaiteriteri near Motueka; starting from either of these places is a good option if you don't want to drive all the way to Totaranui. If you do choose one of these starting points, you get to see the magnificent coastal scenery on the way. The beginning of the walk at the Marahau River estuary is very tidal and attracts a good number of wading birds.

Without using a water taxi, Coquille Bay is the most accessible attractive beach from the park's southern entrance, and it will take around one hour to get there. Named after the ship commanded by French navigator Dumont d'Urville, who arrived in the northern part of the South Island in early 1828, Coquille Bay is a sheltered sandy beach backed by dense native bush and is ideal for swimming.

Another popular option is kayaking around the coast; numerous operators at Motueka and Marahau offer kayaks and equipment for hire.

3 Riwaka Resurgence

Return 16 km to SH 60 via Riwaka Road (this goes inland rather than back via Kaiteriteri). Turn right and drive 2.5 km to the Riwaka Valley Road at the base of Takaka Hill. The Resurgence is at the end of this road, 6 km from SH 60.
A short bush walk through mature beech and fern leads to the base of a cliff where the crystal-clear waters of the Riwaka Stream emerge from under Takaka Hill, after flowing underground for 4 km. The cave is popular with divers, who can penetrate the stream underground for up to 800 metres, reaching a giant chamber with limestone formations. Although the water is very cold even in summer, there is a pleasant picnic spot by the car park for those not contemplating a dip.

4 Takaka Hill Road

Return to SH 60 and turn left. While not particularly difficult to drive, the Takaka Hill is 25 km of slow winding road.

Twisting and turning, this road between Tasman and Golden Bays has both spectacular views and fascinating geology. Famed for its distinct marble, the hill is also known as 'Marble Mountain', with stone quarried from the area used to build Nelson Cathedral, and both the old Parliament Buildings and the Beehive in Wellington. The highest point on the road is 972 metres.

5 Hawkes Lookout

From Riwaka Valley Road this lookout is 10 km up the Takaka Hill Road, on the left.

A short easy walk through bush and a landscape of rocky tors leads to a marble outcrop high above the Riwaka Valley, with dramatic views over Tasman Bay towards Nelson and the Riwaka Resurgence lying in the valley directly below. Almost directly across the road are the Ngarua Caves. The remains of numerous moa have been found in this cave system and you can view a complete moa skeleton there (an entry fee applies). Sadly, there is also evidence of damage to the caves by nineteenth century souvenir seekers.

Flax/harakeke

New Zealand flax, unrelated to the northern hemisphere true flax, is in fact an ancient member of the lily family and most closely related to day lilies. Easily recognised by its long handsome leaves and distinctive flower spikes (see image), harakeke is endemic to New Zealand and Norfolk Island. Within this country there are two identifiable species: common flax or harakeke (*Phormium tenax*), and mountain flax or wharariki (*Phormium cookianum*) that is much smaller. In spring the red and yellow flowers on tall stems produce large quantities of nectar that is particularly attractive to birds, and it is not uncommon for tui to fly a considerable distance to feed on them.

While flax is often prolific in wetlands, it will grow in almost any situation to around 1200 metres. In the past, huge areas of lowland New Zealand were covered by dense swathes of flax, and in 1900 the lower section of the Manawatu River supported no less than 70 mills processing enormous quantities of the plant into fibre.

Now a popular and virtually indestructible garden plant, harakeke has numerous cultivars in every colour and shape imaginable. The extensive Rene Orchiston Collection at Paynes Ford is an impressive show of the marvellous variety of this native species.

Low tide, Marahau Beach.

6 Harwoods Hole and Gorge Creek Lookout

One km from Hawkes Lookout turn right into Canaan Road. Follow this gravel, rough and narrow road for 10 km to the car park at the very end.

A dramatic tomo over 170 metres deep, Harwoods Hole is the deepest vertical cave shaft in the country. The hole wasn't properly explored until December 1958 and the following month the Starlight Cave, which leads from the bottom of the hole, was also discovered.

The track to the hole is an easy 45-minute walk through beech forest, though the path does become a bit of a rocky scramble towards the end. There are no barriers and the edge of the hole is a jumble of boulders that require a reasonable degree of fitness to negotiate. It is actually quite hard to see into the hole, but soaring cliffs on all sides give a very good idea of its extent. Cavers regularly use the hole so don't be tempted to throw rocks into the shaft.

Worth the time, a short side track leads up to the Gorge Creek Lookout. This lookout is located on top of a sheer escarpment with views over Gorge Creek and back towards the hole, a view that gives a better idea of the giant tomo's scale. In the bush keep an eye out for tomtit, kakariki and robins.

7 Harwoods Lookout

Return to SH 60 and turn right. The lookout is 4.5 km on the left, just below the summit on the Takaka side of the hill.

Only a two-minute walk from the road, Harwoods Lookout has great views north over Takaka and Golden Bay as far as Farewell Spit. To the west are the peaks of the Lockett and Devil Ranges. Excellent information boards detailing the geology and ecology of the region make this short stop worthwhile. For the more energetic the Takaka Hill Walkway from the summit is a 5-km loop track that clambers through marble outcrops dating back over 400 million years.

8 Paynes Ford

Continue north on SH 60 for 28 km to Paynes Ford Bridge, which is 3 km south of Takaka township.

Following an old coach road, this track skirts spectacular limestone bluffs along the Takaka River and is an area popular with rock climbers. A maze of rough tracks that lead to dramatic cliff faces, rocky overhangs and clefts in the limestone bluffs are worth exploring. An erratic numbering system for them must mean something to someone, though there isn't any information regarding the numbers anywhere nearby. 'Number Four' heads up a short track to a cliff face where a rare native forget-me-not makes its home. A swampy piece of ground along this track is home to the Rene Orchiston Collection of flax featuring dozens of varieties of harakeke that will not fail to impress. When you reach the bend in the river the walk becomes a lot less interesting, so return to the car park from this point.

9 Wainui Falls Track

Continue 3 km to Takaka and take the road to Totaranui via Pohara for 23 km to the Wainui Inlet. Clearly marked on the right is Wainui Falls Road; turn into this road and travel 1 km to the end and park.

The Wainui Falls are within Abel Tasman National Park and thunder over a 20-metre

Anapai Bay.

drop into a deep pool. While the falls are the main attraction, the stream and bush are impressive in their own right. The forest is a lush mixture of mature beech, rata and nikau and the stream tumbles over huge water-worn rocks the size of small trucks. It is 30 minutes one way to the falls and the track is in good condition, though the wire suspension bridge might pose a minor challenge for those a bit unsteady on their feet.

10 Abel Tasman National Park, Totaranui entrance

From the Wainui Falls it is just 12 km to Totaranui, though all of this is winding, narrow road and at least half the distance is gravel. It can get busy so take it easy.

The national park is named after Dutch explorer Abel Janszoon Tasman, who arrived in the area in December 1640. The superlative 'golden' used to describe its sandy beaches does not really do the colour justice, though Golden Bay in fact takes its name from early gold strikes in the district and not the colour of the sand. All the bays along this coast possess a hemline of coarse sand the colour of burnt gold, made even more striking by the contrasting clear azure waters lapping their shores. Typical is Totaranui Beach, a long stretch of beautiful coast with a huge camping ground, an information centre, and a boat ramp at its

northern end. Totaranui is a particularly popular holiday destination and despite the size of the camping ground it is often booked out during summer.

From here several other bays are within easy reach. Anapai Bay, a 45-minute walk to the north through native bush thick with rimu, rata and beech, is a beautiful untouched beach with dark golden sand and stunningly clear water, ideal for swimming after a hot walk.

From the southern end of Totaranui Beach a good track follows the coast to Skinners Point and then on to Goat Bay (20 minutes), a small sandy beach backed by native bush and also ideal for swimming. Waiharakeke (one hour) is a much longer beach with shimmering golden sand and features the lush subtropical bush for which this area is justifiably famous.

11 Te Waikoropupu (Pupu) Springs

Return to Takaka and take SH 60 for 4 km west. After crossing the Takaka River turn left and continue for a further 2.5 km.

Claimed to be the clearest spring water in the world, these springs are not a single outlet but a series of eight interconnected vents in the main pool that discharge up to 14,000 litres per second at a constant temperature of 11.7°C. The water is a mixture of salt and fresh water as the huge underground water system that supplies the springs extends far out under the sea. An innovative underwater mirror system allows the visitor a peek at life below the surface. What is not so well known is that the springs are set in native bush that includes some fine old totara and rimu, and is home to native birds such as bellbird, tui and kereru.

12 Farewell Spit

From Te Waikoropupu Springs, return to SH 60 and turn left, continuing 22 km to Collingwood. Take Puponga Road north for 23 km to Farewell Spit.

Over 30 kilometres in length, Farewell Spit is one of the longest recurved sandspits in the world. The delicate ecosystem of the area is home to a rich variety of bird life (over 90 species have been recorded), including migratory birds such as godwits, which arrive in their tens of thousands in the spring and feed in the shallow waters of Golden Bay. But the extremely shallow water is also a death trap for whales and the bay is the site of regular strandings, mainly by pilot whales. At the end of the spit are an old lighthouse and a gannet colony.

Puponga Farm Park, a working farm at the base of the spit, acts as a buffer to preserve the fragile ecosystem and is an area of outstanding beauty in its own right. Only 2.5 kilometres of the spit is accessible to the casual visiting public and a loop walk that takes less than two hours includes the 'inside' beach of Golden Bay and the 'outside' beach, fronting the Tasman Sea.

Eroded rocks on Wharariki Beach.

At the southern end of the outside beach are rocky cliffs known as Fossil Point, where fossils are clearly visible in the mudstone. Little blue penguins and fur seals are also common. There is an information centre and café with displays on the natural history of this unique locale (closed June to August).

In order to preserve the unique environment access to the entire spit is limited to two tour operators, Farewell Spit Eco Tours (www.FarewellSpit.com) and Farewell Spit Nature Experience (www.farewell-spit.co.nz).

13 Pillar Point Lighthouse

From the Farewell Spit car park return 1 km. Turn right into Wharariki Road and continue for 3 km.

Winding through wind-stunted manuka, this track is a 30-minute uphill walk to a modern lighthouse with the best views over the area. To the west is Cape Farewell, directly north Farewell Spit curves far out into the sea, while to the east lie Golden and Tasman Bays. On a clear day Taranaki is just visible.

14 Cape Farewell Walk

Continue 1 km to a farm road to the right; the car park is just beyond the woolshed.

A 10-minute walk up a farm track leads to a coastal lookout point atop sea cliffs with a huge rock arch and giant sea caves pounded by the waves far below. At 40 degrees 30 minutes south, this is the most northerly part of the South Island and lies directly east of the Manawatu in the North Island.

15 Wharariki Beach

Follow Wharariki Road for 1 km to the car park at the very end.

Facing the heaving Tasman Sea, Wharariki is in marked contrast to the sheltered Golden Bay to the east. This beautiful wide sandy beach is flanked by dramatic rock formations blasted into shape by the wave-driven action of fierce and relentless westerly winds. Keep an eye out for lolling fur seals. This beach is definitely not safe for swimming.

Te Waikoropupu Springs.

25 Marlborough and Kaikoura

Dramatic coastline • Whales • Coastal mountains • 200 km

From the wide expanse of Cloudy Bay to the dramatic mountains towering over the Kaikoura Peninsula, this region is rich in sea life that includes whales, dolphins, seals, and birds.

INFORMATION
Picton i-SITE, The Foreshore,
Picton, ph (03) 520 3113
Blenheim i-SITE, Blenheim Railway
Station, SH 1, Blenheim,
ph (03) 577 8080
Kaikoura i-SITE, Westend,
Kaikoura, ph (03) 319 5641

Getting there
While the route begins at Picton, this area is just as accessible from Christchurch to the south. The roads are good, but slow in parts.

Best time to visit
The whales at Kaikoura have become an international draw card and on some days in summer close to a thousand visitors go out to see them. Whales are visible during all months of the year, but March through to May often has settled, cooler weather and there are far fewer people. If you're planning to visit from mid-December through to early March you will need to book activities well in advance. The road through Molesworth Station to Hanmer Springs is only open from late December to the beginning of April.

Facilities
Picton, Blenheim and Kaikoura all have good accommodation, services and places to eat, but there is very little in between. Kaikoura is a pretty town in a spectacular setting, though the ugly modern sprawl north along SH 1 does the town no favours. Just north of Kaikoura, a number of roadside stalls sell the town's most famous sea delicacy — crayfish.

1 Whites Bay
Drive south from Picton towards Blenheim on SH 1 for 18 km. At Tuamarina turn left and drive 9 km to Rarangi Beach. Continue along the road to Port Underwood. From the point where the road starts climbing uphill at Rarangi it is 4 km to Whites Bay.

While the coast of Cloudy Bay is not known for its beaches, tucked away on the road to Port Underwood are a number of very picturesque bays including Whites, which was named after an African-American slave, Black Jack White, who jumped ship in 1828.

Due to forest clearance in times past there are no very large trees, but today the bush does support a good variety of native birds such as fantail, kereru, tui and bellbird. Birds are most common on the easy 20-minute Pukatea Loop Walk. Two longer tracks (maximum one hour 15 minutes) are the Black Jack Loop Walk and the Port Underwood Lookout that both wind uphill to a viewpoint over Cook Strait. The tracks begin near the historic cable station and there is a good camping site and safe swimming at the bay.

An alternative drive to Whites Bay is from Picton via Port Underwood, although this road is winding and slow. The section between Picton and Port Underwood is sealed, but the 20 km stretch from Port Underwood to Whites Bay is rough, gravel and badly corrugated.

2 Cloudy Bay
From Whites Bay drive 4 km back to Rarangi Beach.
Best known these days as a wine label, Cloudy Bay is in fact a broad bay at the mouth of the Wairau River. This river, 275 kilometres long, originates in the Spenser Mountains near Nelson Lakes National Park and drains the Wairau Plain. The long beach is mainly shingle and only broken by the mouth of the Wairau River, where it forms wide lagoons at the southern end of the bay below White Bluffs.

At Rarangi a short track leads over to tiny Monkey Bay with excellent views south over Cloudy Bay and Cape Campbell. The small cove is pounded by the southerly swells and a sea arch pierces the rock behind the bay, booming in heavy weather as waves crash into the little opening.

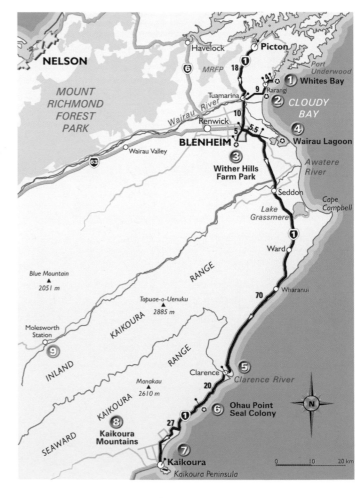

3 Wither Hills Farm Park

From Rarangi head back to SH 1. Turn left and drive 10 km to Blenheim. At Blenheim take Maxwell Road and turn into Taylor Pass Road where the main entrance to the park is located, a total distance of 5 km.

The strikingly beautiful and bare Wither Hills form a dramatic backdrop to the burgeoning town of Blenheim. This open landscape is now such an integral part of Marlborough that it is difficult to believe that these hills were once carpeted in dense native forest. Either deliberately or accidentally, early Maori destroyed much of the initial forest by fire, and what little was left was cleared by early European settlers. Once gone, the bush never recovered, and a fire in 2000 demonstrated the extremely fragile nature of this landscape in a climate of dry summers coupled with strong warm winds.

Numerous tracks and access points from the town provide walks of every type, though for most visitors the Taylor Pass Road entrance is the most accessible. A popular short walk winds up through a gully to the Rotary Lookout from where the hills, tawny brown in summer, provide an impressive backdrop to views over Blenheim and the grapevine-covered Wairau Plains below. To the northwest are the rugged Richmond Ranges, while to the east are Cloudy Bay, the turbulent Cook Strait and, visible in the distance beyond (except in the very worst weather), the North Island.

4 Wairau Lagoon

Return to SH 1 and travel south for 5.5 km to Hardings Road, on the left. The entrance to the lagoon area is at the end of this road.

Unfortunately, the access track to the lagoon begins through the middle of Blenheim's sewer treatment plant, but it quickly emerges onto a vast salt marsh of interlacing waterways that throngs with aquatic bird life and provides a home to some unique salt-tolerant plants.

The Wairau Bar is one of New Zealand's most significant archaeological sites. Maori used the bar as a base for moa hunting, and evidence suggests that they slaughtered over 8000 of these giant birds and consumed more than 2000 moa eggs in the area. The bar was the main port for Blenheim until an earthquake in 1855

Clarence River with the Seaward Kaikouras in the distance.

dropped the level of the entire Wairau Plain, deepening the Opawa River in the process and allowing shipping access further inland.

5 Clarence River

SH 1 crosses the Clarence River 86 km south of the Wairau River.

Originating at Lake Tennyson in the Spenser Mountains just south of Nelson Lakes National Park, the Clarence River first flows south and then, just north of Hanmer Springs, shifts direction and flows northeast between the Inward and Seaward Kaikoura Mountains. Near the ocean, the 160-kilometre-long river gouges a 10-kilometre gorge through the

foothills of the Seaward range before finally reaching the sea.

6 Ohau Point Seal Colony

Continue south on SH 1 for 20 km to the seal colony.

On a rocky shore on the northern side of Ohau Point a large fur seal colony has established itself below the main road. A safe viewpoint immediately above the colony provides the perfect spot for a very close-up peek at daily life among the seals. While many lounge and snooze on rock ledges, others dart and dive between the rough breakers, swirling kelp and tidal pools. Pups are most likely to be seen early in the year.

New Zealand fur seal.

7 Kaikoura Peninsula

From Ohau Point drive 27 km south to Kaikoura.

Originally an island, the Kaikoura Peninsula was joined to the mainland by debris washed down the Hapuku and Kowhai Rivers from the mountains. Formerly heavily forested, the peninsula was long occupied by Maori, with at least 11 different pa sites identified. Sealers and whalers were attracted to the area early in the nineteenth century, followed later by farmers. Even without the whale watching, the close proximity of the mountains to the sea makes Kaikoura one of New Zealand's most spectacular locations, and the open farmland on the peninsula provides endless views of both coast and crests.

The Kaikoura Walkway follows the coastland at the end of the peninsula and eventually ends in the town, though shorter versions of this walk may be more manageable. Right by the car park at the end of Fyffe Quay (an extension of the Esplanade) is a fur seal colony — but you'll need to keep a sharp eye out as the animals easily blend into the surrounding landscape. Most folk only go up to the lookout, but it is worth continuing along the cliff-top as there are views of the mountains to the west and you can see seals and seabirds on the attractive rocky shoreline below.

The deep waters of the Kaikoura Canyon create a unique nutrient-rich environment that sustains a huge range of aquatic life,

Rocky shoreline and seaward Kaikoura Ranges, Kaikoura Peninsula.

Whales

The presence of whales in the outlying waters has been instrumental in transforming Kaikoura from a sleepy seaside fishing and farming village to a bustling tourist centre that annually attracts tens of thousands of visitors from all over the world. Once hunted to near extinction, today whales are jealously protected in the waters around New Zealand, and while Kaikoura has become justifiably famous, a wide variety of these wonderful cetaceans is now seen frequently around our coasts. At Kaikoura the most common species are the giant sperm whales (see image) that live in the coastal waters all year round, while pilot, blue, southern right and humpback whales migrate along the coast and through Cook Strait at different times of the year.

Sperm whales are normally creatures of the open ocean, but at Kaikoura they are attracted to the deep waters of the Hikurangi Trench, which lies 80 kilometres offshore. An extension of this trench known as the Kaikoura Canyon comes as close as 2 kilometres offshore and drops to a depth of 1000 metres. These waters are also a meeting point of warm and cold currents, and consequently the area contains a rich food source not for only whales, but for a host of other marine animals including dusky, Hector's, bottlenose and common dolphins, orca, fur seals, albatross, petrels and shearwaters. Whale Watch Ltd is the only operator licensed for on-water viewing (www.whalewatch.co.nz), though there are aerial viewing options also available. Other operators cater for swimming with and viewing dolphins, scuba diving and fishing.

including Hector's and dusky dolphins, fur seals, seabirds, fish of every kind — and, of course, whales.

8 Kaikoura Mountains

The physical location of Kaikoura is nothing short of spectacular. Within a short distance of the coast, the rugged Kaikoura Mountains climb to nearly 3000 metres, and offshore the seabed drops steeply into the Kaikoura Canyon. The Kaikoura Mountains are in fact two separate ranges, divided by the Clarence River. The highest point of the Seaward Kaikouras is Manakau at 2610 metres; while the higher, Inland mountains peak at the 2885-metre-high Tapuae-o-Uenuku ('the footprint of the Rainbow God').

A northern extension of the Southern Alps, these ranges formed along New Zealand's Alpine Fault and initially rose out of the sea some 30 million years ago. More recent mountain-building activity over the past 200,000 years has seen them rise sharply, a process that is still continuing today. The endemic Marlborough rock daisy (*Pachystegia insignis*) is common in these mountains.

A popular day hike to the top of Mt Fyffe (1602 metres) will take seven hours return. But if the summit seems just a bit too much, an alternative is the Fyffe Hut at 1100 metres, which is five hours return.

GOT TIME? (+182KM)
9 Molesworth Station

Open only through summer, the road from SH 1, 22 km south of Blenheim, runs 182 km through the heart of the station to Hanmer Springs, and the 1437-metre-high Island Saddle is the highest point in New Zealand on any public road. While mostly gravel and often winding and narrow, it is not a difficult road and it makes a comfortable day's drive. The station is more accessible from Hanmer.

New Zealand's largest station, covering over 180,000 hectares of inland high country, has had a mixed history. This is tough country at best, with hot dry summers and icy winters. Ranging in altitude from 500 to over 2000 metres, this station is the source of the Acheron, Clarence, and Waiau Rivers. Mountainous and rugged, Molesworth has a beauty and appeal all its own, with vast unpopulated vistas, a subtle landscape of muted colours, and a quiet solitude rarely found elsewhere.

Established as a merino sheep station in the middle of the nineteenth century, the run initially flourished, and in 1900 it supported 50,000 sheep. However, by 1925 the station's flock had dropped to just 1400, its pastures devastated by rabbits. When the lease ran out on the station in 1938, Molesworth and neighbouring Tarndale Station reverted to the Crown. Through careful management of stock and land, Molesworth slowly returned to productivity and now supports the largest herd of cattle in New Zealand.

On the Acheron Road there is camping at both Acheron and Molesworth, but no other accommodation or facilities. The Acheron Road is open from 28 December to 1 April, from 7 am to 7 pm, but may be closed without warning due to weather conditions or fire danger. The road's status can be checked out in advance by contacting the DoC South Marlborough Area Office (ph (03) 572 9100).

26 North Canterbury and the Lewis Pass • Kaikoura to Reefton
Snowy mountainscape • Thermal pools • Impressive rock formations • 355 km

Winding along the coast and through the Lewis Pass, this route draws fewer visitors than the other Southern Alps crossings and with it comes a more subtle landscape and greater solitude.

INFORMATION
Kaikoura i-SITE, Westend,
Kaikoura, ph (03) 319 5641
Hanmer Springs i-SITE,
42 Amuri Avenue, Hanmer Springs,
ph (03) 315 7128
Reefton i-SITE, 67–69 Broadway,
Reefton, ph (03) 732 8391

Getting there
Beginning at Kaikoura, this route, on a good sealed road, first heads south and then west through the Southern Alps at the Lewis Pass. An alternative road, which bypasses the coastal part of the trip, goes inland from Kaikoura and follows the Amuri Range via Waiau to join SH 7 near Culverden. Although this road isn't fast, it is sealed and does make a pleasant change from SH 1. The Lewis Pass is seldom closed by snow in winter.

Best time to visit
The hot springs at both Maruia and Hanmer make this a good all-year-round trip. While summers can be very hot and winters extremely cold, the added attraction of cooler months in these places is the stunning snow-covered mountainscape. Of course, if it *is* very cold then it's not too hard to figure out how to spend your time in either Hanmer or Maruia. Naturally, Hanmer Springs is a very popular spot for Canterbury folk during school holidays and long holiday weekends and you will need to book accommodation ahead at these times. On the western side of the Alps, Reefton can have stretches of bleak, foggy and wet weather in the winter months.

Facilities
This is empty country, and apart from Kaikoura, Hanmer Springs and Reefton, none of which are particularly large, facilities along this route are light. Cheviot and Waipara, in the heart of the North Canterbury wine country, have limited accommodation. That said, there is plenty of accommodation at Kaikoura, Hanmer Springs, and to a lesser extent Reefton. Both Kaikoura and Hanmer are popular in the summer months and accommodation at Hanmer tends to be on the expensive side. Hanmer Springs Thermal Pools and Spa was voted Best Visitor Attraction at the 2004, 2005 and 2006 New Zealand Tourism Awards. Popular with families, the springs include a wide number of pools and attractions ranging from hydroslides to quiet spa pools. At Maruia Springs there is a unique, Japanese-style alpine resort, while Reefton, an old coal and gold-mining town, is much more down-home.

1 Gore Bay
From Kaikoura, head south on SH 1 for 67 km to Cheviot. Turn left into McQueen Road (which becomes Gore Bay Road) and travel 8.5 km to reach the bay.

A wide open bay, Gore Bay has a sand and boulder beach backed by steep hills with regenerating bush. At its southern end is the Gore Bay Scenic Reserve and The Cathedrals, a 'badlands' formation of eroded cliffs and pinnacles. A rough track follows the coast from Manuka Bay at the southern end of Gore Bay through to the Hurunui Mouth, though the track is not marked at either end. There is a good sheltered camping ground right on the beach, along with a very attractive picnic area.

2 Motunau Beach
From Gore Bay head south on a loop road via Port Robinson that after 12.5 km returns to SH 1 at Domett. Continue south for 26 km to Greta Valley and turn left into Motunau Beach Road, driving 15 km to the river mouth.

The traditionally accepted boundaries of the words 'beach' and 'river' are stretched at Motunau, where the Motunau River

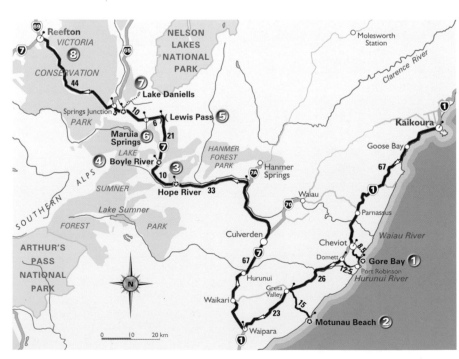

Clay pinnacles, Gore Bay.

is the size of a small stream and Motunau Beach is rocky, with only scraps of sand. Even so, this is a special place and the views south are intriguing. Across Pegasus Bay on the horizon Banks Peninsula floats like an island and it is simple to see how Captain James Cook made one of his very few mistakes when he wrote on his maps, 'Banks Island'.

Just offshore is tiny Motunau Island, an off-limits wildlife reserve and stronghold of the white-flippered penguin. One of the smallest of the species, standing around 35 centimetres tall, the white-flippered penguin is closely related to the common blue penguin. Like their near relatives, these penguins are a blue-grey colour, but with a distinctive narrow band of white around the edge of the flippers. A native to Canterbury, this endangered bird nests only on Banks Peninsula and Motunau Island, and less than 10,000 of them remain. In summer they head to the southern coastal areas of the South Island, returning to their rocky roosts in Canterbury in winter to nest and breed from August to November.

3 Hope River

Return to SH 1 and drive 23 km south to Waipara, turn right into SH 7 and continue 67 km to the Hanmer Springs junction. Continue on SH 7 for 33 km.

The road west initially follows the wide and braided Waiau River and then its tributary, the Hope River, towards Lewis Pass. Along the southern bank of the Hope River natural 'badlands' formations are a feature of the steep cliffs. Here the fragile stony soils have been eroded unevenly to create the intriguing narrow peaks and pinnacles with deep gullies in between known as 'hoodoos'.

4 Boyle River

The Boyle River lies 10 km west of the badlands formations on the Hope River.

From the road below the Lewis Pass, there are excellent views over the wide braided river flats of the Boyle River. Here, the vegetation of the region starts to alter dramatically. As the road leaves the Boyle and follows the Lewis River, the prickly matagouri, manuka and tussock of inland

Canterbury are left behind and quickly replaced by beech forest. Entering the pass, the forest becomes lusher, responding to the increased rainfall, and on the western side bears no resemblance at all to the dry scrubland less than 20 km east.

5 Lewis Pass

From the Boyle River continue on SH 7 for 21 km.

At a lower altitude than Arthur's Pass, at 864 metres the Lewis Pass is an old Maori greenstone trail that follows the Lewis River south of the pass and the Maruia River to the west. Today the pass is the main route from North Canterbury to the Buller region, and attracts fewer visitors than many other South Island regions.

The subalpine vegetation is predominantly beech and there are several good walks in this area. For the more serious tramper, the St James Walkway is a medium-graded tramp, 61 km long. It takes around five days and begins from the car park just below the pass. A three-hour return walk to Cannibal Gorge along the St James is also an option. Meandering through subalpine beech forest

Rugged section of the Boyle River.

8 Victoria Conservation Park

From the Lake Daniells car park continue 5 km to Springs Junction and then turn left and follow SH 7 west 44 km to Reefton. Encompassing the Victoria and Brunner Ranges and the headwaters of the Grey, Inangahua and Maruia Rivers, the Victoria Conservation Park is the largest of its type in New Zealand and covers an enormous area of 206,000 hectares. The landscape is mixed and ranges from pristine terrain through to areas that were once the sites of feverish mining activity for gold and coal. The forest is particularly famous for its beech and this is the only area of the country where all five types of the tree are found in one location.

Cutting right through the park, just after leaving Springs Junction SH 7 crosses the southern foothills of the Victoria Range at the Rahu Saddle. The road follows the Inangahua River through to Reefton and some of the most accessible tracks into the park. Just before Reefton, around Blacks Point there are numerous tracks of various lengths that mainly follow old gold-mining trails. At the Swingbridge picnic area (on the left just before Blacks Point) there is an attractive two-hour walk through splendid beech forest along the dark, tea-coloured Inangahua River.

thickly hung with moss, the short 20-minute Tarn Loop passes a reflective mountain tarn and has labels to assist with the identification of alpine plants along the way.

Right at the pass itself is a 30-minute walk to a lookout point with views of the Maruia River, Cannibal Gorge, Gloriana Peak and the Freyberg Range. Just 12 km on (past Maruia Springs) is the 20-minute Waterfall Track through ancient beech trees to an elegant waterfall that drops 40 metres.

6 Maruia Springs

From Lewis Pass follow SH 7 west for 6 km. Just east of Lake Daniells is Maruia Springs, hot water pools in a magnificent alpine setting overlooking the Maruia River. In use for over a hundred years, the water in the pools is drawn, untreated, from a natural hot spring on the other side of the river. Free from additives, the water is high in mineral content and reputed to have healing properties, particularly for the skin. The pools are drained every day and can vary considerably in mineral content and colour. Under Japanese ownership, Maruia Springs Thermal Resort has private pools, a segregated Japanese-style bathhouse, and small outdoor rock pools designed to resemble a miniature mountain tarn.

7 Lake Daniells

The Lake Daniells car park is 10 km from Maruia Springs and 5 km from Springs Junction on SH 7. Lake Daniells is a small pretty alpine lake at the head of the Alfred River, a tributary of the Maruia. The easy walk of three hours return is through dense beech forest along the Alfred River, while another track circumnavigates the lake. There is a large camping area at the beginning of the walk to the lake and near the entrance by the road is an intriguing fence — not to keep in stock, but to monitor any movement in the Alpine Fault. If time is tight then the short walk to The Sluice Box, where the wide Maruia River runs deep and clear as it is forced through a narrow gorge of marble, takes only 15 minutes.

The Maruia River flows through a narrow gorge.

27 Canterbury Foothills • Rangiora to Geraldine

Alpine vistas • Beech forest • Bellbirds • River gorges • 230 km

The foothills of the Southern Alps are accessible as easy day trips from Christchurch and have surprisingly leafy forest, diverse native bird life and challenging walks.

Getting there

Although the route starts near Rangiora in the north, all of this trip can be reached from any part of Canterbury. The main east–west highway along SH 73 cuts through the middle of it. The roads are good, sealed and mainly straight, making for very pleasant driving. Although not an official state highway, this route has been christened 'Inland Scenic Route 72'.

Best time to visit

A good trip for any time of year. Summer days can be very warm, making the cool bush an appealing option, while on a clear and sunny winter's day when the snow is thick on the peaks the views here are hard to beat. While some spots attract more people in summer, it is seldom crowded anywhere along here, even in peak months.

Facilities

Accommodation, places to eat and services are relatively thin along the actual route, but major centres such as Rangiora, Ashburton, Geraldine and Christchurch are never too far away. There is some accommodation and always a café to be found in the smaller centres such Oxford, Sheffield, Staveley, Darfield and Methven.

1 Mt Thomas

From Rangiora take the Loburn–Glentui Road on the north side of the Ashley River for 26 km to Hayland Road. The car park and camping ground are 3 km at the end of this road.
At 1023 metres Mt Thomas is the most accessible of the small peaks in the range of hills extending west to east above Oxford. While the top is open and often snow-covered in winter, the lower slopes are characterised by fine beech forest and lush valleys. The tramp to the summit will take around five hours return, but the area has a number of excellent short walks ranging from 40 minutes to two hours.

The bush here is alive with bellbirds and if you are lucky you might spot the rare native parrot, the kakariki. There is an excellent camping ground and picnic area at the beginning of the tracks, with great views over the Canterbury Plains.

2 Mt Richardson

Return to the main road, turn right and travel 6 km and then turn right into Glentui Road. Continue 4.5 km to the end of this road.
Mt Richardson is part of the 10,800-hectare Mt Thomas Forest. Just west of Mt Oxford, this 1047-metre peak is reached by a six-hour return walk to the summit. The terrain is a mixture of tussock and beech forest, with many of the trees damaged by the fierce northwest winds, and the top is surprisingly flat. At the beginning of the Mt Richardson track, the Glentui Waterfall is just a short bushwalk from the attractive picnic area through cool beech forest.

The camping ground at Ashley Gorge, 4.5 km from the Glentui turnoff, is superbly located on the south bank of the Ashley River.

3 Mt Oxford

Return to the main road and continue south for 13 km to Oxford. Turn right into Main Street and after 2 km right again into Woodside Road. Continue on Woodside Road for 7 km and then turn right into Mountain Road; the car park is 2 km at the end of this road.
The highest of these three peaks at 1364 metres, Mt Oxford is a challenging

eight-hour return tramp to the summit. The track begins through beech forest and gradually gives way to more open vegetation and finally to snow tussock on the top. This area is exposed to the fierce northwest winds that frequently reach gale force in the Canterbury region. Known as a foehn wind and locally as a 'Nor'wester', these powerful winds occur when westerly weather off the Tasman Sea is forced to drop moisture in the foothills of the Southern Alps. As the winds rise they become drier and warmer, before finally sweeping into Canterbury as a strong, hot blast. The winds are accompanied by a cloud formation in the shape of a wide crescent known as the 'Nor'west Arch'. Winds of a similar type are the Chinook in the North American Rockies, the Terral in Spain and the Helm in Britain.

4 Waimakariri Gorge

Return to Oxford, turn right and drive 12 km to the gorge (clearly signposted).

A classic example of a braided river, the Waimakariri rises in the Southern Alps west of Arthur's Pass, flowing for 150 km to reach the ocean just north of Christchurch. At the Waimakariri Gorge this mighty river is confined to a narrow rocky ravine spanned by an historic bridge built in 1876. Rising over 30 metres above the riverbed, the piers of the bridge are a very early example of the use of concrete in bridge construction. The area has a very popular picnic spot, with good access to the river for boaties, kayakers and fishing folk.

5 Rakaia River Gorge

From the Waimakariri Gorge continue south for 5 km to SH 73. Turn left and then after 1 km turn right into Deans Road, which after 8 km joins SH 77. Turn right into SH 77 and drive south for 33 km to the Rakaia Gorge.

Much like the Waimakariri, the Rakaia is a braided river with its headwaters deep in the Southern Alps below Mt Whitcombe, and is joined by the Wilberforce River from the north near Lake Coleridge. At Rakaia Gorge the river cuts deeply into the light shingle soils of the foothills before surging through narrow rock cliffs spanned by a bridge built in 1884. A walkway along the northern bank has grand views of

Waimakariri River at the Gorge.

the river and the mountains. Although vegetation is generally sparse, there are many fine old kowhai trees overhanging the swirling turquoise waters.

6 Mt Somers and the Sharplin Falls

From Rakaia Gorge continue south on SH 77 and then take the Arundel Rakaia Gorge Road for 25 km to Staveley. Turn right into Boyds Road and drive 4 km to the car park at the end of the road.

The cool beech forest of the Canterbury foothills around Mt Somers and Staveley is in stark contrast to the open plains below and the dry tussock mountain country further inland. At 1688 metres, Mt Somers is not the usual greywacke rock of the Southern Alps but is actually an old volcanic dome. In addition there are geological remnants of the ancient seabed of Gondwanaland. Although the forest here is mainly beech, there is the occasional southern rata, and on the lower slopes, rimu and kahikatea. Bellbirds are common in the bush.

The tramp to the top is a demanding seven hours return, though the lower peak of the Duke Knob is a more manageable option. At the foot of the mountain a one-hour return walk through beautiful forest follows the Bowyers Stream to a rocky gorge and the picturesque Sharplin Falls.

Mt Oxford Range at dawn.

7 Peel Forest Park

Continue south through Mayfield for 47 km (over the Rangitata River) to Peel Forest Road. Turn right and drive 10 km to Peel Forest village. From here it is 31 km to Geraldine.

Covering over 700 hectares on the southern bank of the Rangitata River in the foothills of the Southern Alps, Peel Forest Park is a fragment of a much larger forest razed by early Maori and milled by Pakeha settlers (Mt Peel itself lies outside the park). The climate here is distinct from both the plains and the high country further inland. With a much higher rainfall, the Peel Forest supports a rich and diverse flora and fauna including a large number of native birds and huge old matai and kahikatea, along with one stupendous totara tree estimated to be over 1000 years old. The variety of ferns is especially surprising, and a third of all native fern types can be found here.

The park has a wide range of walking tracks, with jet boat and raft companies providing trips through the Rangitata Gorge. A number of short tracks start at two main areas, Blandswood and Te Wanahu Flat, both clearly signposted and within 2 km of Mt Peel village. These walks include Dennistoun Bush (45 minutes), Big Tree Walk (30 minutes), and Acland Falls

Rakaia River from Rakaia Gorge, looking towards the Mt Hutt Range.

Bellbird/Korimako

Unique to New Zealand, bellbirds are today one of the more common native birds, successfully adapting both to regenerating bush and exotic forests. The only surviving member of the *Anthornis* genus, the bellbird (*Anthornis melanura*) is a member of the honeyeater family, though it is in fact a generalist feeder and will eat nectar, insects and fruit. Bellbirds are vital to the pollination of many native species including flax, tree fuchsia and kowhai. The Three Kings bellbird, confined to the offshore islands of the same name, is a subspecies and differs in size and plumage.

Known for its distinct bell-like song, not only do the male and female of the species have song differences, but the birds are very unusual in that their song also has distinct regional dialects. Dull olive-green in colour, and so perfectly camouflaged in the New Zealand bush, it is usually their song that first signals the bellbird's presence. Individuals often retain the same mate and territory season after season.

In the late nineteenth century bellbird populations started to decline rapidly, along with a number of other native birds, and it was widely thought the korimako would become extinct. Mysteriously, the population started reviving from the middle of the twentieth century, although the mainland population north of Hamilton has never recovered.

(1 hour 20 minutes). There is also a large camping ground at Te Wanahu Flat.

GOT TIME? (+45 KM)
8 Lake Coleridge Basin

Lake Coleridge Road heads inland for 45 km to the Harper River.

Following the Rakaia River inland, the road to Lake Coleridge penetrates deep into the mountains of the Southern Alps and is an easy drive from SH 77 at Windwhistle. The basin was formed by massive glaciers, long since melted and replaced by the wild rivers of the Rakaia, Wilberforce, Harper and Avoca Rivers.

Once a glacier lake, Lake Coleridge was raised in 1912 to generate electricity for the country's first state hydroelectric scheme. Within the basin are Lakes Ida and Lyndon, two small lakes that are important bird habitats and often freeze over in winter. Almost entirely surrounded by mountains and attracting just a small handful of visitors, the Lake Coleridge Basin is definitely a location away from it all.

28 Christchurch City

Urban wetland paradise • Bird-watching • Ancient volcanic landscapes

Although Christchurch is New Zealand's second-largest city, this urban area contains some of the country's most important wetlands, along with several hidden natural gems.

INFORMATION
Christchurch i-SITE Visitor Centre,
Old Chief Post Office, Christchurch,
ph (03) 379 9629

Getting there
These trips are all easily accessible from central Christchurch.

Best time to visit
With a relatively dry climate and urban attractions for a wet day, Christchurch is a good all-year-round destination. Summers can be very hot with temperatures over 30°C, and winters decidedly cool, though snow in the city is rare. Temperatures can plummet quite suddenly with a southerly change, but climatic extremes are uncommon. The beaches are exposed to cool easterly winds even in summer.

Facilities
Christchurch is an easy city to get around and has an excellent range of accommodation, cafés and shopping. In addition to an international and domestic airport, all major (and many local) rental vehicle companies are based there. The city is mainly flat, so cycling is also a good option. Large sporting events can put pressure on accommodation, but unlike many other centres there is usually something available.

1 Avon–Heathcote Estuary
City to estuary via the Sumner Road, southern side, is 8 km. City to estuary via Rockinghorse Road, northern side, is 13 km.
This vast haven for wading birds is easily accessible from several points on both the north and south shores. For the more serious bird-watcher, McCormacks Bay, enclosed by the main road to Sumner, is the best place to spot seabirds such as gulls, terns and shags; while Raupo Island at the mouth of the Avon is the breeding ground for pied stilt. During the summer months godwits cluster at the end of Southshore Spit, a small wilderness area of dune and stunted vegetation on the northern side of the estuary entrance.

2 Brooklands Lagoon and Waimakariri Beach
The Brooklands Lagoon is in Spencer Park, 20 km from the central city.
Situated just south of the mouth of the Waimakariri River, this 270-hectare wetland attracts a range of shore birds. Over 70 species have been recorded here including oystercatcher, red-billed gull, spotted shag, white-faced heron, Caspian tern, banded dotterel and pied stilt. The tidal lagoon is fringed by a shallow salt marsh and hardy native trees, including ngaio. High dunes protect the lagoon from the sea and the relentless easterly breezes.

Accessible on both sides by good tracks, there are bird hides on the west side of the lagoon as well as a raised viewing platform with good views over the tidal flats. The Waimakariri Walkway to the river mouth runs parallel to the vast beach along the lagoon's eastern side.

3 Riccarton Bush
Riccarton Bush is in Kahu Road, in the suburb of Riccarton, 3.5 km from central Christchurch.
Riccarton Bush is a small remnant of the extensive kahikatea forests once common on the swampy plain around Christchurch, but later felled by Maori and European settlers. Now protected by a predator-free fence, the 12-hectare reserve is too small to sustain much native bird life, although the vegetation is surprisingly diverse. In addition to kahikatea — some of which are estimated to be over 600 years old — the bush contains totara, rimu, beech, matai and kowhai. The Deans family preserved the bush with great foresight, and their cottage is the oldest surviving building on the plain.

4 Travis Wetland
Located in the suburb of Burwood, 9 km from the central city. The main entrance, with information, parking and toilets, is in Beach Road.

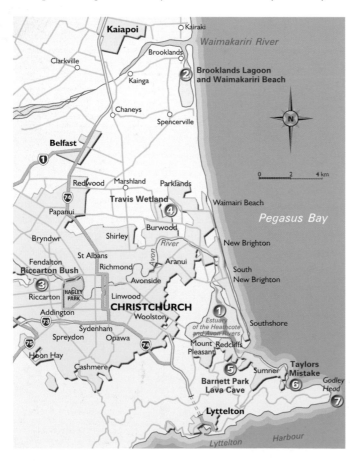

Brooklands Lagoon, Spencer Park.

Much modified by human activity over the past 750 years and now encircled by suburbs, this wetland is home to both native and introduced birds. Over 50 species have been recorded including black swan, shoveler, pukeko, grey duck, mallard, Canada goose and scaup. Thirty-five species of native bird have visited the lagoon, and five species of native duck breed here. In addition to native fauna, the wetland is home to 60 native plant species.

A large bird hide overlooks the deep ponds at the heart of the large reserve, now undergoing restoration with an energetic planting and weed-removal programme. Some of the 112 hectares of wetland are still farmed. From the car park it is a short walk to the bird hide and another 20-minute walk to a tall viewing tower with a wide view of the wetland over the treetops.

5 Barnett Park Lava Cave

Barnett Park is 11 km from the city at Moncks Bay via the Sumner Road.

The rugged landscape of the Port Hills was formed during the Pliocene epoch 10 to 15 million years ago during the eruption of the Lyttelton volcano. Subsequent erosion has left the hills steep and cut by short streams and deep gullies. Barnett Park is a flat area of playing fields backed by a deep steep-sided valley with high rocky bluffs.

The Avon–Heathcote Estuary before Southshore Spit.

Avon–Heathcote Estuary

Within the confines of Christchurch City, the estuaries of the Avon and the Heathcote Rivers join to form a vast tidal salt marsh that is an important habitat for native flora and fauna. Today, only 10 per cent of New Zealand's original salt marsh remains. Although compromised by human habitat, this estuary is now recognised for its high ecological value, and in recent years both the city authorities and local interest groups have restored the river and estuary margins with a substantial replanting programme and improved water quality.

Geologically the estuary is very young and was formed only 450 years ago when the build-up of sand south of the Waimakariri River mouth formed the New Brighton Spit that now protects the mouths of the Avon and Heathcote Rivers from the open sea. The estuary is very shallow with just the river channels remaining at low tide and the tidal influence extends 8 km up the Avon and 11 km along the Heathcote. Numerous small flat islands such as Naughty Boys Island and Rat Island are safe havens for aquatic birds. The flora is mainly hardy salt-tolerant plants such as sea rush, glasswort, sea blite, buck's-horn plantain, oioi, bachelor's button and the rare native primrose and native musk. On higher ground coastal shrubs such as ribbonwood dominate.

Vast mud banks are a rich food source for both young fish and wading birds that feed on crabs, snails, whelks and marine worms. Eels, flounder, mullet and whitebait are common. Bird life is prolific and over 110 species have been recorded here including migratory and breeding birds. Commonly seen species are pied stilt, heron, grey teal, shag, geese, black swan, gull, tern, shoveler, oystercatcher, duck and dotterel. Eastern bar-tailed godwits number around 2000 birds through the summer months.

Godley Head from above Taylors Mistake Beach.

At the head of the valley a flight of wooden steps leads up to a marvellous lava cave. While the cave is relatively shallow, there are wonderful prospects over the estuary, the New Brighton Spit and Pegasus Bay. On the western side of the valley a narrow rough track leads through bush to another, larger cavern called Paradise Cave, tucked away in a side valley and popular with rock climbers. The valley once supported a wide range of birds including kiwi, weka, kaka and the long-extinct moa, but bird life rapidly declined with the destruction of the forest. The small bush remnant is now home to bellbirds and the native harrier hawk.

6 Taylors Mistake

Taylors Mistake is 6.5 km from Barnett Park via Sumner.

A small open bay just over the hill from Sumner, Taylors Mistake is a good starting point for two excellent walks. The first follows the coast back towards Sumner and skirts the high volcanic cliffs of the Giant's Nose with extensive views over Pegasus Bay. Above and below, seabirds including southern black-backed and red-billed gulls and sooty shearwaters wheel in the winds, and hardy native and exotic plants cling to

the dry and exposed rock faces. The walk takes one hour one way.

In the other direction a wide coastal path leads to Boulder Bay, where wind and tide have created a shoreline of cliffs, boulders, sea caves and rocky platforms. While native plants have long been superseded by open grassland here, the area is home to the rare white-flippered penguin.

7 Godley Head

Sumner to Godley Head is 9 km via Evans Pass and the Summit Road.

The Lyttelton volcano, which erupted over 12 million years ago, is much older than its larger neighbour, the Akaroa volcano. Originally the land was a lot higher, but much of the outer volcanic material has eroded away over time, leaving a distinct crater rim of which Godley Head is a part.

The head rises high above the entrance to Lyttelton Harbour, which was formed around 15,000 years ago when rising global temperatures at the end of an ice age caused the seas to rise and flood the old crater. While the dense native forest that covered these hills has long gone, small patches of native vegetation that still cling to rocky bluffs and steep gullies include the native sedge, kawakawa and star lily. Harrier hawks are common, as are seabirds.

Rocky coastline, Taylors Mistake.

29 Banks Peninsula

Hector's dolphin • Volcanoes • 2000-year-old totara • Dramatic coastline • 120 km

At the heart of this peninsula are the water-filled craters of two ancient volcanoes surrounded by mist-shrouded hills offering endless vistas. Offshore, Hector's dolphins are a common sight, while to the south shallow Lake Ellesmere is a haven for aquatic wildlife.

INFORMATION

Lyttelton i-SITE , 44 London Street, Lyttelton, ph (03) 328 9093
Akaroa Information Centre, 80 Rue Lavaud, Akaroa, ph (03) 304 8600
Christchurch i-SITE, Old Chief Post Office, Christchurch, ph (03) 379 9629

Getting there

Banks Peninsula is easily accessible from Christchurch, but be warned: the terrain is steep and rugged and the peninsula contains some very demanding roads. While most are sealed, the driving is slow so take your time. Direct access to Akaroa is easiest from the south via Little River.

Best time to visit

Exposed to southerly weather, especially on the peaks along the Summit Road, in winter the peninsula can be cold, wet and bleak, so this is not the best place to visit in the middle of the year. However, on a clear sunny Canterbury day, from spring through to autumn, its open hilltops and sheltered bays possess a special magic. Akaroa is very popular as a day trip from Christchurch, but most visitors do not seem to venture too much further afield than the township itself. The hills overlooking Christchurch are a favoured recreational destination for cyclists, walkers and runners, so take extra care when navigating the narrow roads.

Facilities

Christchurch offers plenty of everything, from every sort of place to stay and eat through to all the shopping you can handle. Elsewhere on the peninsula, Akaroa, with its historic French connection, Lyttelton and Little River have a reputation for excellent cafés. Akaroa has a good range of accommodation including several historic hotels, although only a small shopping centre. Barrys Bay on the shore of Akaroa Harbour is famous for the long-established cheese factory.

1 Lyttelton Harbour

From central Christchurch follow Colombo Street directly south. This street becomes Dyers Pass Road at the foot of the Cashmere Hills and continues over the pass to Lyttelton, a total distance of 12 km.

One of two volcanic craters on the Banks Peninsula, Lyttelton Harbour extends 18 km inland from the entrance at Godley Head and is surrounded by steep hills rising to Mt Herbert at 919 metres on its southern side. Older than Akaroa, the Lyttelton volcano erupted more than 12 million years ago and it is believed that the original summit was over 1500 metres high. The hills surrounding the harbour are in fact the old crater rim; the crater itself was flooded 15,000 years ago by rising sea levels. Once, the entire Banks Peninsula was cloaked in dense forest, but since the arrival of humans around 700 years ago only 2 per cent of the bush cover remains.

2 Quail Island/Otamahua, Lyttelton Harbour

Black Cat Cruises runs regular trips to the island through the summer months.
Phone (03) 328 9078, www.blackcat.co.nz

Rather than a single geological entity, Quail Island has been built up by three distinct volcanic eruptions. The oldest rocks on the island date back to an eruption at the head of the harbour 14 million years ago, while the youngest rocks derive from lava flows during the Mt Herbert/Te Ahu Patiki eruption 6 million years ago. The island's volcanic origins are clearly evidenced by the distinct cliffs of columnar basalt rock on its eastern side.

The European name for this island arose from the former existence of native quail that appear to have been confined to its environs but which quickly became extinct once the land was cleared for farming. For many years Otamahua was used as a quarantine station and several buildings from this period still remain. While today the island is virtually devoid of native trees, it is slowly being replanted by volunteers, although these plantings are still at an early stage. A complete circuit takes around two hours, with the option of a shorter walk of about 50 minutes.

3 The Crater Rim, Summit Road from Dyers Pass to Gebbies Pass

This section of the Summit Road begins at the Sign of the Kiwi at the top of Dyers Pass; from there it is 14 km to Gebbies Pass.

The Summit Road follows the crater rim from Godley Head to Gebbies Pass. This section from Dyers Pass not only presents marvellous views over the harbour and the plains, but also features some of the most significant bush remnants left on the peninsula. The Crater Rim Walkway, which can be walked in sections, winds along the tops for 14 km and is easily accessed from the road.

At Dyers Pass a short walk (40 minutes) through tussock and regenerating bush leads up to the summit of Mt Sugar Loaf, with amazing views over Banks Peninsula, Christchurch City, the Canterbury Plains and the Southern Alps beyond. Kennedy Bush/Sign of the Bellbird, 4.8 km from the Sign of the Kiwi, is a small forest of dense mahoe with some totara and kowhai and, as the name suggests, bellbirds. There is a superb view of Lyttelton Harbour from the road. Gibraltar Rock, 9 km from the Sign of the Kiwi, is a small patch of regenerating bush below a tussock-clad volcanic outcrop with great views over the city, plains and south to Lake Ellesmere.

The 'Signs' are part of a series of rest-houses along the tops of the Port Hills planned by the conservationist and politician Harry Ell in the early twentieth century — of which only a few were actually built. At one end of the scale, the Sign of the Takahe is a grand gothic restaurant, while at the other the Sign of the Bellbird is a mere stone shelter.

4 Lake Ellesmere/Te Waihora

From the Summit Road at the top of Gebbies Pass, turn right into Gebbies Pass Road and continue for 5.5 km to SH 75. Turn left and continue 12 km to the lake.

This huge brackish coastal lake covering 20,000 hectares is New Zealand's fifth-largest lake and one of the most important wildlife habitats in the land. As much lagoon as lake, Ellesmere is fed by the Selwyn/Waikirikiri and Halswell Rivers. The narrow gravel spit separating the lake from the sea often closes and has to be regularly reopened by bulldozer.

Only 1.5 metres at its deepest, Lake Ellesmere supports an incredible array of bird life, with over 160 species recorded here including over 130 natives, of which 35 breed along the shores. Total bird numbers can reach over 100,000 individuals during summer. In addition, the lake supports over 40 fish species in its nutrient-rich waters. However, its shallow nature renders it particularly vulnerable to pollution.

The 28-km-long Kaitorete Spit between Lake Ellesmere and the ocean was formed 6000 years ago by gravel washed along the coast from the mouth of the Rakaia River, just to the south. Pingao, a yellow/orange-coloured native dune grass, is common here. Birdlings Flat, a small seaside settlement at the outlet for Lake Forsyth to the east, has a long shingle beach and is a popular spot to fossick for semi-precious stones.

5 Akaroa Harbour

Continue on SH 75 for 43 km to Akaroa township.

Once an island, Banks Peninsula was gradually joined to the mainland by alluvial gravels washed down from the mountains by the Rakaia and Waimakariri Rivers. Like Lyttelton, the harbour at Akaroa is the crater of an old volcano subsequently inundated by rising sea levels. Younger than Lyttelton by 3 million years, this crater erupted some 8 million years ago and opened to the sea at Timutimu Head.

Surrounded by rugged steep hills, tiny bays and beaches, only fragments of bush remain here including a small grove of nikau that are at their southern limit, making these trees the most southerly growing palms on the planet. The waters of the harbour are also home to Hector's dolphins, the world's smallest (and rarest) marine dolphin and native to New Zealand.

6 Summit Road

From Akaroa return along SH 75 for 3 km to Long Bay Road. Turn right and proceed up the hill for 5 km to Summit Road. From here turn left and continue 20 km along Summit Road back to SH 75 at Hilltop.

Narrow and winding, the Summit Road offers magnificent views over Akaroa Harbour and the outer bays. Along the road are a number of small reserves including the Ellangowan Scenic Reserve, a short walk through tussock to an amazing viewing point; the Otepatotu Scenic Reserve, where you can take a one-hour return walk through mountain totara to a 755-metre peak; the Hay Scenic Reserve, one of the finest surviving bush remnants, containing large totara, miro and kahikatea; and Montgomery Park Scenic Reserve, with a gnarled old totara estimated to be 2000 years old.

Side trips can also be made to Le Bons, Okains, Little Akaloa, and Pigeon Bays,

Quail Island/Otamahua, Lyttelton Harbour.

Farmland surrounding Akaroa Harbour.

Hector's Dolphin

Endemic to New Zealand, the Hector's dolphin is one of the smallest marine dolphins in the world, growing to a maximum of 1.5 metres and weighing an average of 45 kg (compare this with bottlenose dolphins, which reach 4 metres long and can weigh over 500 kg). Their distribution is rather patchy, with two separate South Island populations and a subspecies, Maui's dolphin, in the North Island. The South Island population estimates are around 7000 dolphins, with the largest concentration of over 5000 in the waters north of Haast on the West Coast. Further concentrations are found on the east coast around Akaroa and in Te Waewae Bay and Porpoise Bay in Southland — although it appears these two populations have remained cut off from each other and the one around the Southland coast may even be a subspecies. Numbering around 100 animals, the Maui's dolphin population in the north inhabits the waters between Kawhia and Muriwai; these are the rarest marine dolphin in the world and have a different genetic and skeletal structure and a slightly different body shape to their Hector's cousin.

Rarely found further than 10 km offshore, these endearing cetaceans favour groups of five to 12 individuals and live for around 20 years (bottlenose dolphins can live up to 50 years), preferring to remain in the same area for life. The greatest danger they face is set nets, which their 'radar' is unable to detect and in which they become entangled and unable to swim to the surface, eventually drowning.

all small and fascinating, and each with a unique history. While the roads down to the bays are winding and narrow, any accesses linking the bays are even narrower, more twisting and unsealed.

GOT TIME? (+ 26 KM)
7 Mt Herbert/Te Ahu Patiki

The Mt Herbert Track starts at Diamond Harbour, a 26-km drive around the harbour from Governors Bay. An alternative is to catch the Black Cat ferry from Lyttelton, which runs regular cross-harbour services (ph (03) 328 9078, www.blackcat.co.nz).

At 919 metres the highest point on the peninsula, Mt Herbert commands splendid views of Canterbury and in particular Lyttelton Harbour. The peak was formed by the Diamond Harbour volcanic eruptions, the last to occur on the peninsula some 6 million years ago. Frequently snow-covered in winter, just below the peak is the Herbert Peak Scenic Reserve where large matai, totara and pahautea/New Zealand cedar are common.

The track to the summit begins at Diamond Harbour and ends about 5 km away at Charteris Bay. Needless to say, it is a steep climb, though the track is well marked and well formed, and takes six to seven hours return.

30 Arthur's Pass

Mountain views • Kea • Alpine passes • Rainforest • Rock formations • 145 km

The route through Arthur's Pass cuts through the heart of the towering mountain peaks of the Southern Alps and traverses unparalleled alpine scenery. Exceptional walks and mountain tracks give access to an area of unique flora and fauna.

INFORMATION
Arthur's Pass National Park Visitor
Centre, SH 73, Arthur's Pass,
ph (03) 318 9211
Greymouth i-SITE, cnr Herbert and
Mackay Streets, Greymouth,
ph (03) 768 5101

Getting there
Beginning at the foothills of the Southern Alps, this route climbs two mountain passes and ends at Lake Brunner near Greymouth on the West Coast. The roads are excellent and, while this does make a comfortable day's journey, Arthur's Pass is such an attractive and accessible alpine region that it is worth considering spending longer here.

Best time to visit
This is true alpine country and even in the summer months the mountains sport a covering of snow and the weather can be very fickle. Summer is a great time to experience the stunning alpine flora and for tramping to the higher slopes. Winter, on the other hand, brings a magical landscape of snow and ice, but often bitterly cold temperatures. Arthur's Pass is occasionally closed by snow, and snow chains may be necessary at other times, although warnings are posted either side of the pass so it's unlikely you will be caught out by unexpected weather.

Facilities
Accommodation and services are thin on the ground on this route and if you want to stay in the mountains you will need to book ahead. There are both motels and backpackers at Arthur's Pass village, but very limited camping facilities, though there are a number of cafés. Jacksons has a camping ground and there are limited motel, campervan and camping facilities at Moana at Lake Brunner. Either side of the pass, the Bealey and Otira Hotels also offer accommodation. It is best to top up your petrol tank at a larger centre before you head into the mountains.

Before you go — check the weather
Arthur's Pass is a popular base for those wanting to go tramping in the mountains. However, the weather is extremely changeable even in summer. If you are venturing further than the short walks off the main road you need to be well prepared. The first stop should be the excellent DoC visitor centre in Arthur's Pass village. The experienced staff can provide up-to-date information on the weather and the walks and are very helpful in offering sound advice as to which track might suit your ability and equipment. You can record your name and intended walk on a Search and Rescue Action Card here — these must be cancelled on your return by crossing off the card or by phoning the visitor centre. The short tracks are suitable any time of year and manageable in lighter clothing, but the longer ones will require warm and waterproof clothing, food and drink and strong footwear, even in summer.

1 Porters Pass
Christchurch to Porters Pass is 80 km;
Springfield to Porters Pass is 18 km on SH 73.
The road to Porters Pass rises steeply from the Canterbury Plains to a height of 946 metres, slightly higher than Arthur's Pass. However, the two passes are remarkably different. Whereas Arthur's is much wetter, dominated by beech forest and more likely to be closed by snow, Porters — which lies in the heart of the 21,000-hectare Korowai/Torlesse Tussocklands Park — is drier, treeless and open. The Torlesse and Big Ben Ranges lie at the centre of this park — and, as the name suggests, the flora is dominated by snow tussock. From the top of the pass there are excellent views over the plains east towards Christchurch and the Port Hills.

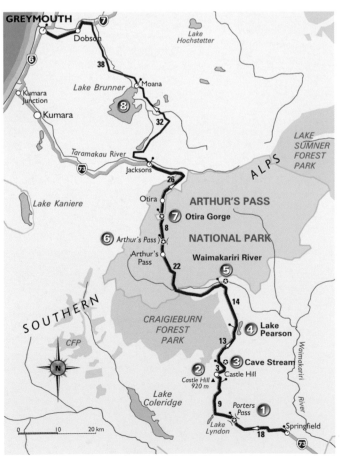

Clouds part over Porters Pass after snowfall.

Limestone rock formations, Castle Hill Scenic Reserve.

2 Castle Hill

From Porters Pass continue west on SH 73 for 9 km to Castle Hill Peak.
At Castle Hill distinctive weathered limestone formations have been worn away by aeons of wind and rain — in direct contrast to the greywacke composition of the surrounding mountain ranges. While the rocks can be easily seen from the road, they are just a 10-minute walk away and worth the stroll as they are impressive close up. Once you reach them there's no set track as such, so take as long as you like to wander around. This is a great place to find some solitary perch and enjoy a bit of rejuvenating mountain quietude.

3 Cave Stream

Cave Stream Scenic Reserve is clearly signposted to the right, 3 km west of Castle Hill on SH 73.
This small reserve in limestone country is best known for one of the more accessible cave systems in New Zealand — and it's free. Dwelling in the shadow of the Craigieburn Range, the 360-metre cave has been formed over thousands of years by the water action of a small stream, creating a long cavern along a fissure in the limestone rock. The system is entered from the lower entrance and involves walking in very cold water with a final clamber up a ladder alongside an underground waterfall. While accessible to inexperienced cavers, you do need warm clothing and a torch (and backup), and do not head in if the water is dirty-looking or it has just rained heavily. The journey through the cave will take around one hour and from the top entrance it is a short distance back to the car park.

4 Lake Pearson

Cave Stream to Lake Pearson is 13 km on SH 73.
A haven for water birds, this small alpine lake is notable for a huge alluvial fan almost cutting it in two. The lake, now a wildlife refuge, has dense reed beds that are the breeding grounds for the southern crested grebe, one of New Zealand's rarest birds, with less than 300 of its kind remaining. There is a basic camping ground by the lake and several good places for picnics under the willows.

5 Waimakariri River

Travel a further 14 km along SH 73 from Lake Pearson to the Waimakariri River. The best views are from a high bluff just before the bridge over the river, but take care when parking.
Braided rivers are formed in mountainous areas and in New Zealand are a particularly notable feature of the South Island, with the Waimakariri, Rangitata and Rakaia Rivers all prime examples. This type of watercourse forms a wide shallow riverbed with numerous channels, most of which are dry throughout the year. However, in spring, fed by melting snow and rain, the river becomes a torrent stretching across the entire bed, with floods radically altering the channels from year to year. The numerous small islands in the riverbed make an ideal habitat for many nesting birds, protected from predators by the swift-flowing water.

With numerous channels stretching across a wide shingle bed, forming small

Cave Stream flowing through a limestone cave.

islands and rocky banks, the upper Waimakariri near Arthur's Pass is the epitome of a South Island braided river.

6 Arthur's Pass

Continuing on SH 73, it is 22 km from the Waimakariri River to Arthur's Pass.

The Arthur's Pass National Park has some of the most dramatic and accessible mountain scenery in the country. At an altitude of 920 metres the climate and vegetation is definitely subalpine. While beech forest hugs the valley floor, the higher vegetation is mainly a mixture of tussock and alpine herbs and shrubs. Stronghold of the kea, New Zealand's cheeky and entertaining (and at times exasperatingly inquisitive) mountain parrot, the park is also home to a significant population of the elusive great spotted kiwi.

Surrounded on all sides by the towering peaks of the Southern Alps including Mt Rolleston (2275 metres), Arthur's Pass village is a great base both for long tramps and short walks, though the weather here is notoriously changeable so check in at the DoC visitor centre if you have any concerns. Longer tramps (all day) include Mt Bealey, Mt Aicken and the popular Avalanche Peak, while Temple Basin and Bealey Valley are good half-day options.

Short walks (under one hour) include Devils Punchbowl, Bridal Veil Track and The Chasm (the first two lead to views of falls, one large the other small, and the last-named is a narrow rocky passage on the Bealey River). The Dobson Nature Walk at the top of the pass is a short walk through fascinating alpine vegetation such as mountain flax, tussock, turpentine bush, hebe and the Mt Cook lily. The best time to see alpine flowers in bloom is from November to February.

7 Otira Gorge

Arthur's Pass to the Otira Gorge is a further 8 km on SH 73. There is a danger of loose rocks falling on to this very winding and narrow road, so it is best to stop at the lookout at the top of the gorge.

The western side of Arthur's Pass is dramatically different from the drier, more open Canterbury side of the pass. The road drops quickly through a deep rocky gorge alive with small waterfalls and streams gushing down from the steep boulder-strewn slopes. Thick native bush clings to the precarious hillsides as the road weaves slowly down through the gorge, although the worst of the old road is now bypassed by the impressive Otira Viaduct.

8 Lake Brunner/Moana

From Otira Gorge continue 26 km west to Jacksons then turn right and drive 32 km to Lake Brunner/Moana. Greymouth is 38 km on.

This large lake covers an area of 40 sq km and is in parts about 100 metres deep.

Mt Cook Lily/Mountain Buttercup

The world's largest buttercup, the Mt Cook lily (*Ranunculus lyallii*) is a perennial plant that grows up to 1 metre high with dark glossy leaves up to 40 centimetres wide and startling pure-white flowers on tall stems. The wide cup-shaped leaves can collect enough water to afford a good drink. A true alpine dweller, this buttercup thrives in the subalpine zone between 700 and 1500 metres and is found throughout the South Island from Stewart Island to Marlborough, in some places flowering in spectaculur prufusion in late spring and summer.

The plant is not a lily, but a buttercup. It was erroneously labelled in 1847 when its discoverer, botanist David Lyall, only collected the leaves, which resembled those of a lily. More than a decade later, when the flowers were eventually examined, the truth dawned but by that time the name had well and truly stuck.

While partially cleared of forest along much of the shoreline, the lake has some very attractive bays. At Moana township the banks of the Arnold River, the lake's outflow, are lined with very handsome forest that includes huge kahikatea, rimu and beech as well as kamahi, a small native tree forming dense groves and recognisable by its beautiful bark, which is a subtly mottled combination of white, grey and brown. The forest is also notable for its ground cover of Prince of Wales fern, which forms large dark-green swathes of delicate feathery fronds.

At Iveagh Bay, 10 km south of Moana, kahikatea grows right down to the very edge of the water, forming an impressive forest backdrop to wonderful views across the lake to the mountains.

Devils Punchbowl Falls, Arthur's Pass National Park.

31 South Canterbury and the Waitaki Valley • Geraldine to Oamaru
Limestone country • Whale fossil • Tussocklands • World's largest fuchsia • 240 km

Often bypassed by travellers, this area conceals some real gems that are well worth seeking out. In particular, the limestone country of the Waitaki Valley and Kakahu is a wonderland of prehistoric fossils and fantastical shapes.

INFORMATION
Geraldine i-SITE, cnr Talbot and Cox Streets, Geraldine,
ph (03) 693 1006
Oamaru Visitor Information Centre,
1 Thames Street, Oamaru,
ph (03) 434 1656
Timaru i-SITE, 2 George Street,
Timaru, ph (03) 688 6163
Waimate Information Centre,
75 Queen Street, Waimate,
ph (03) 689 7771

Getting there
While this route begins at Geraldine, any point of the trip is easily accessible from SH 1. The roads in this area are good with the exception of the Danseys Pass Road, which is in a class of its own. Winding, narrow and rough gravel for a considerable distance, Danseys Pass Road is nevertheless a rewarding motoring experience through some magnificent country.

Best time to visit
With the exception of Oamaru, this region is not a tourist hotspot so there is considerably less pressure on facilities than in many other parts of the country during the warmer months. Summers are generally warm and dry, though the region does experience sudden southerly changes that can drop the temperature as much as 10°C in just a couple of hours. The Waitaki Valley can experience strong northwesterly winds that howl down from the Mackenzie Country in spring and summer. Snow in winter is rare.

Facilities
Both Timaru and Oamaru are small cities that offer plenty of accommodation, places to eat and good services all year round. Geraldine is rapidly growing as a tourist service centre on the main highway to Mt Cook and has numerous cafés and places to stay. Waimate is smaller and, being just off SH 1, a little forgotten, but at the same time considerably less pricey.

1 Kakahu Escarpment and Bush
From Geraldine take SH 79 for 15 km towards Fairlie and turn left into Hall Road. Kakahu Bush and Escarpment is 3.5 km down this gravel road.
The limestone landscape around Kakahu is an area of fascinating rock formations combined with a rare lowland bush remnant. Just a short 10-minute walk from the road, the Kakahu Escarpment is a marvellous smooth wave of rock sculpted by wind and water and rising around 30 metres above the surrounding farmland. Huge weathered mushroom-shaped boulders lie at the base of the escarpment. Nearby a walkway following the swift-flowing Kakahu River leads to the Kakahu Bush, a 365-hectare reserve that protects mature and regenerating lowland podocarp forest and intriguing geological formations

Kakahu Escarpment.

Waves crashing over the Dashing Rocks, Caroline Bay.

that include fossils and the fascinating 'balancing rock'.

This area also contains the largest colony of long-tailed bats in the eastern South Island. One of just two native bats, this bat is closely related to other long-tailed bats in Australia, New Guinea, New Caledonia and Norfolk Island, and is thought to have arrived in New Zealand well over 1 million years ago. Unlike short-tailed bats, these bats are aerial feeders and have a home range of around 100 sq km.

2 Dashing Rocks, Timaru
From Kakahu Bush follow Winchester Hanging Rock Road for 9 km over the Opihi River and turn left into Opihi Road. Take this road for 10.5 km to Pleasant Point, then travel 18 km on SH 8 to Timaru. Dashing Rocks Walkway is on Pacific Street, which is off SH 1, 3.5 km north of the city centre.
Just north of Caroline Bay a small tree-topped promontory faces the full wrath of the Pacific Ocean when a heavy easterly

swell is running. The base rock has been formed by an old lava flow from Mt Horrible, inland from Timaru, and the striking geometric patterns in the rock make their volcanic origins obvious. Above that is a much finer soil known as loess. Loess is not unusual in the eastern areas of the South Island and was formed by wind-blown dust creating loose, easily eroded yellow soils. The walk to Dashing Rocks takes about 10 minutes.

3 The Hunters Hills
Drive south of Timaru on SH 1 for 36 km and turn off on to SH 82, continuing 8 km to Waimate.
The Hunters Hills are a long low range, primarily made up of greywacke rock, a hardened mixture of compressed marine sand and mud, subsequently raised well above sea level by tectonic uplift. Stretching from Tengawai River in the north to the Waitaki River in the south, the highest point is Mt Nimrod at 1525 metres.

While the tops are subalpine with tussock, the foothills were once densely blanketed in native forest of which small areas that include totara, tree fuchsia, matai, kowhai, mahoe, and to the north, silver beech/tawai, still remain.

There are various access points to the Hunters Hills including Kelcey's Bush and Studholme Bush, 8 km west and 16 km northwest of Waimate respectively, and Otaio Gorge and Mt Nimrod/Kaumira Scenic Reserves, southwest of Timaru.

4 Kapua Moa Site
From Waimate continue south on SH 82 for 9 km to Kapua, just through the Waimate Gorge.
While there isn't too much left to see today, this old swamp site has yielded one of the richest troves of moa bones in New Zealand — with an extraordinary 2.5 million bones belonging to at least 10 species of moa, the most common being the Eastern moa (*Emeus crassus*), unearthed here.

Discovered in 1894 by T. McDonald who was clearing a spring for water, the find was described at the time as 'the largest and most varied collection of bones ever obtained from one place'. Given that the oldest bones date back nearly 3000 years — i.e. long before human occupation — the most likely explanation for so many remains in one place is that the moa became bogged down in the deep swampy water and soft mud and were unable to extricate themselves.

5 Waitaki River
Continue south and then west on SH 82 for 54 km to Kurow township.
Over 100 km long, the Waitaki River is the main outflow draining the Mackenzie Basin and is fed by Lakes Pukaki, Tekapo and Ohau as well as major tributaries the Hakataramea and Ahuriri Rivers. A classic braided river with a wide shallow bed comprised of numerous channels, the Waitaki has been dammed at Benmore, Aviemore and Waitaki, though its lower reaches are free of development. An excellent view of the river is obtained from the top of Kurow Hill.

6 Duntroon
From Kurow, head back east on SH 83 for 24 km to Duntroon.
North Otago is home to some of New Zealand's most interesting geology and

Oamaru Stone
The limestone country west of Oamaru provides a building material that has created one of New Zealand's most unique urban landscapes. The distinct light-cream limestone, named 'Totara limestone' by geologists, has been formed from fragments of the calciferous shells of fossilised marine animals and plants dating back 30 to 40 million years to a time when this area was submerged by sea. On occasion, tiny fragments of shark's teeth and whale bone are found in the stone. Soft enough to be cut by huge chainsaws, it hardens when exposed to air. As you would expect, the town of Oamaru is famous for its numerous fine buildings made of this material, which has been quarried at Weston for over a hundred years.

the area around Duntroon, on SH 83 west of Oamaru, features fascinating rock formations and fossils that are easily accessible from the road. The Vanished World Centre in Duntroon is an excellent starting point to brush up on your palaeontology. Here you will find a collection of impressive fossils up to 30 million years old including ancient penguins, whales and dolphins, and other species yet to be classified (www.vanishedworld.co.nz; a small entrance fee applies). A short loop drive from Duntroon covers three of the more outstanding geological formations, all with an easy walk of the road.

7 Earthquakes

From Duntroon Village turn off SH 83 by the church on to Earthquakes Road. Earthquakes is 6.5 km down this road, on the left.

At Earthquakes huge rocks have broken away from the cliffs to expose ancient seabed fossils, the highlight of which is a well-preserved whale specimen from the Oligocene epoch, between 23 and 28 million years ago. Huge time-weathered boulders along the base of the cliffs remain a rich source of fossils today. Take care as rocks still fall and there are sudden drops and crevasses concealed in the long grass. The exposed cliff face was in actuality the result of a massive landslide and not an earthquake, as the name might suggest.

Tree Fuchsia

The bush clothing the Hunters Hills contains fine examples of the native tree fuchsia, of which New Zealand has four species that encompass either extreme of the fuchsia family. Three of the native fuchsia are very small and include the small creeping plant *Fuchsia procumbens*. Right at the other end of the scale, the fourth fuchsia is the largest of its kind in the world. *Fuchsia excorticata* is in fact a small tree that grows to 10 metres in height and is easily recognised by its thin, flaking and easily peeled off bark. While the tree is large, the flowers are pale and insignificant but definitely fuchsia-shaped, and its timber is strong, extremely tough and has very high tannin content. Another unusual feature of the tree fuchsia is that it is one of just two deciduous native trees.

8 Elephant Rocks

Continue for 3.5 km to the Livingstone–Duntroon Road and turn left. After 1 km turn right into Island Cliff Road; the Elephant Rocks are 2 km on the right.

Also dating from the Oligocene epoch and subsequently shaped by water and wind, these large weathered limestone rocks take their name from both their grey colouring and general elephantine shape. Protruding bare and stark from the short grass, the rocks are a pensive monument to the ravages of time.

9 Anatini Whale Fossil

Anatini is 1 km from Elephant Rocks. From here it is 40 km to Oamaru via Ngapara and Weston.

Just a short walk from the road is the fossil of an ancient baleen whale. Protected by Perspex, the fossil is very clear and an interpretive board helpfully explains which parts of the whale are visible. It's also worthwhile strolling down to the valley, which is lined with ancient limestone rock formations, if you have the time.

GOT TIME? (+45 KM)
10 Danseys Pass

From Duntroon to Naseby is 45 km.

The Danseys Pass Road links the Waitaki Valley to Naseby and was originally a coach road supplying the goldfields of the Maniototo Basin. Winding initially through the limestone farmland along the Maerewhenua River, the road climbs to the pass, reaching a height of 934 metres, then traverses stunning wild tussock country before dropping down into Naseby. This is wild empty country and the home of the native falcon and paradise ducks — the latter easily recognisable by the distinct white head of the male and the darker plumage of the female.

The road is rough, narrow, winding and gravel, dusty in summer and frequently closed by snow in winter, but take your time and enjoy an undeservedly forgotten corner of New Zealand. There is a camping ground 14 km from Duntroon.

Limestone cliffs and boulders at Earthquakes, location of fossilised whale bones.

32 Mackenzie Country and Aoraki/Mt Cook • Tekapo to Wanaka
Aoraki/Mt Cook • Glaciers • Tussocklands • 340 km

This is big country — a region of open plains, glacial lakes, tussocklands, towering mountains and wide rivers. Dominating the skyline and rising above them all is Aoraki/Mt Cook, soaring to 3754 metres, while far below is Tasman Glacier, New Zealand's longest glacier at 30 km.

INFORMATION
Geraldine i-SITE, cnr Talbot and Cox Streets, Geraldine,
ph (03) 693 1006
Tekapo Information Centre, SH 8, Lake Tekapo, ph (03) 680 6686
Lake Pukaki Visitor Information Centre, SH 8, Lake Pukaki,
ph (03) 685 6194
Twizel Information Centre,
61 Mackenzie Drive, Twizel,
ph (03) 435 3124
Wanaka i-SITE, 100 Ardmore Road, Wanaka, ph (03) 443 1233
Aoraki/Mt Cook DoC Information Centre, Mount Cook Village, SH 80, Mt Cook, ph (03) 435 1186

Getting there
All the roads in this area are excellent, although occasional snow can close the Lindis Pass and, more rarely, the Burke Pass. The road through Lindis Pass is moderately winding over a distance of 40 km, but it is beautifully built and the motoring is easy.

Best time to visit
Despite the cold winters this is a trip that can be made at any time of the year. The summers are hot and temperatures over 30°C are common, but with sudden southerly changes that can drop down to 12°C and will have you reaching for your warm jacket. While the Southern Alps are snow-covered even in summer, the winter scene to low levels is truly magical. However, on occasion the weather around the mountains can clag right in and is so wet and miserable that you won't see a thing. Annual rainfall in this area is low (575 mm), though considerably heavier in the vicinity of Aoraki/Mt Cook. During the peak of the summer season the area around

Aoraki/Mt Cook is also packed with tour buses and independent travellers, but this is big country so it isn't too hard to get away from the crowd.

Facilities
While a popular tourist destination, the Mackenzie Country is a large area so facilities are somewhat scattered. Geraldine, Fairlie, Tekapo, Mt Cook, Twizel and Omarama are all small towns with a handful of motels, hotels, backpackers and camping grounds. While there are cafés and modest shopping centres, there isn't too much else. Tekapo is becoming a popular summer destination in its own right and the large attractive camping ground is often full through late December and January. If you're planning to stay in the area in mid-December through to early March it is best to plan ahead.

1 Lake Tekapo
Tekapo is 87 km from Geraldine via Fairlie and the Burke Pass.
At 700 metres above sea level, covering 87 sq km and 120 metres at its deepest point, Lake Tekapo is the largest of the three Mackenzie Basin lakes. Formed by ancient glaciers long since melted,

the lake is today primarily fed by the Godley River but also by the Mistake, Cass, and Macaulay Rivers. Its distinctive turquoise colour is the result of finely ground rock suspended in the melting ice water, meaning that even on the hottest summer's day swimming in this lake is only for the very hardy. While some exotic trees have been introduced around the shores, the primary vegetation is tussock, although the area is also home to two rare native brooms: *Carmichaelia curta* and *C. kirkii*.

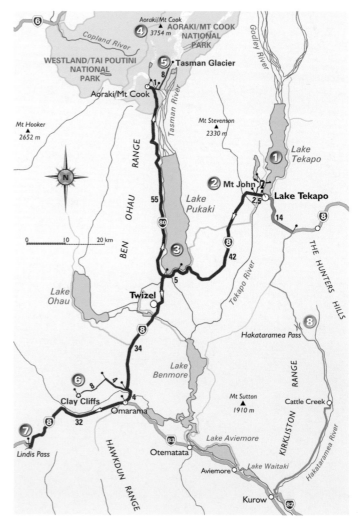

Boulder-strewn shoreline, Lake Tekapo.

2 Mt John

From Tekapo head 2.5 km west on SH 8 and turn right. The road to Mt John is 1 km on the right; the 1-km road to the summit is narrow but sealed.

Rising 1031 metres above the icy waters of Lake Tekapo, Mt John is renowned for ultra-clear night skies, especially in winter. The University of Canterbury operates an astronomical observatory on the summit, and tours can be arranged through Earth and Sky (www.earthandsky.co.nz).

Sitting isolated from any other high point, the unsurpassed views from the top of Mt John encompass the entire Mackenzie Basin, Lake Tekapo, Lake Alexandrina, tiny Lake McGregor, the headwaters of the Godley River and the Southern Alps. At over 1000 metres, the climate is definitely alpine and the exposed tops can be extremely windy. In fact, this is officially the country's windiest spot — on 18 April 1970 a wind gust at Mt John reached 250 kph, the highest wind strength ever recorded in New Zealand.

From the shores of the lake a track leads up the mountain and a shorter easy track circles the tussock-clad summit. An excellent information board on the summit's west side details all the natural landmarks, while right on the summit itself, along with the observatory buildings, is a very good café.

3 Lake Pukaki

Return to SH 8 and follow the highway south for 42 km to Lake Pukaki.

Fed by the Tasman River, the source of which is the Tasman and Hooker Glaciers at the foot of Aoraki/Mt Cook, Lake Pukaki was created by the terminal moraine of a receding glacier blocking the valley. The lake's icy waters are an iridescent blue, the result of minuscule particles of rock ground to a fine powder and washed down by the glaciers.

The road to Aoraki/Mt Cook follows the Lake Pukaki shoreline for 32 km and the views out over the water to the mountains are unrivalled.

Lake Pukaki before Aoraki/Mt Cook.

Tussock

New Zealand has nearly 200 native grasses of which around 30 can be classed as tussock. These include four main types: snow tussock, red tussock, short tussock and lowland tussock, and most of these belong to the genera *Carex*, *Chionochloa*, *Festuca* and *Poa*.

Before Maori arrived in New Zealand, tussock grasslands were confined to the drier and colder regions that could not support forest. Extensive burning of native forest by Maori in the more fragile environments, particularly in the eastern South Island, significantly increased tussock grasslands and they reached their greatest extent in the early nineteenth century, covering as much as 30 per cent of the landmass. With the advent of European colonisation, and the virtual disappearance of lowland tussock, today the most common tussocks are the higher-altitude varieties such as red and snow tussock.

4 Aoraki/Mt Cook

Continue south for 5 km on SH 8 to SH 80/Mt Cook Road. Mt Cook Village is 55 km along this road.

New Zealand's highest mountain at 3754 metres, and known in Maori as Aoraki or 'the sky piercer', sits at the head of a dramatic glacial valley in the heart of the Aoraki/Mt Cook National Park, which covers an area of over 70,000 hectares and contains all but one of New Zealand's peaks standing over 3000 metres. Before a massive landside in December 1991 — in which 12 million cubic metres of rock and ice hurtled over 7 km down the slopes at a speed of 200 kph — the mountain was actually 10 metres higher. The flora is alpine dominated by tussock, with patches of prickly matagouri and mountain totara. The Mt Cook lily and the spiky wild Spaniard are also common here.

While graceful Aoraki/Mt Cook at the end of the Hooker Valley dominates the scene, Mt Sefton looms high above the Mueller Glacier, with the Huddlestone Glacier clinging to its rocky slopes. Popular walks include the Hooker Valley Walk (four hours), the Red Tarn Walk (two hours), and Kea Point (one hour and overlooking the Mueller Glacier). Behind Mt Cook Village is the dark-green swathe of Governors Bush, a small patch dominated by silver beech and home to native birds such as the tomtit, tui, bellbird and fantail (one hour — and ideal if the weather's not so good).

5 Tasman Glacier

Backtrack along SH 80 for 1 km and turn left into Tasman Valley Road, which is gravel but in good condition. Continue 8 km to the car park.

Tasman Glacier, 30 km in length, is the longest glacier in the country and reaches far into the mountains. However, this is no spectacle of shimmering blue, but a torn landscape of deep ice up to 100 metres thick covered by a layer of rocks and gravel left behind as the glacier slowly melts. Great piles of raw, jumbled raw rock left in its wake make the valley look more like a working quarry than anything else.

Large blocks of broken ice float in the frigid icy-green waters of the terminal lake at the head of the Tasman River. A short walk of just 20 minutes leads to a fantastic view point overlooking the glacier and Aoraki/Mt Cook.

Aoraki/Mt Cook reflected in Hooker Lake.

Black Stilt/Kaki

For over 50 years the black stilt has teetered on the brink of extinction, and despite conservation efforts it remains one of the world's rarest and most threatened birds. Down to just 23 individuals in 1981, the population has slowly recovered although today is still less than 100 birds, including just 10 breeding pairs. The only stilt endemic to New Zealand, kaki were once widespread throughout South Canterbury, but as they nest on the ground and rely entirely on camouflage for protection, they have been particularly vulnerable to predators such as cats, stoats and dogs. During the seven years from 1992 to 1999, only eight out of 189 chicks reached adulthood.

Black stilts have a distinctive all-black plumage, a bright red bill and long bright red legs. Until 18 months of age, young birds are black and white and are often confused with the pied stilt, a close relation.

The primary location of the black stilt is the Ahuriri River, but the birds range widely throughout the Mackenzie Basin. While low in numbers, the chance of seeing the birds foraging along the roadside is still reasonably high.

6 Clay Cliffs

Retrace your route down SH 80 to SH 8 and turn south towards Twizel. After 34 km (4 km north of Omarama), turn right into Quailburn Road and after 4 km turn left into Henburn Road. The gate is another 4 km along this road, while from the gate it is a further 4 km to the car park.

Water eroding the soft gravelly soils creating deep gullies and tall pillar-like formations over many thousands of years has created this unique example of a 'badlands' landscape at the Clay Cliffs. Known as hoodoos, these unusual structures are formed when rock protecting the soil prevents the soft gravel beneath from eroding, in turn serving to create the high fluted formations. The cliffs are on private land and there is a small fee.

Clay cliffs near Omarama.

7 Lindis Pass

Return to SH 8, drive 4 km south to Omarama and continue on SH 8 for 32 km to Lindis Pass. From the pass it is 80 km to Wanaka.

The main route between South Canterbury and Central Otago reaches 971 metres at Lindis Pass, the saddle between the Lindis Valley to the south and the Ahuriri River to the north. This is stunning landscape, wide open with rolling hills carpeted in golden tussock interspersed with the occasional patch of matagouri and coprosma. Overshadowing the northern approach to the pass is the 1494-metre peak of Mt Longslip, where native falcons are common. Much of the region is protected by the Lindis Conservation Area and the Lindis Scenic Reserve, the combined area covering nearly 3000 hectares.

While there are no formal tracks, the open nature of the terrain makes for easy walking. However, this is definitely alpine country and even in summer warm clothing is essential. Snow is common in the pass during winter, and on occasions heavy falls close the road, though usually not for long.

GOT TIME? (+100 KM)

8 The Hakataramea Pass *This back-country road begins 14 km east of Tekapo and runs 100 km over the Hakataramea Pass and down the valley to Kurow.*

Rising to 965 metres at its highest point — which is 45 km from Tekapo and 62 km from Kurow — this road is gravel for over 40 km. Although it crosses a number of shallow fords and you are met with closed gates, it is able to be navigated in an average family car. This is not grand mountain country, but a more subtle and minimalist landscape of rolling hills enveloping tussocklands of delicate colours under a huge sky. Eventually the road winds down into the farmland of the Hakataramea Valley and finally crosses the Waitaki River in Kurow by way of an old war-weary bridge, the battered survivor of countless river floods. Note that there are no facilities whatsoever between Tekapo and Kurow.

Tussocklands, Lindis Pass.

33 North Otago • Oamaru to Dunedin

Little blue penguins • Yellow-eyed penguins • Moeraki boulders • 125 km

Known as one of the best regions in New Zealand for viewing penguins, North Otago also boasts the magnificent coastline stretching out north of Dunedin, including the unusual Moeraki boulders.

> **INFORMATION**
> Oamaru i-SITE, 1 Thames Street,
> Oamaru, ph (03) 434 1656
> Dunedin i-SITE, 48 The Octagon,
> Dunedin, ph (03) 474 3300

Getting there
Starting at Oamaru, this trip runs parallel to the coast and never strays far from SH 1 down to Dunedin. The roads are excellent, sealed and easy travelling.

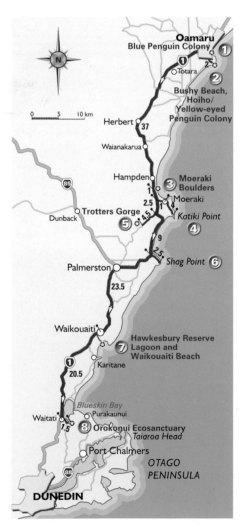

Best time of year
Spring through to autumn is a good time along this stretch of coast. Seal and penguin numbers are higher in summer and autumn, although yellow-eyed penguins do not migrate so are in residence all year. Winters can be cold and wet, and the summers mild at best.

Facilities
Both Oamaru and Dunedin offer a wide range of facilities including shops, places to stay and cafés, but there is not too much in between along SH 1. Dunedin has several good and historic hotels right in the city and not many motels, but as a student city it has some great and inexpensive places to eat (especially along George Street, north of the Octagon). Palmerston, on SH 1 and about halfway between Oamaru and Dunedin, has limited accommodation, a handful of cafés and a small shopping centre.

1 Blue Penguin Colony
Waterfront Road, Oamaru (by the harbour).
The smallest of all the penguins, the little blue penguin is common throughout New Zealand and Australia, but Oamaru is the only place here where numbers are reasonably large and the birds are easy to see as they make their way back from the sea at dusk to nests in the old quarry. The penguin colony, now a major attraction in the area, was established relatively recently, with only 33 breeding pairs in 1992. Today there are over 150 pairs, along with a further 100 pairs in a nearby colony.

The visitor centre at the colony presents superb information on both the birds and the natural history of the area, with a special viewing stand that allows an excellent view of the penguins without disturbing them (there is an entry fee to the stand, which opens just before sundown, when the birds return for the night). The number of penguins coming ashore each night varies considerably depending on the time of year, so check when buying tickets as to how many penguins are expected that evening (www.penguins.co.nz).

2 Bushy Beach, Hoiho/Yellow-eyed Penguin Colony
From the blue penguin colony return to Tyne Street and turn left into Bushy Beach Road; drive 2 km to the car park at the end.
The hoiho, or yellow-eyed penguin, is much larger than the blue penguin and considerably less sociable, preferring nesting spots that are isolated from other penguin neighbours. At Bushy Beach a small colony of these rare birds has established itself in the low-growing vegetation above the beach and a special hide has been constructed to allow public viewing. As these penguins come ashore late in the afternoon, the beach is closed after 3 pm as the birds will not return if there are people positioning themselves on the shore between the sea and their nests. This facility is free.

Yellow-eyed penguin.

The unusual volcanic boulders on Moeraki Beach.

3 Moeraki Boulders

Return to SH 1 and drive south for 37 km to Moeraki Beach.

Volcanic in origin, the Moeraki boulders are an unusual geological formation known as septarian concretion. This is the result of erosion of softer outer rock exposing the more resistant stone in the shape of almost perfect round boulders. Now lying scattered along Moeraki Beach, the boulders are best seen at low tide. Moeraki is an attractive beach that is long and undeveloped, backed by dunes and exposed to the open sea.

4 Katiki Point

From Moeraki Beach drive 1 km south on SH 1 and turn left into Moeraki township. After 1 km turn right into Tenby Street, which becomes Lighthouse Road; drive 4 km to the end of this road.

Just below the historic wooden lighthouse and above a small sandy cove in the rocky coastline is a little area of protected coastal vegetation. Both blue and yellow-eyed penguins nest here, coming ashore late in the day to rest and feed chicks. Fur seals also make this cove home. An excellent public hide that looks right down on to the small beach comes complete with binoculars. From the top of the hill by the lighthouse the views are amazing: north

to Cape Wanbrow near Oamaru, south to Shag Point and beyond that, even further south, a glimpse of the Otago Peninsula.

5 Trotters Gorge

Return to SH 1 and drive 2.5 km south of Moeraki, turn right into Horse Range Road and the access to Trotters Gorge is 4.5 km on the right.

Established in 1864, Trotters Gorge is a 152-hectare reserve on the southern end of the Horse Range and a popular picnic spot and walking area. The deep gorge is surrounded by high rocky bluffs that look like limestone but are in fact a greywacke/breccia conglomerate. The creek itself is home to 12 native species of fish and in the thick bush that thrives in the deep moist soils of the gorge there is a surprising number of native birds, with the song of bellbirds almost constant. An easy 20-minute walk leads to a grassed picnic area and shelter by a deep swimming hole in the stream.

6 Shag Point

Back at SH 1, turn south and continue 9 km along Katiki Beach to Shag Point Road (9 km north of Palmerston). Continue 2.5 km to the end of the road.

Shag Point is a high bluff just to the north of the Shag/Waihemo River that in pre-settlement times supported a rich forest and a large moa population. The main attractions today are the colonies of fur seals and yellow-eyed penguins that make Shag Point their home. The small narrow coves, offshore rocks and kelp-encrusted reefs make the point an ideal playground for seals and a sheltered spot to raise their pups.

Walking tracks weave along the windswept bluffs giving several excellent views of the seals below as they lounge on rocky ledges or duck and dive in the rolling waves. A viewing hide is the ideal spot to watch yellow-eyed penguins come ashore in the late afternoon.

Seals at Shag Point.

Penguins

New Zealand has six penguin species of which three are found on the mainland: the little blue penguin (*Eudyptula minor*), the hoiho or yellow-eyed penguin (*Megadyptes antipodes*), and the Fiordland crested penguin (*Eudyptes pachyrhynchus*). The other three penguins are found on the subantarctic islands and are the erect-crested penguin (*Eudyptes sclateri*), the Snares penguin (*Eudyptes robustus*), and the Eastern rockhopper penguin (*Eudyptes chrysocome moselii*). There is some debate as to whether the white-flippered penguin, found only in Canterbury, is a separate species or a subspecies of the little blue penguin.

The most common penguin in New Zealand, and also the smallest penguin in the world, is the little blue penguin (see image), so named because of its blue-grey colouring. Weighing 1 kg or less and only 40 cm long, the little blue penguin only comes ashore at dark to nest in burrows after spending the day feeding at sea. The little blue is also found in Australia, where it is called the fairy penguin.

Hoiho, or the yellow-eyed penguin, is found on the east coast of the South Island from Banks Peninsula to Stewart Island and the Subantarctic Islands. Hoiho weigh up to 4 kg, are 70 cm long, and have a striking yellow band around their eyes. Solitary birds that prefer to nest away from other birds in coastal bush and scrub, yellow-eyed penguins come ashore earlier in the day than the little blue, usually in the late afternoon before dusk. Hoiho numbers have been severely reduced due to loss of habitat and predation by the likes of cats, dogs and stoats. The world's rarest penguin, fewer than 1000 survive on mainland New Zealand, though these numbers are rising with the protection of both the birds and extension of their habitat.

Much the same size as hoiho is the Fiordland crested penguin, found on offshore islands, in south Westland, Fiordland and on Stewart Island. Also like the hoiho, these penguins nest in thick coastal vegetation, but are not so solitary and form loose colonies. Fiordland crested penguins are distinguished by a long yellow crest along the side of the head. Today there are fewer than 3000 of these birds left.

Before you go — watching the penguins

While interest in New Zealand's wildlife has led to greater conservation efforts, visitors often unwittingly threaten the very wildlife they have come to see. Hoiho are easily upset and once disturbed they will return to the sea, leaving chicks unfed and the adults tired and stressed. Here are a few simple rules for when you visit.
- Don't get between the penguins and their nesting area. They are nervous birds and will return to the sea if they feel at all threatened.
- Use a hide, and if one is not available keep your distance and stay still. Penguins will often pass within a few metres of you if you are still.
- Leave your dog at home. Dogs are one of the penguins' worst predators.
- Stick to the tracks and don't disturb the nesting area.

7 Hawkesbury Reserve Lagoon and Waikouaiti Beach

Return to SH 1 and head south via Palmerston for 23.5 km to Waikouaiti. Turn left into Beach Road and then right into Scotia Road, at the end of which is the lagoon.

The Hawkesbury Lagoon at the mouth of the Patonga Creek is the perfect habitat for wetland and wading birds including stilt, paradise duck, Canada goose, black swan, mallard, heron and the occasional grey teal. The lagoon is adjacent to Waikouaiti Beach, a magnificent stretch of white sand running from Cornish Head at the northern end to the mouth and lagoon of the Waikouaiti River, just below the Huriawa Peninsula. Volcanic in origin, this peninsula features several blowholes in the cliffs on the southern side.

With unobstructed views both north and south along the coast and over the estuarine marshes to the east, it's easy to appreciate Huriawa's former strategic value to Maori as a fortified pa. Hooker's sea lions and fur seals are common along the shore.

8 Orokonui Ecosanctuary

Continue south on SH 1 for 20.5 km to Waitati and turn left into Harvey Street and then left again into Orokonui Road; continue to the car park on the left just before the end of the road, a distance of 1.5 km.

This newly established 'mainland island' is a 300-hectare reserve of old and regenerating forest that includes mature podocarps as well as kaikawaka or New Zealand cedar. An ancient type of conifer that can be traced back to the Gondwana supercontinent, in New Zealand the 'big five' podocarps are totara, rimu, kahikatea, matai and miro. The weeping form of the juvenile rimu, the tapering shape of the kahikatea and the small hard leaves of the totara are all typical traits of conifers. While conifers usually reproduce by means of cones, the New Zealand trees differ in that they have berries, an important food source for many native birds.

Orokonui is now protected by a predator-resistant fence and the plan is to gradually reintroduce rare native birds. Several South Island kaka have been released and pukeko and paradise ducks have since established themselves in the safe area.

34 Otago Harbour

Pristine beaches • Seal and penguin watching • Outstanding coastal scenery • Royal albatross • 150 km

In recent years the Otago Peninsula has gained a reputation as one of New Zealand's best and more accessible areas in which to see wildlife such as penguins, seals and seabirds. However, the peninsula and the harbour are an area of outstanding natural beauty in their own right, and all within a short drive of Dunedin City.

INFORMATION
Dunedin i-SITE, 48 The Octagon, Dunedin, ph (03) 474 3300
Department of Conservation, Coastal Otago Area Office, 77 Lower Stuart Street, Dunedin, ph (03) 477 0677

Getting there
Both sides of the harbour are easily accessible from central Dunedin. However, the peninsula is hilly and steep, and the roads correspondingly winding and often very narrow. Sealed for the most part, some roads around Hoopers and Papanui Inlets are gravel. The road out to the albatross colony can at times be very busy with camper vans and buses.

Best time of year to visit
Late spring to mid-autumn (November to April) is definitely the best time to visit this area. The coastal Otago weather is capricious to say the least, alternating between warm sunny days and cold wet windy weather that stems from the heart of Antarctica. Once again, summer is the best time if it is the wildlife you have come to see.

Facilities
Dunedin is both an old historic city and a lively student town. Over the peak of the summer season, when the students are on holiday, a restful atmosphere prevails. There are plenty of good eateries and bars, but accommodation can be sticky though. Like Wellington, Dunedin has little flat land and the short motel strip at the northern end of George Street can often be booked out. The city and Port Chalmers do have some good hotels ranging from

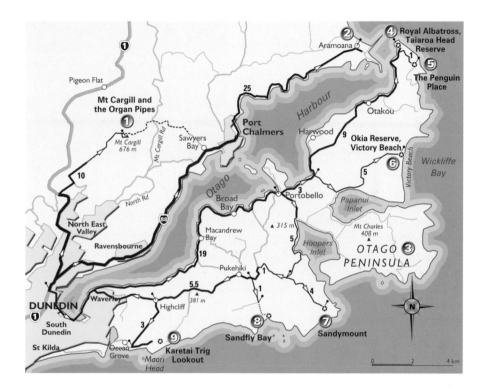

luxurious and historic to budget. There are also several camping grounds handy to the city, including one at Portobello on the peninsula.

1 Mt Cargill and the Organ Pipes

To drive to the top of Mt Cargill from the city centre, travel north on Great King Street and follow Pine Hill Road to Cowan Road, which then continues to the top; a distance of 10 km. This last section of road is very rough.
Looming over Dunedin from the north, 676-metre Mt Cargill is very exposed and often shrouded in cloud, creating a unique subalpine environment on the summit just a short drive away from the city. While there is a road to the top (very rough on the final section), the best way to experience Mt Cargill is by foot via the Organ Pipes. This two-hour return walk is not difficult (most

of the climbing is in the first 15 minutes) and the track winds through fine bush, ferns and mosses. What look like carefully shaped steps are in fact natural formations of broken rock from the Organ Pipes. The mountain is part of the rim of a volcano and the Pipes are basalt rocks that have been shaped into very precise geometric forms during the cooling process. The views from the top are superb.

If you want to walk to the top then follow North Road in the North East Valley until it eventually morphs into Mt Cargill Road, a distance of 8 km. The car park is 3 km from here on the left, but there is very limited parking space.

2 Aramoana

From the city centre take SH 88 to Port Chalmers and then continue following the coast on the Aramoana Road to the end; a distance of 25 km.

Essentially, Aramoana is a large sandbar protecting the sheltered waters of the Otago Harbour from the open sea. Facing the ocean is a wide sweep of white sand broken by the long breakwater, constructed to stop the harbour channel from silting up. Directly opposite Taiaroa Head, Aramoana is a good spot to watch albatross in flight (binoculars will come in very handy), and fur seals and blue penguins are not uncommon on the beach. Just inside the breakwater a track and boardwalk lead through the wide tidal salt marshes, home to numerous wading birds including godwits in the summer months.

3 Otago Peninsula

Like Banks Peninsula in Canterbury, Otago Harbour is the drowned crater of a large ancient volcano formed during the Miocene epoch between 13 and 10 million years ago. The rugged peaks surrounding the harbour are the relics of the old crater rim, and the basalt columns at the Organ Pipes on Mt Cargill and at the Pyramids in the Okia Reserve are graphic reminders of this region's turbulent geological past. On the peninsula itself the highest peak is Mt Charles (408 metres) near Allans Beach and on the mainland Mt Cargill reaches over 600 metres. Two shallow inlets on the southern side of the peninsula are a haven for aquatic birds, while the undeveloped beaches are famed for wildlife such as seals and penguins.

The sea cliffs of Taiaroa Head.

4 Royal Albatross, Taiaroa Head Reserve

From Dunedin take the Portobello Road 19 km east; at Portobello continue east for a further 12 km on Harington Point Road to the very end. The site of an unusual mainland colony of northern royal albatross, there are albatross at Taiaroa Head all year round. Although numbers vary considerably and the colony itself is closed during the breeding season from mid-September to mid-November, there is every chance of

seeing birds in flight. The best time to view the birds is from December to February and you are more likely to see them on the wing when the weather is rough and windy. The only access to the colony is by guided tour and bookings are recommended as this is a very popular spot to visit (ph (03) 478 0499, www.albatross.org.nz; check the prices beforehand). While the albatross are the undoubted stars of the show, the reserve is home to another 11 bird species, including the rare Stewart Island shag.

5 The Penguin Place

The Penguin Place is 1 km from the albatross colony on Harington Point Road. Otago Peninsula is home to both blue and yellow-eyed/hoiho penguins, but in recent years the popularity of penguin watching has placed undue stress on the birds with visitors unintentionally diminishing the very wildlife they come to see. There is a viewing hide at Sandfly Bay near Sandymount, and little blues come ashore at Pilots Beach just below the albatross colony.

However, an alternative is to visit the Penguin Place. A working farm with a colony of rare yellow-eyed penguins as well as some blues, the Penguin Place offers a one-and-a-half-hour tour of the breeding colony, with specially constructed hides that permit very close viewing of these stand-offish birds that prefer to keep their

Surf at Allans Beach, Otago Peninsula.

distance from neighbours by nesting in thick scrub. The Penguin Place has substantially replanted the dunes, and while the replanting takes hold, they have provided private nesting boxes for the birds. Groups comprise no more than 15 people, and if there are no penguins the tours don't go. Only afternoon and early evening viewings are available in winter, with all-day tours from October to Easter; chicks can be seen November to February (ph (03) 478 0286, www.penguinplace.co.nz).

6 Okia Reserve, Victory Beach

Return towards Portobello village and after 9 km turn left into Weir Road. Follow this road, which is gravel but in reasonable condition, 5 km to the end.

This large coastal reserve comprises an extensive area of dune, wetland and a pristine beach, wide open to the Southern Ocean and about as wild as it gets on the Otago Peninsula. The dunes behind the beach are nesting grounds for both hoiho and little blue penguins and a resting area for Hooker's sea lions. Easily camouflaged in the scrub-covered dunes, be aware that the sea lions can be quite aggressive and dangerous when disturbed.

The volcanic origin of the Pyramids, two aptly named small hills guarding the approach to the coast, is evidenced by the geometric basalt columns on the seaward side of the smaller pyramid (similar to

The Chasm.

Northern Royal Albatross

Twelve of the world's 20 albatross species breed in New Zealand, mainly on offshore and subantarctic islands. Of the 12, seven are endemic to this country, the best known — the royal albatross — being second only in size to the wandering albatross. There is some scientific debate as to whether the royal diverges into two separate species, the southern and the northern, but it is the northern royal albatross (*Diomedea sanfordi*) that breeds on Taiaroa Head at the entrance to Otago Harbour.

The albatross first established themselves on Taiaroa Head between 1914 and 1919 and this is the only mainland colony of any albatross in the southern hemisphere, with an established population now of around 150 birds. The birds arrive in September to breed, though the eggs are not laid until November, with the chicks hatching 11 weeks afterwards in late January and early February. Albatross only breed every two years and care for the chick for as long as 12 months. In between breeding they spend most of their time along the South American coast, often living up to 65 years of age. With a wing span reaching 3 metres, these noble petrels can achieve speeds of more than 115 km/h in favourable winds.

the Organ Pipes on Mt Cargill). There is a short scramble to the top of the smaller pyramid that gives a lovely view over the dune country.

7 Sandymount

Return to Portobello village, but instead of heading back to Dunedin along the coast veer left into Highcliff Road, which runs along the spine of the peninsula. After 5 km turn left into Sandymount Road and continue 4 km to the car park. Watch for loose sand over the road.

As the name suggests, Sandymount consists of wind-blown sand driven up from Sandfly Bay to cover the rocky summit that rises to 319 metres. A rough track leads up from the car park to the top, with spectacular views south to Nugget Point and north to Moeraki and a glimpse of Dunedin City. However, the area is best known for the Chasm and Lovers Leap, dramatic coastal cliffs over 200 metres high, both reached by a short easy walk.

The Chasm is a huge slash in the hillside dropping to a rock base and beyond that to the sea, while at Lovers Leap a sheer cliff face plunges to a large sea arch. From both lookout points the views along the high cliffs on the southern coast of the peninsula are fantastic, but in windy weather it can be very exposed so come prepared.

8 Sandfly Bay

Return to Highcliff Road and turn left, and after 1 km turn left again into Seal Point Road and continue 2 km to the very end.

Taking its name not from the bloodsucking insect but from the exposed nature of the coast that has driven sand high on to Sandymount, this beautiful wide white-sand beach is flanked by steep cliffs at either end, while offshore lie several small rock stacks. Yellow-eyed penguins nest in the extensive dunes and seals are common on the beach. You can also walk from Sandymount to Sandfly Bay in under an hour.

9 Karetai Trig Lookout

Continue west along Highcliff Road towards Dunedin and after 5.5 km turn left into Centre Road. Follow Centre Road for 3 km and turn left into Tomahawk Road. The track to the trig starts at the end of Tomahawk Road.

A steady uphill trudge through farmland leads to a cliff-top trig with excellent views west over the city beaches: Smaills, Tomahawk, St Kilda and St Clair. Far to the south lies Nugget Point, and to the east along the coast dramatic sheer-faced cliffs descend into a rugged sea. This is a good spot to watch seabirds wheeling far below along the wave-lashed cliffs, while offshore is the tiny and appropriately named Bird Island.

35 South and Central Otago • Dunedin to Alexandra

Unique wetlands • Wild coast • Desert landscape • Fossils • 225 km

Renowned for its wild beauty, the South Otago coast stands in direct contrast to the unique Sinclair Wetlands further inland. Turning away from the coast the route heads inland to New Zealand's driest region and our own special desert country.

INFORMATION

Alexandra i-SITE, 22 Centennial Ave,
Alexandra, ph (03) 448 9515
Clutha i-SITE, 4 Clyde Street,
Balclutha, ph (03) 418 0388
Dunedin i-SITE, 48 The Octagon,
Dunedin, ph (03) 474 3300
Department of Conservation,
Coastal Otago Area Office,
77 Lower Stuart Street, Dunedin,
ph (03) 477 0677
Lawrence Information Centre,
17 Ross Place, Lawrence,
ph (03) 485 9222
Milton Information Centre,
53 Union Street, Milton,
ph (03) 417 7480

Getting there

This trip begins in central Dunedin and initially winds southwards down the coast before heading inland. The roads are sealed and in good condition, though the side trips are on gravel roads.

Best time to visit

Summer through to autumn is the best time of year as this part of the country is at its most attractive then. While the coastal areas are wet and cool, further inland the climate becomes markedly drier. Central Otago is both New Zealand's driest region and the coldest, with minus 22°C recorded at Ophir just north of Alexandra and annual rainfall of around 300 mm. The winters are cold but dry and the heavy frosts and snowy ranges make Central Otago in this season immensely appealing.

Facilities

Outside of Dunedin facilities along this stretch of road vary considerably. Although there are cafés and small shopping centres at Milton, Lawrence and Roxburgh,

accommodation is light. In particular, historic Lawrence is a very appealing spot to stop on the way to 'Central'. Alexandra is a prosperous town with plenty of places to eat and to stay at, a substantial shopping centre, and is also part of a burgeoning grape-growing area.

1 Tunnel Beach

Not easy to find from central Dunedin, the simplest way to get here is to head south on SH 1 and after 2.5 km turn left into South Road and follow the clearly marked signs that say 'Southern Scenic Route'. This route winds through suburban streets to Blackhead Road; Tunnel Beach Road is on the left. The distance from SH 1 is 4.5 km.

In an area with a surfeit of wonderful coastal vistas, it is hard to go past Tunnel Beach. A short walk over farmland tends downhill to a large sea arch, from the top of which are marvellous views, especially along the coast to the south. In wild weather massive waves thunder against the rocks below — and the rougher the weather, the more impressive the wave action.

From the top of the arch a low tunnel with shallow steps leads down to a small boulder-strewn cove. The tunnel was built by John Cargill, son of the prominent settler William Cargill, so that his daughters could go swimming away from the more public beach at St Clair. Unfortunately, one of his daughters drowned here. Needless to say, this is not a safe place to swim.

2 Taieri Mouth

Return to Blackhead Road and turn left, continuing on to Brighton Road and turning left again to follow the coast to Taieri Mouth; a total distance of 29 km.

This really is a wonderful piece of coastline. From Brighton down to the mouth of the Taieri River extends a combination of long sandy beaches and small rocky coves of white and gold sand fringed by toetoe, flax, coprosma and hebe. Just south of the river mouth is a striking dune-backed beach of beautiful white sand along a wide shallow bay, safe for swimming. Offshore, tiny Taieri/Moturata Island is joined to the mainland by a sandbar that is accessible at very low tide and is a haven for fur seals, titi/sooty shearwaters and even royal spoonbills. Right behind the dunes is a very pleasant camping area.

3 Sinclair Wetlands

From Taieri Mouth return 10 km to SH 1 via Finlayson Road and then turn right. Continue on SH 1 north for 7 km and turn left into the

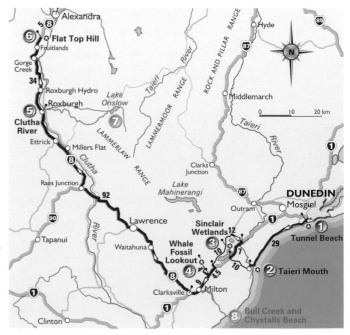

Tunnel Beach.

Henley–Berwick Road and left again on Berwick Road to the wetlands; a distance of 12 km.

Covering 315 hectares, and adjoining Lakes Waihola and Waipori, these wetlands are all that remains of the vast swamp — long since drained for farmland — that once covered most of the Taieri Plain. This portion has only survived due to the far-sighted actions of Horrie (Horace) Sinclair, who purchased the land in 1960 and allowed it to revert to its original condition.

In addition to the 40 bird species that breed here, a further 45 have been recorded in the wetlands. A causeway through its

heart links two small islands, both of which have excellent views over the entire reserve. There is camping and backpacker accommodation on site (ph (03) 486 2654; an entry koha/donation is requested).

4 Whale Fossil Lookout

Head south for 10 km on the Berwick Road until it rejoins SH 1 and continue for 4.5 km. Turn right into Limeworks Road and right again into Jensen Road. The lookout is on the right; a total distance of 4 km from SH1.

Tucked away in the limestone country just west of Milburn is a curious display of fossils. Protected by a small shed is a collection of large limestone rocks from

Taieri Mouth, Dunedin coast.

Pukeko

The pukeko (*Porphyrio porphyrio*) is a member of the rail family, and is closely related to the other five rail species in New Zealand: the takahe, weka, banded rail, spotless crake and marsh crake, as well as other similar rails scattered throughout the world. A relative newcomer to New Zealand, it is believed to have arrived here from Australia around a thousand years ago.

These bold birds have a reputation for being particularly fearsome. Pukeko will band together to fight off hawks, stoats and cats, using a considerable degree of shrieking and squawking, though their swampy nesting sites do give them a certain level of protection. Although awkward in the air, they can fly some distance, though they prefer to either run or swim to safety. Widespread throughout New Zealand and favouring wet and rough ground, pukeko are one of the few native birds to have thrived since the arrival of humans, having now become so common that they even live beside busy motorways in central Auckland.

the nearby Milburn Limeworks Quarry, all containing ancient marine fossils dating back about 25 million years. The most significant is the whale fossil, which at the time of discovery was an unknown species, and there are also fossilised dolphins and shellfish. Great views over the Tokomairiro Plain and Lake Waihola are an extra bonus, as is the extensive information board.

5 Clutha River
Return to SH 1 and continue south for 9 km to the junction of SH 8 to Central Otago. Drive 92 km via Lawrence to Roxburgh.
New Zealand's second-longest river, the 340-km Clutha begins as the major outlet for Lake Wanaka and even at that point is a waterway of consequence. Further downstream the swift-flowing river is joined by numerous tributaries, the most substantial of which are the Kawarau, Manuherikia, Teviot and Pomahaka. Below Balclutha the river divides around a large fertile island known as Inch Clutha, and even after reaching the sea makes its presence felt by creating a deep underwater trough that extends 100 km out into the open ocean.

Draining a large catchment area, the water flow can vary considerably and the river is notorious for its history of numerous and serious floods.

6 Flat Top Hill
Follow SH 8 towards Alexandra for 34 km; the Flat Top Hill Reserve is on the right, 5 km before the township.
Flat Top Hill lies at the foot of the Old Man Range and is the driest place in New Zealand, with less than 300 millimetres of rain a year. The rocks here are ancient by New Zealand standards, dating back 100 million years and now forming schist.

The Flat Top Hill Conservation Area protects 813 hectares and is characterised by layered rock tors and flat-topped stone outcrops. The vegetation is equally unique and is a rare surviving example of dry short tussock grassland. While at first glance the flora seems rather dull and uniform, over 180 native plants have been recorded here, most of which are highly localised and rare. Moreover, given the exceptionally dry conditions, it is surprising that 12 native ferns are found here too.

A loop walk with excellent interpretive panels takes around 30 minutes, while a walk up the slope to the summit of Flat Top Hill is longer than it looks and will take up to two hours return. From the top there are great views over Alexandra and the Clutha River.

GOT TIME? (+40 KM)
7 Lake Onslow
The lake isn't easy to find as it is not signposted from Roxburgh. From the main street of Roxburgh (SH 8) turn down Jedburgh Street (signposted Roxburgh East) and cross the Clutha River. At the T-junction turn right and after 1 km turn left into Wright Road. From this point on the route is reasonably signposted the rest of the way.
Although the trip to Lake Onslow is 40 km of gravel and winding road, it rises up and over some wonderful open high tussock country broken by narrow deep valleys that together make an immensely appealing and unique natural design. This man-made lake was originally known by the very descriptive name of the 'Dismal Swamp'. It was first flooded in 1888 to provide water for mining operations and later for irrigation and power. This is an open and very exposed landscape with only tawny tussock to impede the path of the wind. The lake itself is equally exposed and only a few rustic fishing cribs dot the wide shoreline.

8 Bull Creek and Chrystalls Beach
(+24 km)
Bull Creek and Chrystalls Beach are about 24 km east of Milton off SH 1.
Quietly forgotten on the South Otago coast, Bull Creek and Chrystalls Beach are remarkably different in character although only a few kilometres apart. Bull Creek cuts deeply through the rolling coastal hills and within the narrow sheltered valley is lush bush, home to native birds and in particular the bellbird. Unlike the long stretches of beach north and south, the coast around Bull Creek is rocky with small sandy coves suitable for swimming if you can brave the water temperature. The cluster of seaside cribs are mostly of the older homebuilt variety that, together with the bush and rocky shoreline, help to create a charming seaside settlement that more than compensates for the decidedly cool climate.

Chrystalls Beach just to the north is quite different. A long stretch of shoreline exposed to the open ocean, it is backed by extensive dunes covered with native grasses. In the middle of the beach is an old volcanic basalt plug known as Cooks Head. Coarse golden sand overlying finer white sand creates an especially appealing beachscape. Although neither location has any accommodation or other facilities at least there is a toilet.

Lake Onslow.

36 The Catlins • Balclutha to Invercargill

Empty beaches • Fur seals and sea lions • Fossil beds • Curio Bay • Magnificent forests • 230 km

In many ways New Zealand's last frontier, this sparsely populated corner of the country might experience some wild weather, but it also features some of New Zealand's finest coastal scenery, wildlife and luxuriant forest.

> **INFORMATION**
> Catlins Information Centre,
> 10 Campbell Street, Owaka,
> ph (03) 415 8371
> Clutha i-SITE, 4 Clyde Street,
> Balclutha,
> ph (03) 418 0388
> Invercargill i-SITE, 108 Gala Street,
> Invercargill, ph (03) 214 6243

Getting there

Most visitors travel north to south, beginning at Balclutha and completing the journey at Invercargill. While generally known as the Catlins, the area straddles both the South Otago and Southland regions, with the southern section of this coast more correctly known as Chaslands. The main road is Route 92 and is sealed making for good motoring. However, many if not most of the side roads are gravel.

Best time to visit

In recent years the Catlins has become one of the more popular driving trips in the country, but it is still uncrowded and does not yet attract the tourist bus trade. With numerous side trips and a very small permanent population, the area retains a remote and empty feel. While summer is definitely the best time to visit, the weather in the Catlins can be cool and wet almost any time of year — all part of the Catlins' special charm.

Facilities

With a short summer season and the majority of travellers doing this journey as a long day trip from Dunedin through to Invercargill, accommodation in the Catlins is scanty. At the beginning of the trip, Balclutha has a good range of shops and accommodation, and it would pay to fill your tank here (or, if travelling in the other direction, at Invercargill). Balclutha has a reasonable range of places to stay and eat, while Owaka, in the heart of the Catlins, is smaller and has just a handful of cafés, motels and bed and breakfast establishments. The camping ground at nearby Pounawea, next to the river and a scenic reserve, is particularly attractive.

1 Nugget Point

From Balclutha drive south for 6 km on the Owaka Highway/Route 92 and turn left into Kaka Point Road, continuing 14 km to Kaka Point. Follow the coast road to Nugget Point for 9.5 km; the last 8 km of road is gravel.
Wild and windswept Nugget Point is named after the group of jagged rocks situated just offshore. A short track out to the historic lighthouse leads to the most spectacular views both north and south along the coast. The point is also a unique seal colony as it is the only place in New Zealand where elephant seals, fur seals and Hooker's sea lions share the same territory.

The Nuggets, at Nugget Point.

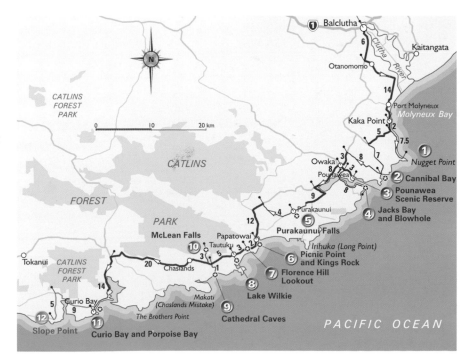

The seals are hard to see as the track is 130 metres above the sea and the animals blend in with the colour of the rocks, so binoculars are very useful.

Just before the lighthouse, a steep path leads down to Roaring Bay (10 minutes one way), where there is a hide to watch both blue and yellow-eyed penguins, which come ashore to nest late in the day.

2 Cannibal Bay

Backtrack towards Kaka Point and after 7.5 km turn left into Karoro Creek Road. After 5 km turn left into Ahuriri Flat Road and then take Cannibal Bay Road to the end; a distance of 7 km.

Cannibal Bay is a magnificent sweep of deserted beach and just one of several equally beautiful beaches in the Catlins area, though unfortunately the water is pretty cold, even in summer. However, the chilly water is perfect for the sea lions and fur seals that are common along the shores of this coast.

A 30-minute walk south along the beach will take you to False Islet and Surat Bay at the Catlins River estuary.

3 Pounawea Scenic Reserve

Take Cannibal Bay Road 8 km back to Route 92 (this road is a partial loop) and turn south and drive 3 km to Owaka. At Owaka turn left into Pounawea Road and continue 4 km to the end.

This small reserve of virgin forest right on the river estuary contains all the important lowland trees including totara, southern rata, rimu, miro and kahikatea. A short flat walk loops through the huge trees, and in addition to the fine forest the birdlife here, especially bellbirds, is prolific. The reserve almost surrounds the pleasant camping ground and the track begins in the camping area.

4 Jacks Bay and Blowhole

Head back along Pounawea Road for 3 km and turn left into Hinahina Bay Road, over the estuary, and into Jacks Bay Road, driving 8 km to the bay.

From the southern end of the beach an easy track leads to the dramatic Jacks Blowhole. The entire track and the blowhole are on private land and there is a donation box at the beginning of the track. Although over 200 metres from the sea, the 55-metre-deep hole is linked to the ocean by an underground cavern through which water is forced at high tide, creating an impressive booming sound.

A track skirts around the blowhole, with two lookouts enabling good views of the crashing waves beneath. In addition there are excellent views of Jacks Bay, a long sweep of beautiful beach dominated by the cliffs of Catlins Heads. The track is closed for the lambing season in September and October.

5 Purakaunui Falls

Retrace your way to Owaka and head south on Route 92 for 8 km. Turn left and follow the Purakaunui Falls Road for 9 km to the falls.

While the waterfalls in the Catlins area are not especially high or dramatic, they are particularly picturesque and set in beautiful native bush. With the water gently cascading down a stepped rock face, Purakaunui Falls is the most popular stop in the Catlins. The walk to the falls is through an especially handsome forest of beech, ferns and mosses, and the best view is from the lower lookout, accessed by a short flight of steps.

6 Picnic Point and Kings Rock

Complete the loop 4 km back to Route 92 via the Waikoato Valley Road, turn left and drive 12 km to Papatowai. Picnic Point is on the southern side of Papatowai village.

Picnic Point is a pleasant spot on the estuary of the Tahakopa River and the starting point for an easy 30-minute loop walk along the beach and through a small but impressive stand of native forest of kamahi, matai and rimu. Further south along the coast, and only accessible at low tide, is Kings Rock, a pillar of rock eroded by the sea to look very much like a chess piece.

7 Florence Hill Lookout

Travel south for 2 km on Route 92 from Papatowai to the lookout car park on the left.

At almost 200 metres altitude, Florence Hill Lookout has spectacular views south over the pristine Tautuku Bay, the Rainbow Isles and Tautuku Peninsula. To the north the blowholes at Long Point/Irihuka are just visible on a fine day.

8 Lake Wilkie

The lake is on Route 92, 3 km south of Florence Hill Lookout.

Tiny but pretty, Lake Wilkie is set in a deep hollow below a rocky escarpment and

The rocky headland of Cannibal Bay.

Curio Bay

Welcome to Jurassic Park! Only this Jurassic Park is the real thing — transfixed in stone and acknowledged as one of the best-preserved examples of a fossilised forest in the world. Fossilisation occurs when silica replaces the wood of trees, creating an exceptionally hard stone. Subsequently, when the surrounding softer rock is worn away by the action of wave erosion, the entire shape of the ancient trees is exposed. At Curio Bay stumps, tree trunks, branches and logs are all easily discernible in the wide rock shelf.

These ancient forests were present over 180 million years ago and include the ancestors of modern kauri and Norfolk pine, as well as numerous subtropical ferns and cycads. Indications are that at least four separate forests were destroyed over a period of 20,000 years by a series of cataclysmic events such as volcanic eruptions or massive landslides. The exposed fossils at Curio Bay also appear to be part of a much greater fossil bed as similar specimens have been found at Waikawa Bay, 12 km distant. A very useful information board and viewing platform help make sense of the fossils, which are only exposed at low tide. The low vegetation above the rock shelf is the nesting ground for yellow-eyed penguins that, late in the day, will suddenly pop out of the water with surprising speed and agility.

11 Curio Bay and Porpoise Bay

From the McLean Falls turnoff head 20 km south on Route 92 to the Waikawa turnoff (which is 75 km from Invercargill) and then follow the road along Waikawa Bay for 14 km to Curio Bay. The last section is gravel.

The fossilised stumps and trunks of trees, up to 180 million years old and only exposed at low tide, are clearly identifiable on the flat rocky shelf that is Curio Bay. Home to a colony of yellow-eyed penguins that pop out of the surf late in the day, fur seals are also seen reclining on the rocks around the bay. Curio Bay is separated by South Head from the much larger Porpoise Bay, which is home to the most southerly population of Hector's dolphin.

GOT TIME? (+15 KM)
12 Slope Point

From Curio Bay drive back 1 km and turn left into the Haldane–Curio Bay Road. Drive west for 9 km, turn left into Slope Point Road and drive 5 km to the car park. This road is all gravel.

There's not too much to see at Slope Point — and in fact it's usually so bleak and windy that even the toughest trees have difficulty growing upright here. It is, however, at 46.4 degrees south, the most southerly point of the South Island and is almost equidistant from both the South Pole and the Equator.

surrounded by mature podocarp trees. In mid-summer the flowering rata are particularly impressive. Keep an eye out for cheeky weka along the track.

9 Cathedral Caves

Signposted 2 km south of the Tautuku River on Route 92, 10 km south of Papatowai.

The main member of this group of spectacular sea caves is over 30 metres high, while others burrow deep into the cliff. It is a 20-minute walk from the car park to the first one, but take some time to explore the other caves along the shore and be prepared to get your feet wet, even at low tide. The walk is very tide dependent and the caves are only accessible for one and a half hours either side of low tide depending on the sea and the sand base.

While the tide times are helpfully posted on the gate, avoid disappointment by checking them beforehand at the Owaka information office or on the website (www.cathedralcaves.co.nz). There is a small entrance fee and the gate is closed if the tide is not right.

10 McLean Falls

Travel 1 km south from the Cathedral Caves and turn right into Rewcastle Road; the car park for the falls track is 3 km on the right.

One of the higher waterfalls in the Catlins, McLean Falls is not one but four interlinked cascades. The highest single fall is 20 metres, with water spreading across a rock face and the stream forced through a narrow gorge for a further three drops. Equally attractive is the stroll along the bush stream to the falls, with trees and rocks covered with thick mosses, and bellbirds and tomtits flitting amongst the foliage.

McLean Falls in the Catlins.

37 Southland • Gore to Tuatapere

Ancient forest • Turbulent coast • Foveaux Strait • 300 km

Southland is a prosperous farming province stretching inland from the wild coast of Foveaux Strait. This route links rare bush remnants and coastal gems away from the hustle of the usual tourist haunts.

INFORMATION
Gore i-SITE, Hokonui Heritage Centre, cnr Hokonui Drive and Norfolk Streets, Gore, ph (03) 203 9288
Invercargill i-SITE, 108 Gala Street (Southland Museum), Invercargill, ph (03) 214 6243
Riverton Information Centre, 172 Palmerston Street, Riverton, ph (03) 234 8260
Tuatapere Information Centre, 31 Orawia Road, Tuatapere, ph (03) 226 6739

Southland either to or from the Catlins or on their way to Stewart Island as the region is not generally considered a major tourist destination in itself. With this in mind, Southland is relaxed and casual and the usual visitor pressure through summer doesn't present such a problem in this region. The summer and autumn months are best as spring and winter here can be cool and wet. Gore, however, hosts a number of popular events such as the Hokonui Moonshine Festival, the Hokonui Fashion Design Awards and the New Zealand Gold Guitar Awards, so accommodation during these times can be at a premium.

too much else. A port town with a singular charm, although rough weather and a tough economy have bashed it about a bit at times, Bluff more than makes up for it with plenty of personality.

1 Dolamore Park and Croydon Bush Scenic Reserve, Hokonui Hills

Take SH 94 west of Gore for 5 km and turn left into Kingdon Road, then right into Reaby Road, and finally right again into Retreat Croydon Road where the reserve is on the right, 11 km from Kingdon Road.

Dolamore Park and Croydon Bush lie adjacent to the Hokonui Hills, totalling an area of nearly 1000 hectares between them. The tracts were never milled and as early as 1895 parts had been set aside as reserve land. Thick forest used to totally cover these hills but most of the trees were milled for timber in the late nineteenth century. What remains, however, is impressive. The bush here is surprisingly dense, with enormous matai, rimu, kahikatea, rata and tree fuchsia to be found. The understorey is lush with ferns

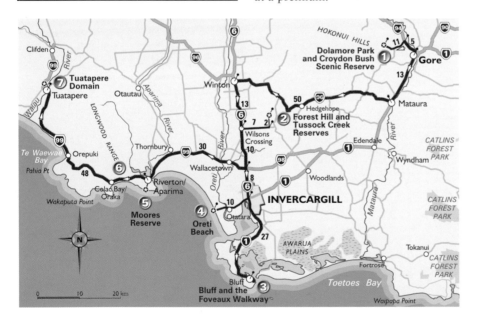

Takitimu Mountains.

Getting there

Starting at Gore on SH 1 in eastern Southland, this route wends its way through inland forest and along the coast, from Bluff to Tuatapere. The roads are sealed, in excellent condition, and the driving is easy.

Best time to visit

Most visitors tend to drive through

Facilities

Invercargill is at the heart of this trip and is a pleasant city with plenty of accommodation, good places to eat and a wide range of services. Gore and Winton are sizeable small towns and both offer a modest range of services. Tuatapere to the west is smaller still, and while the range might not be great there are still places to stay and eat, although not

Paradise Duck/Putangitangi

Paradise duck (*Tadorna variegata*) are an endemic species of shelduck — a curious mix of duck and goose that is just as happy away from water as near it. With their handsome plumage and distinct male and female colouring, these large birds are impossible to miss. The females have a striking white head and a brown chestnut-coloured body, while the male is dark all over with a black head and dark grey body. Always seen in pairs, the ducks often mate for life and will occasionally form large flocks if the feeding conditions are right.

Feeding on grasses, the birds were relatively rare in pre-European times, but have flourished in today's open farmland and crop fields and are one of the few native birds that can be hunted in season. Paradise ducks have a loud distinct call, with males giving a deep 'honk honk' sound, while the females make a similar call but in a much higher pitch.

and mosses hanging from and covering the trunks of trees.

The Dolamore Park area has been more formally developed, with an arboretum, rhododendron garden, picnic areas and very good camping facilities along with starting points for a number of walks. Two short walks of less than an hour loop through the giant trees and up to a lookout 304 metres high with views south over the plains to Bluff Hill. A longer two-hour walk leads to Poppelwell's Viewpoint at 460 metres via the Whisky Falls.

2 Forest Hill and Tussock Creek Reserves

Return to Gore and take SH1 for 13 km to Mataura. Just south of Mataura turn right into SH 96 and drive 50 km to Winton. Turn south on to SH 6 and after 13 km turn left into Wilsons Crossing Road. Drive east for 7 km and at Pettigrew Road turn left and continue 2 km to the car park.

These two adjoining reserves just southwest of Winton harbour are the only native bush left in central Southland. This bush contains a number of native birds, a 500-year-old rata tree and huge native tree fuchsias. Among the limestone outcrops are a number of small caves, perfect habitat for the native cave weta. The views from the lookout extend over the rich central Southland plains, south to Stewart Island and Bluff, west to the Longwood Range and northwest to the Takitimu Mountains.

3 Bluff and the Foveaux Walkway

Return to SH 6 and drive 18 km to Invercargill where the road joins SH 1 to Bluff; a further distance of 27 km.

Rising to 265 metres, Bluff Hill is a very old volcanic cone dating back to the Permian period well over 200 million years ago, when New Zealand was part of the Gondwana supercontinent. Mt Anglem/Hananui on Stewart Island, the Longwood Range and the Takitimu Mountains all date from the same period. The hill is the source of a hard volcanic stone called norite, locally known as 'Bluff granite', and the material of which the Bluff War Memorial is made. While Bluff is the end of State Highway 1, it is not the South Island's most southerly point; Slope Point to the east is just slightly further south.

The Foveaux Walkway is a superb coastal walk that winds around the rocky shore of Bluff Hill through salt-resistant flax and hebes to a lookout point with views both far to the west and to the offshore islands. Despite exposure to

constant sea winds, the even temperature and consistent rainfall has created a forest that is amazingly lush and contains many fine old trees including kamahi, kahikatea, rimu and rata. Stewart Island looms across the wild waters of Foveaux Strait and it is likely that the island was joined to the mainland during the Pliocene ice ages, when the sea level was much lower. The small islands in the strait are a haven for nesting seabirds, including the sooty shearwater or mutton bird.

4 Oreti Beach

Return to Invercargill and at Tweed Street in the city centre turn left and continue via Dunns Road 10 km to Oreti Beach.

Lying between the New River Estuary and Riverton to the west, Oreti Beach is a wonderful wide sweep of white sand, known for the toheroa (*Paphies ventricosa*), an endemic shellfish. Considered a delicacy, toheroa occupy the inter-tidal zone between high and low tide. Found between 10 and 20 centimetres below the sand, these shellfish form large colonies and feed by siphoning plankton out of the water.

At the southern end of Oreti Beach is Sandy Point, a wide sand peninsula that has a rare coastal forest with dense stands of totara and matai, both uncharacteristically diminutive in size owing to the poor soil and salt-laden winds.

5 Moores Reserve, Riverton

Retrace your route to Invercargill and drive north for 8 km on SH 6. Turn left on to SH 99 and head west for 30 km to Riverton. Continue over the Jacobs River Estuary Bridge and turn immediately left on to Bay Road; after 750 metres turn right into Richard Street and take the gravel road up to the car park at the end.

This reserve of lush bush centres on two small rocky outcrops that were once used to spot whales passing through the Foveaux Strait when Riverton was a whaling station. From the top the islands of the strait are all clearly visible, including Stewart, Codfish, Centre and Pig Islands. Below is the estuary of the Jacobs River, formed by the confluence of the Aparima and Pourakino Rivers. To the west the view extends along the coast to Colac Bay, the Longwood Range and, in the distance, the mountains of Fiordland. To the north lie the Takitimu Mountains, Eyre Mountains and the Hokonui Hills, while to the east can be seen the long white sweep of Oreti Beach and beyond that Bluff Hill.

6 The Longwood Range

Dominating the horizon north of SH 99 is the Longwood Range.

Volcanic in origin, the Longwood Range runs north to south between the Aparima and the Waiau Rivers and has a low rounded profile, rising to just 804 metres at Bald Hill. With a reliable rainfall, the range is home to a rich forest dominated by podocarps (predominately rimu) on the lower slopes and by beech at higher levels. The tops are subalpine shrubland, and while snow frequently falls on the hills, it very rarely settles for any length of time.

Extensively milled in the past, large areas of this range have been planted in exotic forest, but today over 23,000 hectares are under the management of the Department of Conservation.

7 Tuatapere Domain

Tuatapere is 48 km west of Riverton on SH 99. Immediately after crossing the Waiau River Bridge, turn right into the domain.

Within the Tuatapere Domain is a small patch of splendid ancient trees that includes totara, matai, kahikatea and beech, the highlight of which is a massive 1000-year-old totara.

Equally impressive is the spectacle of a mighty felled tree that was lifted back onto its stump by the power of flood waters in 1984.

The walk is flat and easy.

Oreti Beach.

38 Stewart Island/Rakiura

Kiwi • Unspoiled wilderness • Rare birds • Coastal scenery

New Zealand's third-largest island is home to the country's newest national park, Rakiura, created in 2002 and covering 85 per cent of the island's total area. The highest point of this exceptional landscape of untouched bush, hidden bays, and rugged mountain ranges is Mt Anglem at 980 metres.

> **INFORMATION**
> Rakiura National Park Visitor Centre (Department of Conservation), Main Road, Oban, ph (03) 219 0009.

Getting there

A day trip from Bluff is manageable and you will be able to visit Ulva Island, take a boat trip and have a wander around Oban, the landing point for the ferry on Stewart Island, all in the time available. Anything more will necessitate an overnight stay. While the ferry is modern and fast, taking just one hour from Bluff to Oban, it is fairly small and frequently booked out, especially in summer, so make sure you plan ahead to avoid disappointment (Stewart Island Experience: ph (03) 212 7660 or 0800 000 511, www.foveauxexpress.co.nz; this company also operates a bus service from Invercargill to Bluff). However, be warned that the Foveaux Strait has a reputation as a wild stretch of water.

Facilities

Oban offers a good range of accommodation from camping and backpackers through to motels and lodges, but there is not a lot of it so if you intend to stay on the island you will need to book ahead. Similarly, places to eat are good though not numerous. Shopping is pretty much restricted to a general store.

1 Short walks around Oban

A number of short walks around the settlement of Oban can be included on the short trip to and from Golden Bay. The Raroa Reserve Track and the Fuchsia Walk are both brief side tracks through the bush and are an alternative to walking along the road. Observation Rock, just 10 minutes' deviation from the road, is a wonderful lookout point over Paterson Inlet and Ulva Island.

2 Ulva Island

Ulva Island is situated in the Paterson Inlet, just around the corner from Oban in Halfmoon Bay. A wildlife sanctuary, the island is a popular destination, especially for day trippers. It is small (you can't really get lost) and relatively flat, with a network of excellent tracks (all well marked) linking a number of very attractive beaches. Near the wharf is Sydney Cove, a beautiful stretch of golden sand and the pick of the beaches, though South West Beach on the other side of the island is also well worth the stroll.

Now cleared of pests, rare native birds have gradually been reintroduced to the island, and while not yet prolific, their numbers will only increase with time. Keep an eye out for kaka, kakariki, saddleback and Stewart Island robin. Inquisitive weka are particularly common, especially on

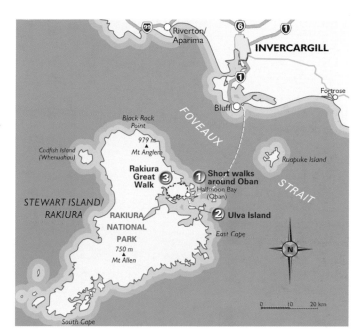

the beaches, where these cheeky birds will peck at your backpack in the hunt for anything of interest. The waters surrounding the island are protected by a marine reserve covering over 1000 hectares.

Ulva Island is a short water-taxi ride from Golden Bay, which is a 20-minute walk from the wharf at Oban, although

Ulva Island.

vehicular transport to Golden Bay is available.

3 Rakiura Great Walk

One of the more popular great walks, the Rakiura Track is a 36-km circuit around the peninsula on which Oban is situated and takes around three to four days. This is not a demanding track and is suitable for anyone of reasonable fitness, with the highest point just 300 metres. A combination of coast and bush, the track meanders through mainly lowland forest that includes rimu and kamahi, though the forest does thin out on the higher sections. Bird life is plentiful and you are likely to see or hear everything from bellbird and tui in the forest to little blue penguins, oystercatchers and shags along the coast. Currently there is no booking system for the Rakiura Track so it's a 'first come, first served' walk.

Kiwi

The kiwi, New Zealand's national icon, is a strange bird indeed. Flightless, with hair-like feathers, it retains only stubs of wings and has no tail. Nocturnal in habit, it has good night vision and a keen sense of smell, using the nostrils at the tip of its bill to locate worms and insects. The stout legs are useful not only for driving off predators, but also for escape: a kiwi can outrun a human.

Of the five species, the most common is the North Island brown kiwi (*Apteryx mantelli*), found in the northern two-thirds of the North Island. The tokoeka (*A. australis*) is found in the South Island. The largest kiwi is the great spotted kiwi (*A. haastii*), found in the Southern Alps and the northwest of the South Island (see image). Smallest is the little spotted kiwi (*A. owenii*), found only on Kapiti Island. The rowi (*A. rowi*) is confined to the area around the Okarito Lagoon in Westland.

On Stewart Island, which has a brown kiwi population of some 20,000 birds, kiwi have developed unusual habits. Usually a solitary bird, here kiwi may form family groups, and they are often active during the day as well as at night. While there is no guarantee of seeing a kiwi, several operators organise viewing trips.

Stewart Island/Rakiura.

39 Southern Fiordland • Tuatapere to Te Anau

Glacial lakes • Wild coast • Virgin forests • Awe-inspiring vistas • 235 km

Often bypassed by busy visitors, this long valley along the Waiau River gives access to some of New Zealand's most impressive scenery, from the wild Foveaux coastline to the marvellous glacial lakes, including the country's deepest lake.

INFORMATION
Fiordland National Park Visitor Centre, Lakefront Drive, Te Anau, ph (03) 249 7924
Tuatapere Information Centre, 31 Orawia Road, Tuatapere, ph (03) 226 6739

Getting there

Tuatapere, the starting point for this trip, is a small township near the mouth of the Waiau River in western Southland, 87 km west of Invercargill and accessible by a good road (from the north the route is southwards from Manapouri). The heart of this trip runs south to north along SH 99, which is a good sealed road although some of the side trips journey through rougher gravel roads.

Best time to visit

Summer and autumn is a good time in this region, and as the area doesn't attract a lot of visitors, the places described are seldom too busy or crowded. Winter and early spring can be cold and wet, and the summers are at best mild.

Facilities

There's not too much of anything along this route so if you intend to stay in the area you will need to bring camping gear and your own supplies. There are basic camping grounds at Lakes Hauroko and Monowai, and while Tuatapere has a sprinkling of places to stay and eat, there's little else apart from a few general stores and a very famous butcher's. However, Te Anau and, to a lesser extent, Manapouri at the northern end of the trip have plenty of accommodation and different services.

Before you go — sandflies

While sandflies (see page 10)are found all over New Zealand, in Fiordland it sometimes feels like they reach plague proportions. Fortunately they are easily deterred by insect repellent readily available from supermarkets, chemists and general stores.

1 Te Waewae Bay

From Tuatapere cross the Waiau River Bridge and turn left into Papatotara Road. Continue 14 km to Bluecliffs Beach.
Te Waewae Bay is a marvellous sweep of wild beach with nothing between its shores and the Antarctic ice. To the west the snow-tipped mountains of Fiordland loom over its frequently storm-tossed waters. The bay is home to a small population of Hector's dolphins and whales are occasionally seen close to shore.

2 Hump Ridge Track

The beginning of the track is at the end of Papatotara Coast Road, 27 km from Tuatapere.
Opened in 2001, the Hump Ridge Track

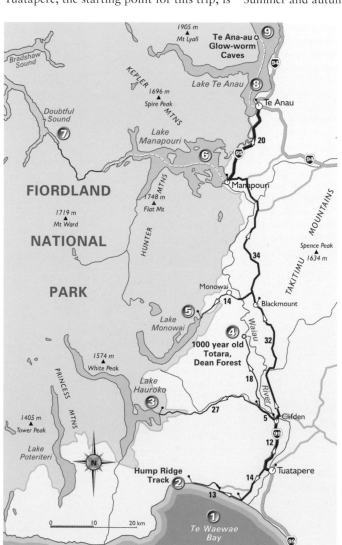

Te Waewae Bay.

is one of the newer walks in the Fiordland National Park and provides access to its southern reaches. Combining coastal vistas and wildlife with several of the few human interventions in the park, highlights are the spectacular Percy Burn Viaduct — the largest wooden viaduct in New Zealand — and the remains of Port Craig, a once lively sawmilling town.

The entire track takes three to four days, but helicopter and boat options can shorten the trip. Track information and permits are available from the information centre in Tuatapere (www.humpridgetrack.co.nz).

3 Lake Hauroko

Return to Tuatapere and drive 12 km north on SH 99 to Clifden. Turn left into Lillburn Valley Road. The lake is 32 km from this point, 20 km of which is gravel and rough in parts.

One of the few accessible points in the southern area of Fiordland National Park, at 462 metres Lake Hauroko is the deepest lake in New Zealand and one of the 10 deepest lakes in the world. Set within the wild and undeveloped mountains, the long gravel road deters most visitors, creating a place of quiet beauty.

There is a three-hour walk through beech forest to a lookout point on the lake's northern side, and the Dusky Track

begins from the head of the lake and can be accessed by (prearranged) boat or guided walk. While there is a boat launching ramp, be aware that the lake is subject to very high winds and can quickly become extremely rough.

4 Thousand-year-old Totara, Dean Forest

From Clifden on SH 99, drive towards Lake Hauroko, and after 5 km turn right into the Lillburn–Monowai Road. The forest is 18 km down this no-exit gravel road.

While it's a long drive down a gravel road for a relatively short walk, the trees in the Dean Forest are truly majestic. A massive 1000-year-old Hall's totara looks every bit its age, but is quite at home among the ranks of other mighty old trees that include rimu, beech and kahikatea. The trees are thickly hung with mosses, the ground is totally covered in lush crown ferns, and the forest rings with the sound of the bellbird. The loop walk is flat and takes no longer than 20 minutes.

5 Lake Monowai

Return to SH 99 and drive north for 32 km to just past Blackmount. Turn left and travel 14 km to the lake; 7 km of this road is gravel.

If for no other reason, this lake should be

visited because it is a prime example of the long-lasting damage wrought to the environment by careless development. The Monowai Power Station was built in 1925 and the lake was raised to provide sufficient water, but over 80 years later the disastrous results of this development are still evident in the stumps and logs of the drowned forest visible along the shoreline.

Created by a long-vanished glacier, the lake is long and narrow and surrounded by high mist-shrouded mountains cloaked in virgin beech forest.

6 Lake Manapouri

Return to SH 99, turn north and continue 34 km to Lake Manapouri.

Much less developed than Te Anau, at 440 metres this is New Zealand's second-deepest lake. With over 34 small islands and numerous bays leading deep into the heart of the Fiordland mountains, the lake maintains a certain air of mystery. In 1970 it was at the centre of one of New Zealand's greatest conservation battles, the 'Save Manapouri' campaign, which opposed plans to raise the level 30 metres to increase power generation. Over a quarter of a million New Zealanders signed a petition to save the lake and the issue had a significant impact on the 1972 general election, which saw a Labour government elected on a platform that included leaving the water level unchanged.

The eastern shore of the lake is drier, more open and flat, radically contrasting with the misty forest-covered mountains to the west. Several operators offer boat trips from the very pretty Pearl Harbour, where kayaks are also available for hire.

7 Doubtful Sound

Several operators run a variety of trips across Lake Manapouri to the West Arm, then by bus over the Wilmot Pass and down to Deep Cove on Doubtful Sound. The largest operator is Real Journeys (www.realjourneys.co.nz).

After Milford Sound, Doubtful Sound is the most accessible of the Fiordland sounds. Yet with far fewer visitors than Milford, this sound has a greater unspoiled feeling. Home to fur seals, Fiordland crested penguins and bottlenose dolphins, the 40-km-long fiord (Milford is just 16 km) is also the deepest at 400 metres.

Deep Cove, Doubtful Sound.

Takahe

The Murchison Mountains, between the South and Middle Fiords of Lake Te Anau, are the last mainland bastion of the rare takahe (*Porphyrio hochstetteri*). There were only four sightings of the bird between 1800 and 1900, so by the early twentieth century the takahe was thought to be extinct. However, ornithologist Dr Geoffrey Orbell was convinced a population still survived and he spent over 15 years searching for takahe, a quest finally rewarded in November 1948 when he rediscovered the birds in the Murchison Mountains.

Closely related to the pukeko, the takahe arrived in New Zealand several million years ago from Australia. Gradually becoming taller and bulkier than the pukeko, in the absence of predators it also became flightless. Takahe plumage is similar to that of pukeko, ranging from turquoise through blue to iridescent purple, with the same distinctive white tail feathers. Once widely spread throughout both islands, the arrival of humans led to the extinction of the North Island species and in the South Island the bird took to its last pocket of refuge in the Murchison Mountains. Even here numbers have dropped radically from the estimated 200 pairs in the early 1950s to just over 100 birds today, mainly due to predation by stoats. Although the birds live a long time and several new populations have been established on offshore islands, unfortunately the small gene pool has resulted in inbreeding and low fertility.

Lake Te Anau.

8 Lake Te Anau

Continue north 20 km on SH 95 to Te Anau.
Covering an area of 344 square km and 65 km long, Te Anau is the largest lake in the South Island and the second largest in the country after Lake Taupo. The east and west sides of the lake could not be more contrasting. To the west the rugged Kepler, Murchison and Stuart mountain ranges climb over 1500 metres and are snow-clad in winter and bush-clad at the shoreline. Three arms of the lake — somewhat unimaginatively named South, Middle and North Fiords — reach deep into the mountains, while to the east the landscape is flat, open and much drier. At the southern end of the lake where the Kepler Track starts there is an easy shore walk through wonderful beech forest to small beaches at Dock and Brod Bays.

The Te Anau Wildlife Centre is an open park on the lakeside in the Te Anau township with various aviaries containing native birds, some of which are not easily seen in the wild. These include takahe, weka, kaka, kea and kakariki. Some of the birds here have been injured in the wild or are part of a bird rearing programme to boost numbers before being returned to their natural habitat.

9 Te Anau Glow-worm Caves

A combination boat and cave trip, the glow-worm caves lie directly across the lake from Te Anau township and are the most impressive caves outside Waitomo. Operated by Real Journeys (www.realjourneys.co.nz), the two-and-a half-hour tour starts with a boat trip to the western side of the lake, followed by a short bush walk, and ends with a trip along an underground river through the caves. While known to early Maori, the caves were only discovered by Europeans in 1948 and consist of caverns, rock formations and a glow-worm grotto accessible by boat.

40 Northern Fiordland • Te Anau to Milford Sound

Spectacular mountain scenery • Milford Sound • Magnificent glacial valleys • Pristine forest • 116 km

Established in 1952 and recognised as a World Heritage Area in 1984, Fiordland National Park is New Zealand's largest national park, covering 1,252,000 hectares. It contains some of the country's most dramatic and unspoilt terrain. Largely mountainous, and with a harsh climate, the park is the stronghold of some of the planet's rarest plants and birds.

INFORMATION
Fiordland National Park Visitor Centre, Lakefront Drive, Te Anau, ph (03) 249 7924

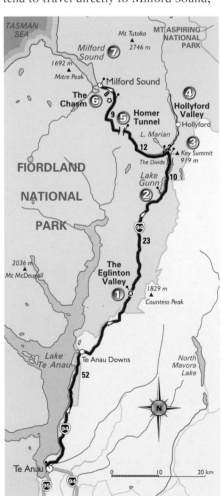

Getting there
The road from Te Anau to Milford Sound covers spectacular alpine scenery and is the only one to give access through the Fiordland National Park. Most visitors tend to travel directly to Milford Sound,
take the boat trip and then return, but it is very worthwhile planning some short excursions along the way. The road is sealed and in excellent condition, although it is subject to road closures during winter mainly due to snow and ice conditions around the Homer Tunnel.

Best time to visit
The Milford Sound attracts vast numbers of visitors every year — approximately 600,000 and growing — many of whom just visit on a day bus trip from Queenstown. If you time your trip outside the busy December to February periods the experience will be all the more pleasant. Winters are cold and wet, and even in early spring and late autumn cold snowy weather is not unusual.

Although the road is extremely busy with buses in the morning to catch the midday lunchtime boat trip, as they only stop briefly at a few selected view points such as the Mirror Lakes along the way, other scenic spots are left in relative peace. Up to 100 coaches per day use the road at the peak of the season, but with most of the vehicles going in the same direction the traffic flows surprisingly smoothly. So, if you want to avoid the worst of the crowds, leave before 8 am and travel direct to Milford Sound, do the boat trip, then take a leisurely drive back, stopping wherever you fancy.

Facilities
Te Anau township on the shores of the lake has a good spread of accommodation, cafés, a sizeable shopping centre and is an ideal base from which to explore Fiordland. There are at least four boat operators offering various day-trip options to the Sound. These can be booked online, in Te Anau, Queenstown or at the visitor

terminal in Milford. Prices and options vary so it's worthwhile checking these out beforehand. Overnight boat trips, kayaking and diving trips are also on offer, while the Milford Deep Underwater Observatory (www.milforddeep.co.nz) has an underwater viewing facility.

Ensure you have a full tank of fuel before leaving Te Anau as there are no petrol stations or other facilities between Te Anau and Milford Sound and cell-phone coverage is limited. Accommodation at Milford is minimal, though there are the usual tourist-type places to eat and plenty of souvenir shops. Iconic Gunn's Camp in the Hollyford Valley has a small store, camping and cabin accommodation in old Ministry of Works huts. Scenic flights are on offer out of Te Anau and Queenstown for those wishing to take in Fiordland's impressive landscape from the air.

Before you go — driving the Milford Road
Statistically, the Milford Road is the third most dangerous road in New Zealand with a 65 per cent higher chance of an accident causing injury than on the rest of the roading network. At first glance this is perplexing as the road does not actually appear that bad by New Zealand standards, but if you want to avoid your vehicle being wrecked and your holiday experience becoming a view of the inside of a medical centre here are a few tips.
• Don't drive the road tired. It's a long way from Queenstown to Milford and back (600 km return) and fatigue leading to lack of concentration can be lethal. If you have no option but a day trip from Queenstown, seriously consider a coach, and if you have time overnight in Te Anau and make the journey to Milford a leisurely day trip (240 km return from Te Anau). The road to Milford is too fabulous to be rushed.

- The first section of the road along the lake and the Eglinton Valley is characterised by long straight sections that can be travelled fast. But the road quickly becomes winding with some tight corners and drivers forget to adjust. Keep your speed down on the second half of the trip, especially after the Homer Tunnel.

- Remember to keep left, and be especially vigilant about it if you are not used to driving on this side of the road. It's really easy to forget this rule when pulling out of a rest stop.

- Winter driving presents a unique set of challenges. If you are not used to ice and snow, take things really carefully, especially around the Homer Tunnel. You will need to carry a set of snow chains. Grit is used to give extra grip on the roads where it is particularly icy, but this material can be slippery as well, so slow down on the corners.

Smithy Creek before the Earl Range, Eglinton Valley.

Lake Gunn.

1 The Eglinton Valley

Head north from Te Anau for 52 km to McKay Creek.

The Eglinton Valley is the quintessential glacial valley with a broad grass-covered flat and very steep beech tree-covered mountains rising on either side. Through the middle of the flat meanders the Eglinton River, fed by Lakes Gunn and Fergus and eventually draining into Lake Te Anau. The best views are from McKay Creek at the valley's southern end.

2 Lake Gunn

Continue north from McKay Creek for 23 km.

Tucked in at the feet of some mountains, the highest of which is Consolation Peak (1851 metres), is this small glacial lake. While the road follows the lakeshore, it is worthwhile stopping at Cascade Creek at the southern end to take in the 45-minute loop walk. Winding through red beech forest thickly smothered in moss, the views of the high snow-capped mountains looming over Lake Gunn's bush-lined shores are spectacular. Helpful information boards along the track aid plant identification.

3 Key Summit

The track to Key Summit begins at The Divide, 10 km from Lake Gunn.

One of the most accessible points to high

The Upper Hollyford River before Mt Talbot.

alpine scenery along the Milford Road, the track to the top of Key Summit (919 metres) takes three hours return and is ideal if one of the longer walks is not an option. From The Divide (515 metres), the walk to the top follows the Routeburn Track for most of the way, branching off for the climb to the summit. Along the way the vegetation changes from beech through to subalpine tussock and shrubs. The views of the Darran and Humboldt Mountains from the top are superb.

4 Hollyford Valley

The Hollyford Valley Road is 2 km on from The Divide.

The Hollyford Valley is an attractive side trip, and while the road is unsealed, it is flat and in good condition and not on the tour bus itinerary. The two key attractions are Lake Marian and the Marian Falls, and the Humboldt Falls. The track to Lake Marian and the falls is 1 km down Hollyford Valley Road.

A mere 10-minute walk from the road, the Marian Falls is a wild cascade of water down a boulder-strewn stream thickly overhung with beech trees. The trek to Lake Marian (three hours return) is a little more demanding, but very worthwhile if you have the time. The lake nestles in an alpine bowl above the treeline surrounded by the towering Darran Mountains that are snow-capped even in summer.

A further 8 km down the road is the access point to the Humboldt Falls, which drop 275 metres in three separate cascades, the highest of which is 134 metres. The walk through beech forest to the falls lookout takes 15 minutes.

5 Homer Tunnel

The Homer Tunnel is 12 km north of the Hollyford Valley Road turnoff.

The area around the Homer Tunnel is 945 metres above sea level and is the highest point on the road. Prior to its construction, access to Milford Sound was either on foot via the Milford Track, or by sea, and there was pressure on the government to build a tunnel through the Homer Saddle to open the area to tourism. Work began on the road in 1929 and on the tunnel in 1935. During the war years work on the tunnel was halted, and it was completed in 1953.

The road on the tunnel's western side is dramatic with its sheer cliffs and hairpin bends dropping precipitously to Milford Sound. The single-lane tunnel is 1.2 km long, slopes steeply down towards the Milford end with a gradient of 1 in 10, and is controlled by traffic lights, although the wait isn't usually too long. Given the altitude, the vegetation here is alpine, so take some time to stroll the short nature walk to the right of the tunnel through a bewildering variety of mountain plants helpfully labelled to assist identification.

6 The Chasm

From the Homer Tunnel continue 9 km to The Chasm.

At this appropriately named gorge the Cleddau River is compressed into a dramatic torrent of water that has worn the rock into smooth sculpted formations over the millennia. Given the area's high rainfall, The Chasm is always impressive viewing.

7 Milford Sound

Milford Sound is 8 km from The Chasm.

At Milford Sound reality exceeds expectation, no matter how many photographs of Mitre Peak you may have seen over the years. The long arm of the Sound snakes 16 km inland from the sea, with peaks rising dramatically out of the water to over 1500 metres. What makes Milford even more remarkable is that the drop below water continues to depths of more than 300 metres, although at the entrance the depth is only 27 metres. Geologically speaking, Milford Sound is actually a fiord formed by glacial action, rather than a drowned river valley as with the Marlborough Sounds.

The spectacular Bowen Falls plunge 165 metres into the sea from a hanging valley, while further along the Sound the Stirling Falls drop 156 metres into the sea, and both falls are spectacular after heavy rain. The Sound is also home to a large seal population, the rare Fiordland crested penguin and dusky and bottlenose dolphins, while underwater black coral grows just 10 metres below the surface (rather than the usual 40 metres) as the water here is heavy with dark tannins, creating the illusion of much deeper water.

FIORDLAND — MAJOR WALKING TRACKS

Fiordland features some of the best walking tracks in the country. To undertake these you need a good level of fitness and proper equipment as the terrain is mountainous and the weather unpredictable and typically extremely wet. Some of the tracks are very popular and can get crowded over the peak summer period, while the Milford Track is booked out months in advance. Bookings open on 1 July and can be arranged online or through any DoC office (www.doc.govt. nz). Before setting out on any tramp, check in with the excellent Te Anau area office for up-to-date track and weather information.

CAPLES RIVER AND GREENSTONE RIVER TRACKS

Although these tracks can be done separately, together they form a loop track from the Milford Road to Lake Wakatipu around the Ailsa Mountains linked via the McKellar Saddle. The track encompasses alpine scenery and two river valleys quite different in character. The Caples is more open and tussock-clad, while the Greenstone is narrower and bush-lined. The round trip takes four to five days and is less demanding than the other Fiordland tracks. A further option is to return on the Routeburn Track.

DUSKY TRACK

This is the most challenging track in the national park, taking eight to nine days to complete and covering 84 km via Dusky Sound. It reaches deep into the core of the mountains and traverses untouched wilderness. There are numerous river crossings, and the terrain is mountainous.

HOLLYFORD TRACK

From the heart of the Fiordland mountains, this track follows the Hollyford River to Lakes Alabaster and McKerrow and through to the mouth of the Hollyford River at Martins Bay. Among the many highlights are excellent views of Fiordland's highest mountain, Mt Tutoko (2746 metres).

From the end of the Hollyford Road the track is 56 km long, with the only options of egress either to walk back or fly out. The trip takes four days, but as the Hollyford Valley is at a low altitude this track is less affected by seasonal weather than other Fiordland tracks. However, it contains numerous crossings and in bad weather trampers can be stranded for days.

TUATAPERE HUMP RIDGE TRACK

This walk in the southern part of Fiordland National Park combines coastal vistas and wildlife with one of its few human-modified landscapes as parts of the track traverse private land. To walk the entire track takes three to four days but helicopter and boat transport options can shorten the trip. Track information and permits are available from the Tuatapere information centre (www.humpridgetrack.co.nz).

KEPLER TRACK

A popular loop track through the Jackson Peaks, this 60-km walk takes three to four days and is accessed either from Rainbow Reach near Lake Manapouri or the Dock Bay Control Gates at Te Anau (a track along the Waiau River also links these two points).

Traversing beech forest and alpine terrain, this medium-grade track has spectacular views over Lakes Manapouri and Te Anau as well as the mountains to the west. The highest Mt Luxmore can be very exposed in windy weather.

MILFORD TRACK

The oldest and most popular of the Fiordland tracks, the Milford Track is a four-day 53-km walk from the north end of Lake Te Anau through to Milford Sound. Only 40 people are allowed to start the track each day. However, for very hardy and experienced trampers, bookings are not required through the winter season (May to October; hut tickets are still required), although the track is often closed because of poor weather.

The track traverses very diverse terrain, from the less wet, eastern side over the spectacular McKinnon Pass (the most demanding section of the track) of the Main Divide, down into the very wet but more scenic Milford Sound section. There is also the option of a short side trip to the Sutherland Falls, a 580-metre tiered waterfall with a main drop of 270 metres.

ROUTEBURN TRACK

The most popular track after the Milford, the Routeburn starts (or ends) from The Divide on the Milford Road and ends (or starts) at the Routeburn Shelter north of Glenorchy, near Queenstown. The track is 32 km long and takes three days through spectacular alpine terrain crossing the Harris Saddle (at 1255 metres, the highest point on the track), then following the Route Burn to the road end. Rather than the road trip back, many trampers return via the Caples or Greenstone Tracks. Another option is a two-day return tramp from the Milford Road to the Harris Shelter, which covers the track's best scenery.

Mitre Peak in Milford Sound.

41 Around Queenstown

Lake Wakatipu • Dart Valley • Alpine vistas • 230 km

Occupying a long glacial valley, Lake Wakatipu snakes through dramatic alpine country and is fed by legendary rivers such as the Shotover and the Dart. Towering mountains rise in every direction, snow-covered in winter and a shimmering hazy blue in the heat of summer.

INFORMATION
Queenstown i-SITE, Clocktower Building, cnr Shotover and Camp Streets, Queenstown, ph (03) 442 4100
Cromwell i-SITE, 47 The Mall, Cromwell, ph (03) 445 0212
Queenstown Regional Visitor Centre (Department of Conservation), 37 Shotover Street, Queenstown, ph (03) 442 7935

Getting there
Whichever way you come, it's a long drive to Queenstown. From Invercargill in the south is 180 km via SH 6 and from Dunedin in the east is 280 km, while from Wanaka via Cromwell in the north is 100 km. However, all the roads are excellent, if somewhat winding in parts. An alternative road from Wanaka is via the Cardrona Valley and Crown Range, a distance of 70 km. This road has an overrated reputation as difficult, when in reality only the steep decline from the saddle below Mt Scott to the Arrow Junction is narrow and twisting. Air New Zealand and Qantas operate direct flights from Auckland, Wellington and Christchurch as well as from Brisbane, Sydney and Melbourne in Australia.

Best time to visit
Only spring and late autumn can be considered off-season in Queenstown. Summer brings the trampers, adventure tourists and holidaymakers attracted by the warm dry Central Otago climate and the alpine scenery. Daytime temperatures in summer are often over 30°C, though the area is also subject to short southerly cold snaps. Autumn is equally appealing, with cooler days and nights, and the deciduous trees turning golden through April and May are a wonderful sight. During winter, the ski fields in the Queenstown area draw snow sport enthusiasts from all over Australasia and further afield.

Facilities
Queenstown is New Zealand's leading resort town and with that comes every sort of hotel, motel, café, restaurant, bar and retail outlet you can imagine. It usually isn't too hard to find a place to stay at any time of year, ranging from five-star luxury hotels to the most basic of backpackers, though the more popular places tend to be booked out ahead and Queenstown is pricey by New Zealand standards. Likewise with food, Queenstown has it all: top-of-the-range restaurants, ethnic food cafés and, surprisingly, plenty of inexpensive places as well. Cromwell, which is 60 km at the other end of the Kawarau Gorge, is a good option if you are watching your dollars, and it's also in the heart of the Central Otago wine country.

Before you go — camper vans
Queenstown is getting tough with casual roadside camping. Local bylaws only allow freedom camper vans that display a 'self-contained' certificate. Yet even these vehicles are not permitted to camp in residential zones or the town centre. All campers that are not self-contained are prohibited from freedom camping anywhere in the Queenstown Lakes District. There are camping grounds in Queenstown and Frankton with full facilities, and more basic campsites at Moke Lake and Twelve Mile Delta on the road to Glenorchy.

1 Moke Lake and Lake Kirkpatrick
From Queenstown take the road to Glenorchy for 7 km and turn right. Continue on this road for 8 km to the lakes; 2 km of the road is sealed and the remainder is gravel.

Just 18 km from the hustle and bustle of Queenstown, these two small alpine lakes make you feel as though you are in another world. Set in a deep valley and enclosed by Closeburn Station, their reed-fringed shores are a haven for water fowl. For independent travellers, there is a basic camping ground with limited facilities.

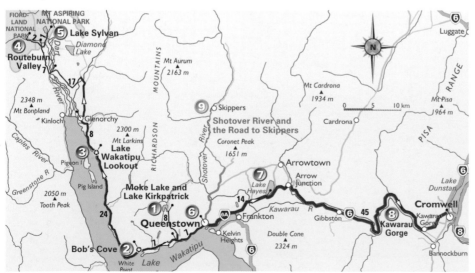

The distinctive S-shaped outline of Lake Wakatipu.

2 Bob's Cove

The cove is 14 km from Queenstown on the Glenorchy Road.

Named after local boat skipper Bob Fortune, Bob's Cove is a small pretty bay edged with white shingle and backed by a mixture of eucalypts and native trees. A short track follows the lake edge past several nineteenth-century lime kilns to a promontory crowned by a low hill. From the top views extend in all directions, with the bush-fringed shore below and the Remarkables rising high on the far side of the lake. These peaks lie directly opposite Queenstown and form a spectacular grey stone rampart along the lake's eastern side. The highest point is Double Cone at 2319 metres, but what makes the mountains so appealing is that they rise in a sheer wall from the lake edge. In winter, when they are covered in snow, the vista of lake and mountains is hard to beat.

3 Lake Wakatipu Lookout

From Bob's Cove continue 24 km to Lake Wakatipu Lookout.

Lake Wakatipu is a glacier lake in the shape of an enormous figure 'S'. Covering 290 sq km, it is New Zealand's third largest lake, and is also very deep, plunging to 420 metres. Strangely, the lake also has mini 'tides'. These fluctuations, known as a seiche, occur in enclosed bodies of water, with the formation of a standing wave that is usually imperceptible to the naked eye. This results in regular variations in the lake level of around 200 mm. The main tributaries are the Dart, Shotover and Caples Rivers.

From the outlook on the road to Glenorchy the views are superb. Not only are the northern and middle sections of the lake spread out before you, but the view extends along the wide braided Dart River and far into the Southern Alps and Mt Aspiring National Park, including a view of the snowy peak of Mt Earnslaw/Pikirakatahi at 2820 metres.

4 Routeburn Valley

From the Lake Wakatipu Lookout, continue 8 km to Glenorchy and continue through the village for 17 km to the Dart River. From the Dart River to the Routeburn Valley is 9 km on an unsealed road that is in good condition, though the last couple of kilometres through the bush is narrow and winding.

In contrast to the dry Central Otago landscape, this basin in the Mt Aspiring National Park is more typical of Fiordland, and if a trip to Fiordland itself isn't possible then this area is a taste of what that region has to offer. A wide montane valley, the lower reaches of the Route Burn river are dense with old beech forest, mosses, ferns, swift-flowing streams and tumbling waterfalls. This is the beginning (or end) of the famous Routeburn Track and a number of short walks. Even if you are not walking the entire track, then a couple of alternatives are a walk along the beginning section for a taste of the landscape (it is four hours return to the first hut) or the short Double Barrel Falls Walk (40 minutes). Keep an eye out for the friendly native robin that is common along the tracks. There is a very attractive picnic area just beyond the car park.

5 Lake Sylvan

From the main car park at the Routeburn Valley entrance return 2 km and then turn left and drive 1 km to the Lake Sylvan car park.

Surrounded by the stark peaks of the Forbes and Humboldt Mountains, this small lake is an easy one-hour return walk. Encircled by beech forest, the lake is a haven for ducks, including paradise ducks and grey teal. At the beginning of the walk there is a basic camping site set among beech trees.

Willow trees in winter colour, Lake Hayes.

6 Queenstown Hill and the Time Walk

Return to Queenstown and just south of the town the walk starts from Kerry Drive.

Queenstown Hill looms 907 metres above the town and presents superb views over the middle and southern reaches of the lake, as well as over the entire Queenstown Basin and the surrounding mountains. It is a solid uphill slog that will take over two hours return, the lower half through pine and Douglas fir, but the track is good and the scenery worth it. A shorter alternative is the Time Walk, though the uphill climb is just as hard — but if you do this loop walk in an anticlockwise direction, the grade is much easier.

7 Lake Hayes

From Queenstown to Lake Hayes is 14 km on SH 6.

In comparison to the cold deep glacier lakes, Lake Hayes is both shallower and considerably warmer. Much loved by calendar companies and landscape artists alike, Lake Hayes is famed for the autumn hues of the willows and poplars along its shores. On the northern side of the lake is a large picnic area that is particularly appealing on a hot summer's afternoon, with large shady trees along the water's edge and a pleasant easy walkway following the eastern shore.

8 Kawarau Gorge

From Lake Hayes continue east for 45 km through the gorge on SH 6 to Cromwell.

The Kawarau River is the outlet for Lake Wakatipu, and it carves its way through rugged mountains to join the Clutha River at Cromwell. In contrast with the usual green and moist image of New Zealand, this unique landscape is a true desert. Dry and barren, the steep mountainsides are bare and brown, with very little vegetation. In more recent times, however, grapes have begun to be grown on the narrow river flats, producing some of New Zealand's finest cool-climate wines.

The gorge winds along the river for 20 km between high peaks that include Mt Scott (1363 metres), Mt Mason (1040 metres) and Mt Difficulty (1285 metres). About halfway through, the Roaring Meg river, true to its name, gushes down to join the Kawarau from the north.

GOT TIME?

9 Shotover River and the Road to Skippers

From Queenstown drive north 12 km via Arthurs Point towards Coronet Peak. The Skippers Road is to the left, off Coronet Peak Road.

Not only was the legendary Shotover River once one of the richest gold-bearing rivers in New Zealand, but it is also a very wild stretch of water. Cutting through steep dry country directly north of Queenstown, the river has gouged deep gorges between sheer cliffs and one of the highlights of a visit to Queenstown is a jet-boat ride up its rapids. Another way to see the river is the equally legendary 'Road to Skippers'.

Built in the 1860s to service the gold-mining settlements along the Shotover, this 15 km of road has barely changed since the old coach days. Largely following the river, the road ends at a camping ground and the restored stone schoolhouse and Mt Aurum homestead. Traversing open tussock country, the views and landscape are superb and timeless. However, this road is definitely not for the faint-hearted. Narrow, winding and gravel all the way, long stretches reduce to a single lane so considerable reversing skills are required when two vehicles meet.

Kawarau River and Gorge, near Queenstown.

Harrier Hawk/Kahu and New Zealand Falcon/Karearea

Widespread throughout New Zealand, Australia and Papua New Guinea, the harrier hawk (*Circus approximans*) is a common sight either circling the open country searching for prey or feeding off roadkill. Handsome birds with dark brown feathers with a lighter underbelly, the female hawk is larger than the male and, unusually, they nest on the ground, most commonly in a protective clump of vegetation such as flax or raupo. When hunting, they glide in wide effortless circles, slowly scanning for ground prey. However, they will often be attacked by other birds, especially magpies and spur-winged plovers, and even on occasion by flocks of sparrows (see top image).

Today roadkill makes up the larger portion of the bird's diet, and in fact its abundance (together with the bush clearances over the last 150 years) has resulted in a large increase in harrier hawk numbers. However, this has a downside as well, for while feeding on roadkill many hawks are themselves killed by cars. For many years the birds were considered harmful to newborn lambs, and it wasn't until 1985 that they became fully protected.

Native falcons (*Falco novaseelandiae*) are half the size of hawks, but have not responded quite as well to human occupation. Estimates are that fewer than 3000 of the birds remain in three distinct populations occupying differing habitats and varying in size and colour; these are the eastern, bush and southern falcons (see bottom image).

The southern falcon is found on the Auckland Islands, Stewart Island and in the mountains of Fiordland, while the eastern prefers the open tussocklands from Southland to Marlborough. The smallest of the three, the bush falcon, is found in the northwest corner of the South Island and the lower half of the North Island. In no area is the bird common, but it is most likely to be seen in open tussock country in the eastern South Island.

In contrast to hawks that feed on carrion, falcons catch their prey on the wing, using their powerful eyesight (six times that of the human eye) and speeds in excess of 200 kph to capture their food. The bird has a reputation for being incredibly fearless and aggressive, especially when defending nests and territory. It is the falcon/karearea that appears on the New Zealand $20 note.

Skippers Canyon, home of the Shotover River.

42 Around Wanaka

Glacial lakes • Alpine scenery • Mt Aspiring • 60 km

Lake Wanaka is the source of the Clutha River and reaches deep into the mountains of the Southern Alps. The Matukituki Valley, scoured by ancient glaciers, offers the best view of the iconic Mt Aspiring/Tititea and the easiest access to the national park of the same name.

INFORMATION
Wanaka i-SITE, 100 Ardmore Street (lakefront), Wanaka,
ph (03) 443 1233
Mt Aspiring National Park Visitor Centre, Ardmore Street (on the road into town), Wanaka,
ph (03) 442 7935

Getting there

Wanaka can be approached from the west via the Haast Pass, from the north over the Lindis Pass, or from the south from Cromwell and Queenstown via SH 6. There are also Air New Zealand flights into the tourist town from Christchurch. The roads in the area are excellent, although occasionally affected by snow in winter.

Best time to visit

Like Queenstown, Wanaka is both a winter and summer destination, and only spring can be considered an off-season in this region. Typical of Central Otago, the climate is dry with cool, clear winter days and hot summers, with the occasional cold southerly snap. The changing of the colours of the deciduous trees in autumn is a particularly attractive time. Every two years during Easter, the Warbirds Over Wanaka airshow attracts huge crowds and casual accommodation is impossible. Wanaka accommodation is also at a premium from Christmas through to early February and during the peak ski season from July to September, so it would be wise to book ahead.

Facilities

While not as frantic as Queenstown, Wanaka has in recent years transformed from a quiet lakeside backwater into a sophisticated alpine town with smart shops, luxury accommodation and modern eating establishments. The range of accommodation is broad, from camping through to five-star hotels, and with a substantial permanent population the town can cater for most travellers' needs. The Glendhu Bay Motor Camp, 13 km west of Wanaka on the road to Mt Aspiring, is an iconic New Zealand camping ground. Situated right on the shores of the lake, the camp has this magnificent bay all to itself and is an ideal spot whether you have a tent, a caravan or a camper van. Lake Hawea, much less developed than Wanaka but just 11 km from town, has limited accommodation.

1 Lake Wanaka

New Zealand's fourth-largest lake, Lake Wanaka covers 192 sq km, is 311 metres deep and was formed more than 10,000 years ago by glacial action. Driving deep into the mountains of the Southern Alps, Wanaka's main feeder rivers are the Makarora, Motatapu and Matukituki Rivers and the lake itself feeds the impressive Clutha River.

One of several small islands at the lake's southern end, Stevensons Island is now a reserve for the rare buff weka. These weka were once common in the eastern South Island, but became extinct in the late 1920s. In 1905, however, 12 birds were transferred to the Chatham Islands where they flourished and today the island weka population is over 60,000. Thirty birds were relocated to Stevensons Island in 2003, though nine immediately escaped by swimming to the mainland, a distance of just 200 metres. Today weka are established on Mou Waho and Mou Taho Islands as well as Stevensons. Several operators offer boat trips out to the islands.

From Wanaka town centre walkways extend a considerable distance in both directions along the shoreline of the lake.

2 Roys Peak

Mt Roy is 5 km from Wanaka, on the Mt Aspiring Road.
The hike to the summit of Roys Peak at 1578 metres is a popular day's outing. While the climb is a slog, the views from the top are panoramic. Spread out below is Lake Wanaka with a glimpse beyond to Lake Hawea, while to the west is Mt Aspiring/Tititea and the Southern Alps. The zigzag track is in good condition and

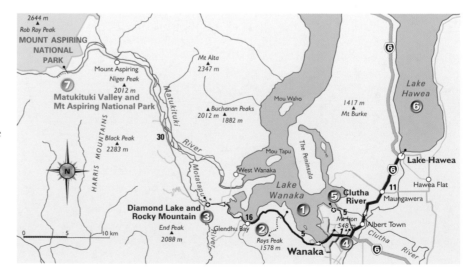

the climb through 1200 metres is on a steady rather than steep grade. The return trip to the summit takes around six hours, though a two-hour return walk will bring you to a good viewing point. The track is closed for the lambing season during October and the first half of November.

3 Diamond Lake and Rocky Mountain

Continue on the Mt Aspiring Road through Glendhu Bay for 16 km. The car park is just before the bridge that goes over the Motatapu River.
Rocky Mountain is a small peak (775 metres) and once lay deep under grinding glacial ice that has given the mountain its distinctive rounded shape. Nestled in the southern lee of the mountain is Diamond Lake, a small raupo-fringed tarn that reflects the surrounding landscape in its limpid waters. Patches of native bush cling to the steep hillside above the lake, which is a 10-minute walk from the car park, while the lookout over Lake Wanaka and the Matukituki River is a further 30 minutes. The track to the top is a bit rough and will take a total of two hours return, but the views over the Wanaka Basin, the broad delta of the Matukituki and the Southern Alps are splendid. But a word of caution: the track to the lookout and the summit can be very icy in winter.

Hooker River before Aoraki/Mt cook.

The Southern Alps

While there is no official definition of the Southern Alps, it is generally recognised that the name applies to the range of mountains that run some 550 km from the Nelson Lakes area through to Fiordland. Geologically young and still actively forming, the Alps rise above the contact zone of the Pacific and Australian tectonic plates along the fault. The tilting of the land along the Alpine Fault is particularly noticeable on the West Coast, where the mountains rise steeply within a short distance of the sea.

Reaching their greatest height around Aoraki/Mt Cook, with 16 peaks over 3000 metres, towards the north the mountains gradually diminish in size. Glaciers have had a major impact on the shape of the Southern Alps, and of the more than 350 glaciers in the area the longest at 30 km is Tasman Glacier, below Aoraki/Mt Cook.

The mountain ranges are also responsible for dramatic differences in the climate and vegetation between the east and west coasts. Westerly winds off the Tasman Sea, laden with moisture, are forced upwards by the mountains, drenching the West Coast in heavy rain. The wettest place in New Zealand is the Cropp River in the mountains east of Hokitika. Warm foehn winds, known in Canterbury as the 'Nor'wester', become warmer and drier as they climb the mountains. The change in rainfall is graphically illustrated as one travels through any of the east–west passes where the open shrub and grasslands of the east give way to the dense and lush rainforests of the west.

Poplar trees in autumn, Lake Wanaka.

Lake Hawea, looking towards Corner Peak.

4 Mt Iron

Mt Iron is 1 km east of Wanaka on SH 6.
Sitting just to the east of Wanaka, Mt Iron (548 metres) stands isolated from the surrounding mountains, offering fantastic views in every direction: south along Cardrona Valley, east to the broad terraces of the Clutha River, north over Lake Hawea, west across Lake Wanaka and beyond to the Southern Alps. Known as a 'roche moutonée', glaciers have ridden over the western side of the mountain, leaving it relatively smooth, while the eastern side has been sharply scraped away, forming steep cliffs and rocky bluffs. The walk to the top will take around 30 minutes, and it is easier to walk the loop track clockwise: up the gentler western slope and down the steeper eastern side. The open nature of the low vegetation ensures endless views all the way.

5 Clutha River

Half a kilometre beyond Mt Iron turn left into SH 6/West Coast Road, then after 500 metres turn left into Aubrey Road. Follow Aubrey Road for 3 km and turn right into Outlet Road, continuing 2 km to the end.
The Clutha River has the largest water flow of any New Zealand river and at 340 km is the second-longest river in the country. At the Lake Wanaka outlet the river flows swift and clean, and just east the lake has created a deep river valley with broad flat terraces (the airport is in fact situated on an old river terrace). There is a good track along the river from the outlet to Albert Town that will take one hour one way.

6 Lake Hawea

Return to SH 6 and turn left, then continue for 11 km to Lake Hawea.
Lake Hawea was formed by the same glacial flow that created Lake Wanaka, from which it is separated by less than 1 km at The Neck. At the base of the lake is an old moraine wall, left behind by the retreating glacier, from where the short Hawea River drains into the Clutha. Covering an area of 141 sq km and 392 metres deep, Lake Hawea has just one main tributary, the Hunter River, which flows into the top of the lake. There are significant areas of bush around its shores and a popular picnic spot is at Kidds Bush, halfway up the lake on the road to Haast. The lake was raised by 20 metres in 1958 to increase capacity for power generation.

GOT TIME?
7 Matukituki Valley and Mt Aspiring National Park

Travel 50 km west of Wanaka on the Mt Aspiring Road. At least half the road is gravel and the last section has a number of shallow fords that in some weathers might prove a challenge for smaller vehicles.
Mt Aspiring National Park, covering 355,000 square hectares, stretches along the Southern Alps from the Haast Pass down to the Routeburn Valley. The park takes its name from the peak of Mt Aspiring/Tititea, which is 3033 metres high. Distinctively pyramid-shaped, this mountain has often been called 'the Matterhorn of the South'. The surrounding area is famous for its glaciers that include the Bonar, Volta, Therma and Rob Roy.

Access to Mt Aspiring National Park is not easy. The Haast Road cuts through the top of the park, while to the far south the Routeburn Road enters for just a few kilometres. The West Matukituki Valley is a stunning unspoiled alpine glen leading to the very heart of the mountains and has the best views of Mt Aspiring/Tititea. Within the valley, Raspberry Flat is the starting point for a number of tracks, including the Rob Roy Track, a three-hour return walk beginning in open grassland before entering beech forest along a mountain stream, and gradually rising out of the bush into an alpine tussock basin with views of the Rob Roy Glacier, waterfalls and the mountains beyond. Keep a close eye on the kea around here as they can be very pushy and will pinch anything if your back is turned even for a moment.

43 Haast Pass • Wanaka to Haast

Boisterous waterfalls • Pristine rainforest • Alpine vistas • 180 km

Following an ever-changing landscape, SH 6 leaves behind the open, glacier-scoured country of the Wanaka Basin and winds through marvellous mountains, along rushing rivers, and through stunning forests, to eventually emerge at the mouth of the Haast River.

INFORMATION
Haast Visitor Centre, SH 6, Haast,
ph (03) 750 0809
Makarora Visitor Centre, SH 6,
Makarora, ph (03) 443 8365
Wanaka i-SITE, 100 Ardmore Street
(lakefront), Wanaka,
ph (03) 443 1233

Getting there

Once a journey of epic proportions, the road through the Haast Pass is now sealed all the way and makes comfortable if somewhat slow driving. As the lowest pass (563 metres) through the Southern Alps the route is rarely blocked by snow, but take care around the Gates of Haast, a narrow section that runs along the Haast River, as there are loose rocks that occasionally roll on to the road.

Best time to visit

While summer and autumn are the ideal times with mild temperatures and less rain, winter snows turn the mountains into picture-postcard scenery. West of the pass, heavy rain at any time of year turns the numerous waterfalls along the road into raging torrents, more than compensating for the limited views.

Facilities

Wanaka has a good range of places to eat, accommodation and services. Haast township has very limited services that include a general store and two petrol stations, but there are no ATM machines or cell-phone coverage. What's more, Haast is a popular overnight stopping point, so if you intend to stay here in the summer months you will definitely need to book ahead. The only facilities between Wanaka and Haast are two cafés, a camping ground and a couple of bed and breakfast places at Makarora. It would also pay to fill the petrol tank before leaving Wanaka.

1 The Neck

Travelling on SH 6, 40 km from Wanaka.
Both Lakes Hawea and Wanaka were formed by glaciers during the last ice age 14,000 years ago that left a narrow strip of land just 1 km wide separating the two bodies of water. From Wanaka to The Neck, SH 6 hugs the shores of Lake Hawea, while beyond The Neck the road follows Lake Wanaka. There are superb views over both lakes.

2 Makarora

On SH 6, 25 km from The Neck.
The dense forest around Makarora contrasts dramatically with the dry landscape only a few kilometres to the east. These flats were once forested in beech, matai, kahikatea and miro, and the township of Makarora originated as a milling centre supplying the Otago goldfields with timber. Despite its small size, a remnant of this great forest still supports a good number of native birds, including the elusive bush parrot, the kaka.

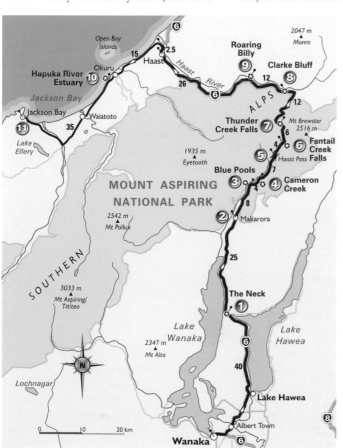

Stewarts Creek Falls, Makarora Valley.

3 Blue Pools

On SH 6, 8 km from Makarora.
On the confluence of the Blue and Makarora Rivers and overhung with old beech trees, the deep clear water of the Blue Pools varies considerably in colour, ranging from a light iridescent blue through to an intense deep green. While an attractive place to swim, the water is very cold at any time of the year, regardless of hue. The Makarora River is one of several main tributaries feeding into Lake Wanaka.

4 Cameron Creek

On SH 6, 4 km from the Blue Pools.
A wooden platform high above the beech forest allows grand views over the Makarora River and, to the west, the mountains and valleys of the Southern Alps. The creek is named after Charles Cameron, the first European to traverse the pass in 1863.

5 Haast Pass

On SH 6, 7 km from Cameron Creek. There is a large parking area with toilets at this location.
Haast Pass, set in deep beech forest, is the lowest pass through the Southern Alps. From the pass the Haast River cuts a narrow valley to the west, while the Makarora River carves a wide path east to Lake Wanaka. A short track zigzags up through the forest to a lookout and offers superb views down the bush-lined pass, both east and west. Stretching in every direction are snow-capped mountains, although the road is seldom affected by winter snow.

6 Fantail Creek Falls

On SH 6, 4 km from Haast Pass, on the right.
Surrounded by ancient beech forest, these picturesque fan-shaped falls are on a side creek of the fast-flowing Haast River. Only 100 km long, the Haast rises just west of the pass and is joined by the larger Landsborough River around 30 km from where the waters empty into the sea.

7 Thunder Creek Falls

On SH 6, 6 km from Fantail Creek, with good offroad parking.
True to its name, Thunder Creek Falls slams into the Haast River with a mighty crash in a drop of 28 metres from a glacial hanging valley. The falls are within Mt Aspiring National Park, the northern boundary of which skirts SH 6 through the pass.

8 Clarke Bluff

On SH 6, 12 km from Thunder Creek, with a good lookout over the river from the car park.
Opposite Clarke Bluff, the wide Landsborough and Clarke Rivers join the Haast from the north to create a classic braided river lying downstream from their confluence. From this point there are excellent views up the valley to Mt Hooker.

Blue Pools, Makarora River.

Rata

New Zealand has 11 species of rata, four of which grow into trees while the remainder are vines. Closely related to pohutukawa, the best known are the northern rata (*Metrosideros robusta*) and the southern rata (*M. umbellata*). And just to confuse things, the southern rata grows as far north as Whangarei (though it is rare in the North Island), and the northern rata grows in the north of the South Island.

Both trees are known for their striking crimson flowers that daub the dense green of the New Zealand bush with a bright splash of red during the summer months. Rata are also the favourite food of nectar-eating birds such as tui and bellbird. A rare white-flowering rata, *M. bartlettii*, is confined to the Cape Reinga area.

The northern and southern species, while closely related, differ considerably in their growth habits. The northern rata starts out in life as a perching vine high in the trees, eventually sending roots down to the ground. Over time the rata overwhelms the host tree and becomes a tree in its own right, albeit with a gnarled and twisted trunk that betrays the tree's viny origin. The southern rata (see image), on the other hand, starts out as a tree and will reach heights of 20 metres, with a broad canopy. The wood of the tree is extremely hard and was previously used in boat building and furniture making. Regrettably, possums have wreaked major havoc to rata as the tree is one of their favourite foods. Unable to tolerate browsing by these pests, it will quickly die back. A mature tree can be killed by possums in just three years.

9 Roaring Billy

On SH 6, 12 km from Clarke Bluff; parking off right-hand side of road.

This is the wettest part of the road, with rain falling on an average of 180 days per year and an annual fall of over 5500 mm. The Roaring Billy is a tributary of the Haast River and at this point crashes down a series of boulder-strewn cascades into the river. This stream is spectacular if it has been raining hard. The short 15-minute walk to the Roaring Billy is through beech forest thick with mosses and ferns.

10 Hapuka River Estuary

Drive 26 km to Haast town, then 2.5 km beyond the town turn left into Jackson Bay Road. Travel 15 km south to the Hapuka Estuary.

The estuary of the Hapuka River encompasses three interlinked ecosystems of forest, wetland and estuary. The bush is dominated by rimu and kahikatea, with a dense understorey of the semi-climbing plant kiekie, creating a distinctive subtropical feel. Some of the rimu are estimated to be between 500 and 800 years old. Between the bush and the river is a wetland thick with flax and manuka, while along the river the tidal salt marshes are overhung with old kowhai trees.

11 Jackson Bay

Continue south 35 km from the Hapuka River.

Jackson Bay is a wide north-facing bay protected from the worst of the southerly weather off the Tasman Sea by Jackson Head and the Burmeister Tops. Home to a small fishing fleet, the bay is the southernmost point of the road network on the West Coast and marks the terminus of the coastal plain. South of Jackson Bay the coastline becomes more rugged and eventually meets the wild coastal mountains of Fiordland. The Wharekai–Te Kou Walk from Jackson Bay to Ocean Beach takes around 40 minutes return and there is a good chance of spotting Fiordland crested penguins in spring and early summer.

Jackson Bay, south of Haast.

44 South Westland • Haast to Hokitika

Glacier country • Fiordland crested penguins • Okarito Lagoon • Virgin forest • 275 km

Sparsely populated, this tour through South Westland is one of the great driving trips in New Zealand. The road follows the dramatic peaks of the Southern Alps all the way, winding through magnificent rainforest and linking glacial lakes and isolated beaches.

INFORMATION
Haast Visitor Centre, State Highway 6, Haast, ph (03) 750 0809
Westland i-SITE, Carnegie Building, Hamilton Street, Hokitika, ph (03) 755 6166
Westland Tai Poutini National Park Visitor Centre, SH 6, Franz Josef, ph (03) 752 0796

Getting there
Beginning in Haast, SH 6 follows the narrow coastal plain, sandwiched between the Southern Alps and the Tasman Sea. The road is in excellent condition and travels for the most part through farmland and pristine forest, only touching the coast occasionally. Surface flooding can be a problem during very heavy rain.

Best time to visit
Summer through to early winter is the best time in this region. Summer temperatures are mild and in winter Westland is cool rather than cold. However, it can rain heavily at any time of the year, though the most settled weather is through autumn and early winter (March to June).

Facilities
Very few people live in this area, and while visitor numbers are high, facilities are patchy. The largest settlements along the route are Fox and Franz Josef and neither of these places is big. Both have a good range of accommodation, from camping and backpackers through to motels and luxury lodges, and a handful of good places to eat, but not too much else. Moreover, these are popular stopping points and the accommodation is often booked out so it would be wise to plan ahead. Camping is much less of a problem, with a good spread of simple camping grounds all along the route.

1 Ship Creek
On SH 6, 17.5 km north of Haast.
Ship Creek is a marvellous combination of kahikatea rainforest and rimu, wetland and dune, all within a surprisingly compact area. Within a small swamp along the creek massive kahikatea rise straight out of the dark waters heavily stained with plant tannin. A high boardwalk weaves through these ancient trees smothered with heavy mosses, creepers and lichens. Closer to the sea the dune country is completely different. Near the beach a dune-top lookout tower offers views all the way south to Jackson Head and inland, over rimu forest, to the splendid mountains of the Southern Alps. A small dune lake fringed by reeds nestles below, while the beach is thick with worn driftwood and the air heavy with salt spray.

2 Knights Point
On SH 6, 7.5 km north of Ship Creek.
Knights Point was the last section of the West Coast Road to be completed and this final link between Otago and Westland was opened in 1965. At 137 metres above sea level, there are extensive views along creeks and coastal ridges and over a small group of rocky islets just offshore, a haven for seabirds, including the sooty shearwater. Keep a sharp eye out for fur seals resting on the rocks below.

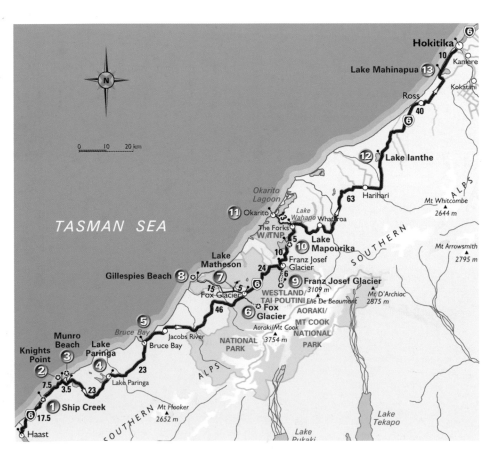

Rimu forest growing on the shores of Bruce Bay.

3 Monro Beach
North of Knights Point 3.5 km.
Flanked by rocky headlands, and pummelled by the wild weather straight off the Tasman Sea, this small sandy cove is home to fur seals and the rare Fiordland crested penguin. Only 1500 pairs remain and, like most penguins, they are somewhat timid. The best time to see them is early morning or late afternoon. A flat walk from the car park through beautiful rimu forest is less than two hours return.

4 Lake Paringa
On SH 6, 23 km north of the Monro Beach car park.
Typical of the numerous lakes on the long coastal plain, Lake Paringa is a kettle lake formed by a retreating glacier. The road skirts the eastern side, but the rest of the lake shore is covered in mature rainforest. The shy bittern can be seen in the wetlands around the lake. When startled, the bittern will stand absolutely motionless with its head and beak pointing directly upwards. Most noticeable at night-time, the deep booming call of this elusive bird resonates across the quiet waters of the lake.

5 Bruce Bay
On SH 6, 23 km north of Lake Paringa.
Consisting of a tiny settlement of just six houses, Bruce Bay is one of the few points where SH 6 touches the coast. Despite being exposed to the pounding surf of the Tasman Sea, rimu forest grows on the dunes almost to the water's edge.

6 Fox Glacier
On SH 6, 46 km north of Bruce Bay.
Fox Glacier lies in a shattered valley that has been torn apart by ice, with high cliffs ripped clean by nature's relentless power. Impressive from a distance, the short walk to the terminal is worthwhile to appreciate still more the sheer force of this glacier. Up close the sharp blue-green ice creaks and groans as it grinds slowly down the valley. However, it is dangerous to walk on the ice or directly up to the terminal without a guide as the melting ice is highly unstable. Guided trips on both Fox and Franz can be organised through the DoC visitor centre at Franz Josef.

7 Lake Matheson
Signposted 5 km west of Fox Glacier township on the Cook Flat Road.
Possibly the most photographed lake in New Zealand, Lake Matheson is renowned for the beautiful mirror images of Cook/ Aoraki, Tasman and La Perouse Mountains that can be captured in its still waters. However, for the best pictures you need to be up early before the wind gets up and ruffles the surface.

Lake Matheson is a kettle lake, formed by a large section of ice left behind when Fox Glacier retreated from its last advance around 14,000 years ago, the depression created by the melting ice filling with water to create the lake. Even without the mountain reflections this lake is worth a visit as it is ringed by handsome kahikatea and rimu forest and fringed with raupo.

8 Gillespies Beach
West of Fox Glacier township, 20 km at the end of the road, which is narrow, winding and gravel for half its length.
Once a thriving but short-lived gold-mining settlement, only a few cribs remain at Gillespies Beach, and walks in this area can be either as short or as long as you like. To the lagoon is two hours return, to the pack track tunnel three hours return, and to the fur seal colony four hours return. There are more seals during the winter months when well over a thousand winter over at Waikowhai Bluff, to the north of the beach. There is also a small camping ground with basic facilities.

Lake Matheson before Aoraki/Mt Cook and Mt Tasman.

9 Franz Josef Glacier

Turn off SH 6 before Franz Josef township,
24 km north of Fox. Drive 6 km to the car park.
While Fox is longer and larger, Franz Josef, the more northern of the two glaciers, is steeper and faster moving. Named in 1865 after Franz Josef, Emperor of Austria, by explorer Julius von Haast, this glacier stretches down to rainforest at the base of the valley. Sentinel Rock is a short uphill climb to a lookout point with great views over the glacier and valley and is a particularly good spot for taking photographs. Late afternoon with the sun setting in the west has the best light.

10 Lake Mapourika

On SH 6, 10 km north of Franz Josef.
Mapourika is the largest of the South Westland lakes and is ideal for swimming, fishing and kayaking. Draining into the Okarito Lagoon, it is also the feeding ground of the white heron/kotuku. There is a good picnic and camping area at the north end of the lake close by MacDonalds Creek.

11 Okarito

Turn off SH 6, 5 km north of Lake Mapourika,
and drive 13 km to the sea.
Okarito lies at the heart of some of the most impressive Westland landscapes. To the west endless driftwood-covered beaches are hammered by the Tasman's rolling surf. To the east rises Mt Elie De Beaumont (3111 metres), with Aoraki/Mt Cook, Mt Tasman and Franz Josef Glacier visible further south. In between lies vast pristine rainforest and the broad Okarito Lagoon. The area is also home to two rare birds: the Okarito brown kiwi and the white heron/kotuku. The elegant kotuku (*Egretta alba modesta*) is distributed throughout the South Pacific, Australia and Asia, and while found in other parts of New Zealand, this is the bird's only breeding colony.

Two outstanding walks begin from the beach. The first, to the Okarito Trig (one hour return), has outstanding mountain views, while the three-hour return Three Mile Lagoon Walk is noted for its coastal scenery (this last walk is tide dependent).

12 Lake Ianthe

On SH 6, 63 km north of the Okarito turnoff
and 22 km south of Ross.

Fox Glacier flows from the Fox Glacier Terminal.

Glaciers

Glaciers are simply rivers of ice. What makes Fox and Franz Josef Glaciers special is that they drop to quite low altitudes — in the case of Franz Josef the terminal is surrounded by rainforest. This occurs for two main reasons. The first is that the winds patterns off the Tasman Sea result in very high levels of precipitation, falling at lower levels as rain and at higher levels as snow; in addition, both glaciers have very large ice fields, known as the névé. The second reason is that both these glaciers move very fast — in fact, ten times faster than most other glaciers. Known as basal sliding, a layer of water beneath, aided by the weight of ice above, causes the glacier to move faster than the ice can melt at these low levels. In 1943 a plane crashed high on the Franz Josef Glacier and the wreckage emerged six years later having travelled 3.6 km from the crash site. In similar circumstances on a glacier on Mt Ruapehu, aircraft wreckage moved just 600 metres in 31 years.

Overall the two glaciers have been retreating for the last 18,000 years, from their point of greatest extent, when they reached far out into the sea. Lake Matheson, 5 km west of Fox Glacier township, is just one of several 'kettle' lakes created by melting blocks of ice left behind by this retreat. In recent years both glaciers have retreated and advanced, with Franz Josef advancing 1 km since reaching its smallest extent in 1982.

Surrounded by mature kahikatea and matai bush, this beautiful small lake is a haven for water birds including the great crested grebe, black teal and grey duck. At the lake's southern end a short boardwalk leads to a giant matai, reputed to be over a thousand years old. Also at the southern end of the lake is a camping ground with basic facilities.

13 Lake Mahinapua

On SH 6, 40 km north of Lake Ianthe and
10 km south of Hokitika.

Unlike most of the lakes in South Westland that are glacial in origin, Lake Mahinapua was originally a coastal lagoon that was eventually cut off from the sea by sand dunes driven up by the relentless westerly winds. Large and relatively shallow, the lake is sheltered from the west by dense bush and its placid waters are popular with kayakers. Bellbirds are common along the forest walks and there is a large picnic area and an attractive camping area beside the shore.

45 Central West Coast • Hokitika to Westport

Pancake Rocks • Pounamu • Fantastic seascapes • Majestic rivers • 265 km

From the pounamu-bearing Arahura River and the glacial Lake Kaniere near Hokitika, this trip traverses some of New Zealand's most spectacular coastal scenery. Expect to encounter superb rainforest, dramatic limestone vistas and an abundance of wildlife.

INFORMATION

Greymouth i-SITE, cnr Herbert and Mackay Streets, Greymouth, ph (03) 768 5101

Paparoa National Park Visitor Centre, SH 6 Punakaiki, ph (03) 731 1895

Westland i-SITE, Carnegie Building, Hamilton Street, Hokitika, ph (03) 755 6166

Westport i-SITE, 1 Brougham Street, Westport, ph (03) 789 6658

Getting there

Although this route starts from the south on SH 6, it can just as easily begin from SH 73 via Arthur's Pass or, coming from the north, via Westport and the Buller Gorge. The roads are all excellent and sealed. The coastal section around Punakaiki cuts through steep hill country and the road is narrow and winding, but the scenery is so breathtaking you will be more than happy to drive slowly.

Best time to visit

At the height of summer the area around Pancake Rocks at Punakaiki is like a shopping mall car park when there's a sale on and appears to be a breeding ground for camper vans. While the summer is definitely warmer, be prepared for heavy rain at any time of year and with it small slips that can occur along the steep parts of the road. Autumn and early winter, while cool, is often a period of settled weather.

If you can wrangle the timing, travel through this area in the late afternoon or the early evening. With the sun going down over the sea, the sunsets along this coast are often magnificent, serving up vistas that are second to none.

Facilities

Greymouth is the largest town on the coast and while it is not beautiful, it has plenty of accommodation even in the busy season. It also has all the services a traveller requires, so if you have anything important that needs doing, take care of it here, as other towns on the West Coast have far fewer facilities. Hokitika, 35 km to the south, is a more pleasant town to stay in, and while it is a touch light on accommodation, it has good places to eat and a handful of lively local pubs. The Wildfoods Festival in early March packs out any accommodation within 50 km of the town. While Punakaiki has greatly expanded its accommodation in recent years, if you plan to stay here it would pay to book ahead and there's not too much else in the way of facilities. Westport in the north is a robust mining town with a good range of accommodation and services, but thin on places to eat. Fuel will be considerably more expensive outside the major towns.

1 Hokitika Gorge

From Hokitika turn off SH 6 and drive towards Kokatahi and Kowhitirangi and then follow the signs to the gorge. The total distance is 33 km. The Hokitika River is wide and broad where it enters the sea just south of the town, but less than 30 km upstream it is compressed through a narrow limestone gorge. Deep in the shade of overhanging trees, the vivid turquoise-coloured water swirls and rushes through limestone that has been sculpted and shaped by the power of nature. The upper reaches of the Hokitika are popular with kayakers, while the wild streams further inland attract the very experienced.

2 Lake Kaniere

From Hokitika turn off SH 6 into Stafford Street and then into Lake Kaniere Road and continue on this road for 18 km to the lake.

Lying to the east of Hokitika in the foothills of the Southern Alps, this deep glacial lake (194 metres) is surrounded by mature forest and overlooked by two small mountains, Mt Graham (828 metres) and Mt Tuhua (1124 metres). Around the lake a 7000-hectare reserve protects the bush that includes fine stands of mature kahikatea growing right down to the water's edge. The views across the water to the mountains are superb, but

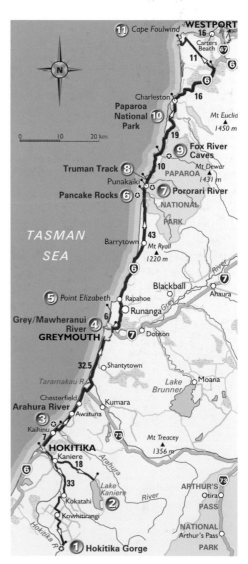

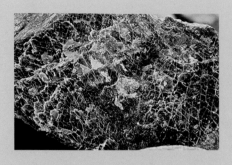

Greenstone/Pounamu/Jade

Pounamu is a mineral called nephrite a calcium magnesium silicate stone containing varying amounts of iron. Formed deep underground in the zone where volcanic and sedimentary rocks are in contact, in New Zealand pounamu is found along the Alpine Fault. Subsequently lifted to the surface, the stone is exposed by river erosion and glacial action and broken down into various forms, from tiny pebbles to large boulders. The intensity of colour is determined by the stone's iron content. In New Zealand there are three main types of pounamu, each with different names and properties: kawakawa (dark green), kahurangi (very rare, translucent, light green and flawless), and kakotea (dark green, streaky with black spots). A fourth type, bowenite, is only found in the Milford Sound. Known as inanga or tangiwai, this pounamu is a pearly, grey-green colour and is often translucent.

The importance of pounamu within Maori culture cannot be overestimated — the very name of the South Island, Te Wai Pounamu, directly relates to this stone. Only found on the West Coast, pounamu in pre-European times was highly valued for both ornamentation and weaponry, in particular patu (hand-held clubs) as the stone keeps a good edge. So treasured were they that many patu had individual names.

The Arahura River near Hokitika is one of the primary sources of New Zealand pounamu and there are several outlets in the town where visitors can see the stone being carved into a variety of objects and purchase a piece. However, be aware that much of the greenstone is in fact from Canada and China, so if you are keen to purchase the genuine article then ask specifically if the stone comes from New Zealand (as even a 'New Zealand Made' tag can disguise the fact that it originates elsewhere). Traditionally, pounamu is given as a gift, and is not acquired for oneself.

the sandflies here can be fierce. A number of very good tracks circle the lake, the longest of which is the Lake Kaniere Walkway, which winds through the bush following the western shoreline and will take four hours one way.

3 Arahura River

Return to Hokitika and continue 7 km north on SH 6.

One of the most important sources of pounamu, the Arahura River rises near Browning Pass in the Southern Alps. The lower reaches run through glacial moraines and low-lying land known as pakihi. Pakihi swamp is peculiar to the high-rainfall areas typical of the West Coast. Characterised by low stunted vegetation, the result of nutrients being rapidly leached from the waterlogged soils, these wetlands are almost permanently flooded. The tannin content of the water, from the high vegetation cover in the area, lends it a distinctive dark brown colouring, very much like tea.

4 Grey/Mawheranui River

On SH 6, 32.5 km north of the Arahura River.

The Grey/Mawheranui River runs 120 km from the Tasman Sea through to its headwaters at Lake Christabel near the Lewis Pass. Joined by several major tributaries, including the Ahaura and the Arnold, the Grey/Mawheranui has carved

Mist rising off Lake Kaniere.

Pancake Rocks.

of excellent short walks, there is good accommodation and cafés, and the sights along the coastal road are stunning. The Pancake Rocks, featured on a thousand calendars, can be very crowded, but when a heavy swell is running this place truly lives up to the hype.

The unusual rock formations began forming 30 million years ago when limestone was overlaid with softer mudstone in a succession of layers. Over the years, sea and wind have eroded the softer mudstone layers, creating the stacked pancake effect seen today. Excellent well-formed paths wend through lush coastal bush to dramatic bluffs, sea caves, arches and surge pools. Numerous narrow fissures in the rocky seascape act as blowholes that are best witnessed at high tide or in rough weather. In a heavy swell the largest blowhole, Putai, can be seen and heard from quite a distance.

a wide valley east of the Paparoa Range, but just before it reaches the sea it narrows considerably to cut through the low coastal hills at Greymouth. It has become infamous for the damaging floods caused when huge volumes of water are forced through the gorge and over the dangerous bar at the river mouth. A cold alpine wind is also channelled along the river valley and is known as 'The Barber' because of its icy cutting edge.

5 Point Elizabeth

From Greymouth drive north to Westport over the Grey River Bridge. Immediately past the bridge, turn left and follow the road along the coast, 6 km to the end.

Point Elizabeth is a marvellous blend of coastal bush and seascapes stretching along an easy walkway. Constructed by gold miners in 1865 to traverse the high cliffs of the point, today the track passes through dense groves of kiekie and nikau palm with the boom of the surf just below a constant companion. Nikau are at their southern limit on the West Coast, but what is surprising is that while at Point Elizabeth the groves are so extensive and dense, the tree does not naturally grow at all a mere 30 km south.

A high lookout has extensive views to the north along the wild coast, while offshore

two small rocky outcrops are home to numerous seabirds and fur seals. Hector's dolphins are commonly spotted.

6 Pancake Rocks, Punakaiki

On SH 6, 43 km north of Greymouth

A stunning combination of heaving sea, luxuriant bush and dramatic rock formations, Punakaiki is more than just the Pancake Rocks. In addition to a number

7 Pororari River

On SH 6, 1 km north of the Pancake Rocks.

Just before entering the sea the Pororari River creates a deep gorge, lined on both sides by magnificent limestone cliffs. High rainfall has resulted in a narrow cleft thick with tree ferns, kiekie and nikau palms overhanging the river and giving the area a distinctive subtropical feel. A walkway along the river is flat and easy.

Ferns

One of the most distinctive features of the New Zealand landscape, of the 200 species of fern that grow here, 40 per cent are endemic. Mamaku (*Cyathea medullaris*), is the most impressive, growing up to 20 metres high with a striking black trunk and broad spreading bright-green fronds. The silver fern or ponga (*C. dealbata*) has become a national symbol; its young spiral-shaped fronds, koru in Maori, are an iconic New Zealand motif.

The most common fern is wheki (*Dicksonia squarrosa*), which forms thick clumps with multiple stems rising from underground rhizomes, allowing the fern to survive bush clearances and fires. While the tree ferns are impressive, smaller ferns are equally attractive in their own right. Common in beech forest are crown ferns that often form huge swathes blanketing the forest floor.

Truman Bay.

8 Truman Track

On SH 6, 1 km north of Pororari River.

Not to be missed, this short 30-minute return track leads through a mature forest of matai, rimu and rata to a short coastal strip of flax and then down to a small sandy cove (not safe for swimming). There are dramatic views along the coast and at low tide it is possible to explore the sea caves and the rocky foreshore. Blue penguins nest here from August to February and the best viewing times are around dawn and dusk.

9 Fox River Caves

On SH 6, 10 km north of the Truman Track.

Following an old gold trail, a track along the bush-lined northern bank of the Fox River leads to limestone caves containing stalactites and stalagmites. The walk takes two hours return and you will need good sturdy footwear as it can be rocky and slippery in parts, plus a torch to explore the caves. Not far from the caves is a huge rock overhang large enough to camp under. Nicknamed 'the Ballroom', it is a formation known as a fluviatile cave. The overhang was once part of the riverbed and was scoured out by the surging waters.

10 Paparoa National Park

Charleston is 19 km north of the Fox River on SH 6.

Covering 306 sq km and established in 1987, the heart of this national park is the granite backbone of the Paparoa Range

Nikau palms, Paparoa National Park.

that stretches from the Grey/Mawheranui River in the south to the Buller River in the north. The drive along the coast road through Punakaiki is particularly spectacular with a most magnificent seascape backed by steep hills covered in dense rainforest. The park is the most southerly point where tree ferns and nikau grow together, while further inland the forest consists of rimu and beech. Near the coast fast-flowing rivers and streams cut deeply through limestone hills, creating dramatic gorges, ravines and caves. A short distance south of Punakaiki is the only breeding colony of the Westland petrel/titi in the world.

Underworld Adventures, one of the most popular and successful ecotour operators on the West Coast, was begun by two cavers in 1987. Located on SH 6 at Charleston, they offer four types of experience, based at the Nile River Canyon and Cave System in the national park, varying from mild to adventurous. These range from an open train ride along the Nile River Canyon to underwater rafting, glow-worm cave walks, and a full-on caving experience (ph 0800 116 686, www.caverafting.com).

11 Cape Foulwind

From Charleston head north for 16 km on SH 6 and then turn left into Wilsons Lead Road. Continue 8 km and turn left into Tauranga Bay Road and drive 3 km to the seal colony. From here to Westport is 16 km via Carters Beach.

Cape Foulwind is the western point of a wide bay that protects Carters Beach from the worst of the southerly weather. A broad surf beach sheltered by headlands at either end, Tauranga Bay lies just to the south of the cape. The walkway around the headland takes around one and a half hours one way from Tauranga Bay to the Cape Foulwind lighthouse, from where there are extensive views to the north. The northern head of Tauranga Bay is a great spot to watch fur seals as the lookout point is directly above the colony. With numerous rock pools, this is the ultimate seal playground, with the best time to see pups between December and March. Be aware that the seals are not confined to the colony and often blend in with the surrounding rocks.

46 Northern Buller • Westport to Karamea

Limestone arches and caves • Empty beaches • Profuse rainforest • 140 km

This often neglected corner of the South Island has a largely unspoilt landscape of bush, beach and limestone. The mild wet climate has created a stunning rainforest, thick with tree ferns and nikau palms. Along the Oparara River dramatic limestone arches and caves are set amidst virgin beech forest.

Getting there
Beginning at Westport, this route follows SH 67 north to Karamea and the Kohaihai River, one end of the Heaphy Track. The main road is sealed and in good condition, although the 30-km section that skirts the Karamea Bluffs from the Mokihinui River to the Little Wanganui River is very winding and slow. Many of the side roads are gravel.

Best time to visit
The coastal area of Buller has a surprisingly mild climate, as evidenced by the lush bush of tree ferns and nikau palms. Summer is warm but rarely hot, and in winter frosts are light and daytime temperatures can be very pleasant. However, like all of the West Coast, it can rain heavily in both summer and winter, though mid-summer through to early winter (January to June) is most likely to bring reliable settled weather. The Buller Marathon in February packs out accommodation within a 75-km radius of the town.

Facilities
Westport is a small port and coal-mining town and certainly no tourist trap. There is a good range of accommodation from camping through to comfortable motels, but the town is light on good places to eat. Likewise Karamea, at the northern end of the route, offers a good range of accommodation, although there isn't much

of it so if you plan to stay here it would be best to book ahead. Karamea also has a handful of very good cafés but there are few shops. Despite the number of small mining settlements scattered along SH 67, facilities are pretty light.

Before you go — surviving West Coast beaches
In many respects the shoreline of the West Coast is one long endless beach. While the weather is rarely scorching, the water with its rolling surf can look very inviting, but like so many New Zealand beaches, the open sea is treacherous for swimming. As well as being exposed to strong westerly winds and swells, the weather can cut up rough anywhere along the coast. What might look like gentle surf from a distance can be a very different story up close. The danger derives from the rapid variations in water depth and the strength of the undertow. One minute you can be standing in knee-deep water, but with the next wave you are up to your neck — or worse, knocked off your feet with the water rushing out to sea at an incredible rate. A related danger is the concealed rips, where the outgoing

rush has scoured deep holes and channels. Once you step into the hole, the strength of the water flow drags you out to sea. Complicating matters even further, rips have the effect of flattening out the surface water, so that what might at first appear a calm and safe stretch of water is actually perilous. Few places along the entire West Coast are safe for swimming, so if you are keen for a dip keep to the lakes or take extreme care, especially if you are not a strong swimmer.

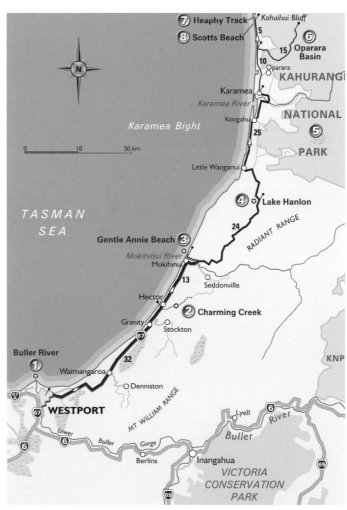

Cabbage tree/Ti kouka

The cabbage tree/ti kouka (*Cordyline australis*) is one of New Zealand's great iconic trees and is the most common of five species of *Cordyline* found in New Zealand. Found the length and breadth of the country, the tree is usually associated with swampy ground, but in fact grows almost anywhere from very wet to very dry situations and even over 1000 metres above sea level. Misnamed a tree, the plant is in fact a lily, similar to agaves and yuccas, and is the tallest member of this family.

Flowers, cream-coloured and small, are produced in profusion on multiple stems and are highly perfumed. Many trees have damaged leaves, a telltale sign of the presence of the native cabbage tree moth that feeds on the unopened leaves, with the holes only revealed once they unfurl.

These are really tough trees. When cut down or badly damaged they will quickly throw multiple stems and readily reproduce from seed. Often seen isolated amid paddocks, these lone trees are the sole survivors of forests long gone, and the trunk is so fire-resistant that early settlers used them to make chimneys.

1 Buller River

From the west end of Palmerston Street in Westport, turn right into Gladstone Street and then left into Derby Street, and finally left into Coates Street, which leads to the beach and breakwater.

On the final stretch to the sea, the Buller River is confined between two breakwaters. With a heavy swell running, the river mouth is a place of great drama, especially if a fishing boat or coal barge is navigating the bar. There is easy access out to the end of the breakwater on the north side and the views along the coast are superb. To the north, misty bush-covered mountains loom over the long sweep of beach, which is littered with bleached driftwood. Off to the south lie the crescent of Carters Beach and the headland of Cape Foulwind. The rare Hector's dolphin is often seen just offshore, and if you are lucky to strike stormy weather you'll witness the heaving swells driving in off the Tasman Sea.

2 Charming Creek

Drive 32 km north of Westport on SH 67 and, just before the bridge over the Ngakawau River, turn into Tylers Road.

The Charming Creek Walkway follows the line of an old railway along the Ngakawau River and through a deep gorge. Broken boulders are testament to the destructive power of water confined to a narrow cleft in the coastal hills, made even more dramatic by the high rainfall common along this coast. Despite the heavy precipitation the gorge is the only location in the country of the mountain daisy *Celmisia morganii*. Although not a rare species, what makes this particular variation unique is that nearly all celmisia are alpine plants and thus a most unusual find in temperate coastal rainforest.

Visible from a bridge on the track are the picturesque Mangatini Falls that plunge into a side creek of the Ngakawau River. Beyond the falls the track goes through a tunnel to Watson's Mills, a pleasant picnic spot at the confluence of the Ngakawau River and Charming Creek. Glow-worms are common in the tunnels and some cuttings along the track, which takes three hours one way or two hours return to the waterfall.

3 Gentle Annie Beach

North of Charming Creek turn left into De Malmanches Road.

Gentle Annie Beach lies to the north of the Mokihinui River mouth and marks the end of the coastal plain and the beginning of the rugged Karamea Bluffs that stretch along the coast to the Little Wanganui

River, just south of Karamea township. Unspoiled and seldom visited, at the end of this wild and open beach is a track up to headlands with marvellous views to the south. North of the river 3 km is a good camping site with toilets and showers, but no cooking facilities.

4 Lake Hanlon

On SH 67, 24 km north of Gentle Annie Beach, 25 km south of Karamea.

From the Mokihinui River, the road climbs steeply through the incredibly rugged terrain of the Radiant Range, laced by deep valleys covered in thick bush. Towards Little Wanganui River and just below the Karamea Bluffs (rising to 400 metres) is tiny Lake Hanlon. Formed by the 1929 Murchison earthquake, this pretty little lake is fringed with beech and rata, a particularly attractive spectacle in summer.

Weka (*Gallirallus australis*), members of the rail family, are common around the lake and indeed throughout northern Westland. Endemic to New Zealand, this flightless bird was once widespread throughout the country, but today is only seen on offshore islands and in the northern part of the South Island. Initially, weka were relatively unaffected by the arrival of people, but the population plummeted in the first half of the twentieth century and all but vanished from most of the North Island and large parts of the South Island. Despite remaining strong around the Gisborne area, in the 1980s that population too mysteriously declined from 90,000 birds to less than 2000 within the space of several decades. The reason for the dramatic decline in numbers is uncertain, nor is anyone quite sure why weka are still common in this one particular region.

5 Kahurangi National Park

Occupying the entire northwest corner of the South Island, Kahurangi National Park covers over 450,000 hectares, making it New Zealand's second-largest national park after Fiordland. Geologically the park contains some of the country's most ancient rocks, dating back 550,000 years to the supercontinent of Gondwana, and it is in this park that our oldest fossils (sponges, trilobites, molluscs) dating back 508 million years have been found.

This park is famous for its dramatic

Oparara Basin, Kahurangi National Park.

limestone landscapes, and the cave systems around Mt Arthur and Mt Owen are the longest and deepest in New Zealand. In terms of flora the park is very diverse, ranging from temperate coastal forest with palms and ferns, through to extensive beech forests in the east with the higher areas home to 80 per cent of New Zealand's alpine plants. Rarely seen, 20 species of the carnivorous land snail are found within its borders. Despite its size this national park is not easily accessible and the tracks that do cross it require both stamina and time. Northern Buller has several access points, including the renowned Heaphy Track.

6 Oparara Basin

Continue north from Lake Hanlon 25 km to Karamea, and from there follow the coast for a further 10 km to McCallums Mill Road. The main car park is 15 km down this road. Narrow, winding and gravel, with stretches where it is difficult to pass other vehicles, the road to Oparara is a challenge. A DoC sign at the beginning advises that it is unsuitable for caravans and camper vans, though the shorter-wheel-based camper vans will manage the road.

Lying within the Kahurangi National Park, the Oparara Basin is an area of outstanding natural beauty. Containing magnificent virgin bush and stunning

Morepork/Ruru

Widespread throughout New Zealand, the morepork (*Ninox novaeseelandiae*) is a small owl, typically no more than 30 cm long, although the females are usually slightly bigger. Like all owls, ruru are nocturnal and are well known for their distinct 'more pork, more pork' call, although their hunting call — a shorter, higher-pitched screech — is quite different. The morepork is one of two native owls; the other, the laughing owl (or whekau), now extinct. The bird feeds mainly on insects but will also hunt mice and other small birds and, while originally a creature of the forest, has adapted to exotic plantings and is even common in densely planted urban areas.

Nikau palms, Karamea.

limestone landscapes, the bird life in the area is also prolific, and there is a good chance of spotting the rare blue duck/whio that makes its home on the boulder-strewn bed of the fast-flowing Oparara River. Weka are common in the car park and are bold enough to jump in your car and steal whatever takes their fancy if you leave the door open.

A number of intriguing caves and arches are easily accessible by short tracks through the beech forest. The largest natural arch in New Zealand looms above the Oparara River and is over 200 metres long. Nearby is Moria Gate, not as grand as the Oparara Arch, but more than making up in beauty what it lacks in size.

About 2 km beyond the arches are the Crazy Paving and Box Canyon Caves. These caves are the home of New Zealand's only cave spider, and while the elusive creature is not itself visible, the delicate egg sacs hanging from the ceilings are plain to see. A torch is necessary for both caves.

7 Heaphy Track
Starts 5 km north of the Oparara turnoff.

One of New Zealand's 'Great Walks', this 82-km track traverses the heart of the Kahurangi National Park and offers a superb range of landscapes, from the tussock-clad Gouland Downs Crossing through to lush subtropical forest at the Karamea end. While the track is well formed and not difficult, there are some long stretches and huts must be booked through the Department of Conservation.

The northern end of the track begins up the Aorere Valley from Collingwood, while the southern end commences from the Kohaihai River, 15 km north of Karamea. Several operators provide return transport from either end — a 460-km trip by road. If walking the whole track isn't an option, there are several shorter trips along the coastal part of the track from the Karamea end.

8 Scotts Beach
From Karamea township head north along the coast for 15 km to the southern end of the Heaphy Track at the Kohaihai River.
For a taste of the Heaphy Track, this easy walk to Scotts Beach is well worth the effort. Just an hour and a half return through beautiful bush, the beach is a stunning stretch of white sand, although the wild surf makes it dangerous for swimming. Bush thick with ferns and nikau stretches up the hillsides from the shore, while a pleasant picnic and camping area with toilets and fireplaces is sheltered from the westerly wind in a grassy glade.

Right after crossing the swing bridge over the Kohaihai River and just off the track to Scotts Beach is a short loop track though dense groves of nikau palm and massive southern rata. Ngaio and karaka, here at their southern growing limit, are also present along this track, and jet-black fantails are common too.

Granite rock formation at Scotts Beach.

47 Buller River and Nelson Lakes National Park • Westport to St Arnaud
Alpine lakes • Unique bird life • Buller River • 200 km

The Buller River winds through some of the most sparsely populated country in New Zealand, three-quarters of which is covered by native forest. At Nelson Lakes National Park two fine glacial lakes huddle in deep mountain valleys rich in flora and alive with native birds.

INFORMATION
Westport i-SITE,
1 Brougham Street,
Westport, ph (03) 789 6658
Nelson Lakes Visitor Centre,
View Road, St Arnaud,
ph (03) 521 1806

Getting there
This route starts at the coast at Westport and ends at Lake Rotoiti in Nelson Lakes National Park. The roads are good but generally winding and slow, so take your time. From Nelson take SH 6 south and from Blenheim take SH 63 west. The area can also be reached from Canterbury via the Lewis Pass on SH 7. Snow is seldom a problem in this area, although heavy rain can cause minor slips. In frosty weather take care through the gorges as these roads are heavily shaded and can be icy.

Best time to visit
Summer and autumn are very pleasant seasons in this area, though you can expect heavy rain at any time. While the winters can be extremely cold, as most of this region is well inland it is often sheltered from the worst of the weather. During February the Buller Marathon packs out Westport and elsewhere within 75 km of the town, so if your arrival unintentionally coincides with this event you could well find yourself sleeping on the beach.

Facilities
Westport is an old coal town with an odd charm of its own and is a good place to stop in northern Westland. While it has a surprising amount of accommodation (seemingly out of proportion to the size of the town), Westport is thin on good places to eat but has a good range of services and shops. Though small, Murchison also has a wide range of accommodation including camping, a hotel and motels, plus some good cafés, but not too much else. At St Arnaud at Lake Rotoiti there is a scattering of places to stay, a café or two and a general store.

1 Buller River
While just 177 km in length, the Buller River passes through some of New Zealand's most scenic landscapes, on its westward journey from the mountainous Nelson Lakes National Park to the rough seas at Westport. Lake Rotoiti is the source of the river, with the Gowan River from Lake Rotoroa joining a short distance downstream. Passing through two bush-clad gorges and skirting the Kahurangi National Park, the river has seven major tributaries including the Maruia and Inangahua Rivers. It also has the greatest flood discharge of any New Zealand river.

2 Lower Buller Gorge
From Westport take SH 6 east for 22 km.
Between Inangahua and Westport the Buller River narrows considerably, cutting through the Paparoa Range to the south and the Mt William Range to the north before reaching the sea. The road through the gorge winds along the river between steep bush-covered bluffs, and at one point, at Hawks Crag, is one way only. Attempts to widen the gorge have been resisted by locals, who value its character over the ability to speed up a journey. Jet boating and white-water rafting options through the gorge are available.

3 Upper Buller Gorge
Continue east on SH 6 for 40 km.
The gorge begins just east of Inangahua and continues for 30 km to just west of Murchison, where the Maruia River joins the Buller and winds through steep bush-covered hillsides of beech forest. The river was completely blocked by a massive landslide caused by the Inangahua earthquake in 1968, although the water broke through naturally a number of days later.

4 Maruia Falls Lookout
Follow SH 6 for 23 km to the junction of SH 65. Turn right and travel 11 km south on SH 65 to the falls.
The most significant remaining feature of the Murchison earthquake, these falls were created by the sharp 1-metre drop across the Maruia River. The rushing water has

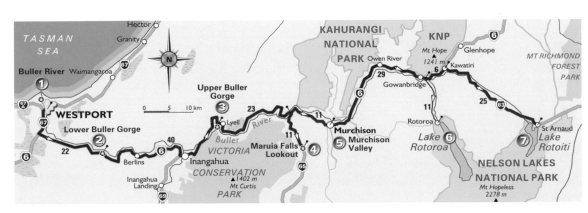

Buller River.

since eroded the riverbed further, so that the falls are now much higher than in 1929. Today they are a popular plunge for adventurous kayakers.

5 Murchison Valley

Return to SH 6 and drive 11 km to Murchison. Nestled in a wide valley surrounded by mountains, Murchison is the point at which the Matiri and Matakitaki Rivers join the Buller. The region is best known for the quality of the white water for kayaking and rafting.

On 17 June 1929 Murchison was hit by a major earthquake of magnitude 7.8, though most damage was caused by massive landslips, including one that blocked the Matakitaki River. The Skyline Track at Murchison is a short but steep walk to a lookout point over the valley that has excellent views of all three rivers.

Maruia Falls.

Earthquakes

An active area of earthquake activity runs the length of New Zealand in a broad band from the Bay of Plenty right down to Fiordland. On average, the islands experience 10,000 to 15,000 earthquakes a year, of which 1 per cent are big enough to be felt. In recent history the biggest quake was the 8.2 Wairarapa earthquake in 1855, while the most significant since instrumental recording began was the 7.8 magnitude Hawke's Bay earthquake of 1931.

New Zealand sits on the boundary of two major tectonic plates, the Australian to the west and the Pacific to the east, and this is one of the world's most active plate boundaries. In the North Island the Pacific plate is sliding under the Australian plate, causing strong shallow earthquakes in the Bay of Plenty area. These gradually become deeper further west, with quakes as deep as 600 km being recorded off the Taranaki Coast. In the South Island the situation is quite different. Here, along the 600-km Alpine Fault the two plates are not only being pushed together, they are also pulling past each other, and the Southern Alps are being squeezed up along the line where the plates meet. However, the South Island quakes are relatively shallow as neither plate is being driven under the other. By geological standards the rate of movement along the Alpine Fault is very fast with a horizontal movement of 30 metres per 1000 years, while the vertical uplift is even faster. Over the course of some 5 million years parts of Nelson and west Otago that were once joined together are now 450 km apart. The Maruia Falls is a graphic example of both the power of earthquakes and the impact of erosion upon the landscape. Created in an instant by the Murchison earthquake in 1929, the bed of the Maruia River dropped by 1 metre, but within the space of a single year it had been eroded a further 4 metres, so that today the falls are 10 metres high.

6 Lake Rotoroa, Nelson Lakes National Park

From Murchison drive north on SH 6 for 29 km and turn right into Gowan Valley Road and travel 11 km to the lake.

Formed during the last ice age, both Lakes Rotoiti and Rotoroa are the result of glacial action in the mountains of the upper Buller River. Reaching into the heart of the most northerly section of the Southern Alps, the lakes give access to both lower forest and true alpine terrain that is deep in snow during winter. The bird life in the 102,000-hectare forest is prolific and includes bellbirds, robins and kaka.

Larger than Lake Rotoiti, Lake Rotoroa attracts fewer visitors and is far less developed. Old kowhai trees overhang the placid water along the shore and huge beech and lofty kahikatea tower over the forest floor, which is beautifully carpeted in handsome crown ferns. A number of short walks begin from the boat ramp along the lake edge and the longer Braeburn Track (two hours return) follows the lake's western shore.

7 Lake Rotoiti, Nelson Lakes National Park

Return to SH 6, turn right and drive 6 km to Kawatiri Junction. Turn right on to SH 63 and continue 25 km to St Arnaud.

The mountains of the Nelson Lakes National Park are part of the Alpine Fault that runs north to south along the spine of the South Island. The highest peak in the park is Mt Franklin at 2145 metres (just 6 metres higher than its neighbour, Mt Travers), and the dense beech forest is comprised mainly of red and silver beech with mountain beech at higher altitudes.

The DoC information centre at St Arnaud has excellent displays on the natural environment and up-to-date information on walks in the area. The Lake Rotoiti Circuit Track around the lake will take a full day, but can be shortened by the use of water taxis from St Arnaud. Other day tramps include the Mt Roberts Circuit, St Arnaud Range Track and the Whisky Falls Track. Several short walks begin from the eastern side of Kerr Bay and are essentially three loop walks, each progressively larger than the other, so it is very easy to find a walk to suit all abilities.

Part of a 'mainland island' scheme whereby predators are eradicated and permanently excluded from a section of the forest, native birds have recovered and flourished in the area. If you keep an eye out you might catch a glimpse of two of New Zealand's more rare parrots, the kaka and kakariki.

The Buller River and Lake Rotoiti.

Index

Photograph acknowledgements

All photography the property of and ©Andrew Fear except for the following, which are the property of and © to the indicated photographers.

Auckland Regional Council: page 31. **Dennis Buurman:** page 103. **Dominic Stephens:** page 40. **Department of Conservation** Te Papa Atawhai, Crown Copyright: pages 28 (top) Paul Schilov; 40 (bottom right); 42 (top); 115 (bottom) Erin Green; 125 (top left) Dick Veitch; 159 (top) ; 164 (top). **Len Doel:** pages 24 (bottom); 43; 45 (bottom); 47; 48 (bottom); 50 (bottom); 67; 81; 90 (top); 97 (top); 109 (top); 121 (top); 126; 131 (top); 133 (top right); 137 (top); 139 (top); 142 (top); 145 (left); 153 (top and middle); 169 (bottom). **Stewart Island Flights:** 141. **Peter Janssen:** pages 18 (top); 22; 23 (top); 45 (top); 46; 56 (bottom); 58 (top); 78 (top); 84 (bottom); 85 (bottom); 127 (bottom); 133 (bottom); 134. **Bob McCree:** pages 32; 33 (top). **Darryn Pegram/Black Robin Photography:** page 82. **Glenys Robertson:** page 63. **Rob Suisted/Nature's Pic:** pages 13 (bottom); 29; 35; 85 (top); 88 (top); 138–139 (bottom); 140 (bottom); 142 (bottom); 143. **Karori Sanctuary Trust:** page 89. **David Wall:** page 30.